SOCIAL JUSTICE, EQUALITY AND EMPOWERMENT

STEREOTYPES AND STEREOTYPING

MISPERCEPTIONS, PERSPECTIVES AND ROLE OF SOCIAL MEDIA

Social Justice, Equality and Empowerment

Additional books in this series can be found on Nova's website under the Series tab.

Additional e-books in this series can be found on Nova's website under the e-book tab.

SOCIAL JUSTICE, EQUALITY AND EMPOWERMENT

STEREOTYPES AND STEREOTYPING

MISPERCEPTIONS, PERSPECTIVES AND ROLE OF SOCIAL MEDIA

CLAUDE FIELDS
EDITOR

nova publishers
New York

Library of Congress Cataloging-in-Publication Data

Names: Fields, Claude, editor.
Title: Stereotypes and stereotyping : misperceptions, perspectives and role of social media / editor, Claude Fields.
Description: Hauppauge, New York : Nova Science Publishers, Inc., [2016] | Series: Social justice, equality and empowerment | Includes index.
Identifiers: LCCN 2015050207 (print) | LCCN 2016005047 (ebook) | ISBN 9781634845106 (hardcover) | ISBN 9781634845410 ()
Subjects: LCSH: Stereotypes (Social psychology) | Social media.
Classification: LCC HM1096 .S73985 2016 (print) | LCC HM1096 (ebook) | DDC 303.3/85--dc23
LC record available at http://lccn.loc.gov/2015050207

Published by Nova Science Publishers, Inc. † New York

CONTENTS

PREFACE

Stereotypes and Stereotyping: Misperceptions, Perspectives and Role of Social Media provides current research on misperceptions, perspectives, and the role of social media on stereotypes and stereotyping. The first chapter assesses implicit and explicit attitudes toward high socioeconomic status (SES) students and links these attitudes to the achievement and personality judgments of a high and a low SES student. Chapter Two reviews current national trends and interdisciplinary research in psychology, sociology, and education documenting educational disparities related to students' gender, race and ethnicity, social class, and college generational status. Chapter Three discusses stereotypes towards people with AIDs in college students. Chapter Four examines if college women's social media usage predicts how they budget their time regarding physical appearance and academic work while in school, and also examines if it predicts their perceptions of the relative importance of appearance related behaviors and domain specific skills for their future careers. Chapter Five studies demographic differences in the level of intercultural sensitivity, English as a foreign language (EFL) interests, and ethnocentrism among college students in Taiwan. Chapter Six uses psychological theories and findings to identify and analyze factors that may have contributed to the deaths in the three shootings of Trayvon Martin, Michael Brown, and Tamir Rice. It considers the roles that physical appearance and shooter bias may have played in all three cases. Chapter Seven evaluates stereotypes in counter-stereotypic occupations. Chapter Eight provides an overview of the current research on the accuracy of national stereotypes and introduce results of a research project on national stereotypes in five Central European countries. Chapter Nine reviews the roles of identity processing styles and self-consciousness in aging and ageism.

In: Stereotypes and Stereotyping
Editor: Claude Fields

ISBN: 978-1-63484-510-6

Chapter 1

THE HIGHER THE SES THE BETTER? IMPLICIT AND EXPLICIT ATTITUDES INFLUENCE PRESERVICE TEACHERS' JUDGMENTS OF STUDENTS

Sabine Glock[1,*], Sabine Krolak-Schwerdt[2] and Thomas Hörstermann[2]

[1]Bergische Universität Wuppertal, School of Education, Wuppertal, Germany

[2]University of Luxembourg, Luxembourg City, Luxembourg

ABSTRACT

Background: Stereotypical expectations of students from families with high socioeconomic status (SES) have been suggested to contribute to the advantages that such students experience in educational systems. Stereotypical expectations are linked to attitudes, which guide behavior and judgments. Research on attitudes makes a distinction between implicit and explicit attitudes. Implicit attitudes are automatic, whereas explicit attitudes are conscious evaluations of an object, and both should contribute to judgments. Educational research has yet to investigate implicit and explicit attitudes toward high SES students.

Aims: This study aimed to close this research gap. More specifically, we assessed implicit and explicit attitudes toward high SES students and linked these attitudes to the achievement and personality judgments of a high and a low SES student.

Sample: 65 preservice teachers from Germany participated in this study.

Methods: Implicit attitudes were assessed via an affective priming task. Participants were presented descriptions of a male student with high SES and a male student with low SES. Their task was to judge each students' academic performance and personality. Afterwards, they were given a newly developed questionnaire for assessing explicit attitudes toward high SES students.

Results: Implicit as well as explicit attitudes toward high SES students were positive. Attitudes predicted the judgments of the students such that more positive attitudes led to more favorable judgments.

---

[*] E-mail: glock@uni-wuppertal.de.

Conclusion: This study provides the first insights into attitudes toward high SES students and the relation of such attitudes to judgments. Teachers' attitudes should not be neglected with respect to their judgments of students of whom they have stereotypical expectations.

INTRODUCTION

Educational research has provided evidence that students from families with high socioeconomic status (SES) experience advantages in educational systems. High SES students have been found to be less frequently recommended for special education than low SES students (Frey 2002; Podell and Soodak 1993). They have been attributed higher educational success than low SES students (Harvey and Slatin 1975), and they have been judged more favorably than their IQ suggested (Alvidrez and Weinstein 1999). Thus, teachers have been found to develop expectations about how high SES students might perform and behave academically (Diamond, Randolph, and Spillane 2004; McCombs and Gay 1988), which in turn has been found to affect the teachers' judgments. Besides stereotypical expectation biases in teachers' judgments, actual teacher behavior has been found to differ depending on the SES of a student, as teachers have been found to behave more favorably toward high SES students (Babad 1993) than toward low SES students. As a result, students' current academic performance as well as their long-term performance has been found to be impacted by stereotypical expectations (de Boer, Bosker, and van der Werf 2010). Stereotypical expectations are related to prejudice (Devine 1989), which is defined as negative attitudes toward a social group or toward a member of a social group (Dovidio et al. 1996). However, positive stereotypical expectations are related to positive attitudes toward a social group. Therefore, positive attitudes may be a factor that drives the advantages of high SES students because attitudes often guide behavior (Fazio 1990) and color judgments (Olson and Fazio 2009; Sanbonmatsu and Fazio 1990). This should hold in particular for preservice teachers. Thus, the aim of our study was to investigate preservice teachers' attitudes toward high SES students and the relations between these attitudes and judgments.

THEORETICAL BACKGROUND

Research on attitudes has made a distinction between explicit and implicit attitudes (Gawronski and Bodenhausen 2006). Explicit attitudes are effortful reflections (Gawronski and Bodenhausen 2006) that are used to make evaluations of attitude objects. That is, whenever people are asked to express their attitudes, they have to retrieve evaluations that are stored in memory, or else they have to construct an evaluation at that point in time (Schwarz and Bohner 2001; Bassili and Brown 2005). Either way, these actions involve controlled and reflective processes (Gawronski and Bodenhausen 2006; Fazio 1990). In this vein, explicit attitudes always depend on a person's ability to engage in such effortful processes (Fazio 1990). Implicit attitudes are automatic evaluations of attitude objects (Gawronski and Bodenhausen 2006). They are stored in memory (Gawronski and Bodenhausen 2006) and are automatically activated whenever the attitude object is present (Fazio 2007; Olson and Fazio 2009). The activation of implicit attitudes does not require reflective or controlled processes

(Fazio and Roskos-Ewoldsen 2005); instead, implicit attitudes are activated without conscious effort (Gawronski and Bodenhausen 2006).

According to the MODE model (*M*otivation and *O*pportunity as *DE*terminants; Fazio 1990), situational factors determine whether the attitude-behavior relation is based on automatic or controlled processes. This relation is automatic whenever people have no motivation or opportunity to think about their evaluations or to act on conscious thinking (Fazio 1990; Fazio and Towles-Schwen 1999). These are situations in which people have to react immediately in order to respond to situational demands (Fazio and Roskos-Ewoldsen 2005) or situations with high cognitive demands so that people have only limited cognitive resources available to reflect on their attitudes and behavior (Fazio and Towles-Schwen 1999; Fazio 1990; Hofmann et al. 2008). In these cases, automatically activated implicit attitudes guide behavior (Fazio 1990; Fazio 1986) and judgments of objects (Fazio et al. 1986). Contrary to these processes, explicit attitudes guide controlled behavior in situations in which people have cognitive resources that are sufficient to allow them to reflect on their behavior (Fazio 1990). If situational demands do not require immediate action but rather provide the opportunity to make a conscious behavioral decision, explicit attitudes usually guide behavior. This path of the MODE model suggests that people consider the consequences of their behavior and think about social norms, thus coming to a behavioral decision by combining these factors with their explicit attitudes. These behavioral decisions can be considered behavioral intentions (Strack and Deutsch 2004). However, it is not only behavioral decisions and behavioral intentions that might be influenced by explicit attitudes but also judgments, which are considered to be a type of deliberate controlled behavior (Fazio et al. 1995). Particularly when people have enough time, cognitive resources, and motivation, their judgments about other people become controlled and reflective. In such situations, judgments are guided by explicit attitudes (Fazio 1990).

In summary, implicit attitudes guide automatic spontaneous behavior, whereas explicit attitudes usually guide controlled behavior (Neumann, Hülsenbeck, and Seibt 2004) such as judgments (Fazio et al. 1995). However, most cognitive processes include spontaneous as well as controlled aspects; that is, both kinds of attitudes affect behavior (Olson and Fazio 2009). Even if there is enough time for a person to engage in a conscious evaluation and controlled behavioral decision making, implicit attitudes may color judgment and behavior.

This should also hold in the educational context. On the one hand, teachers in their classrooms are often confronted with high cognitive demands under time constraints (Santavirta, Solovieva, and Theorell 2007), and interactions with students usually require immediate behavioral responses. On the other hand, teachers can take their time and use their cognitive resources for activities such as grading. Nevertheless, even when teachers are able to reflect on their judgments, their implicit attitudes may still unconsciously affect them. Hence, there are many situations in the educational context in which behavior may be guided by both implicit and explicit attitudes. Implicit attitudes play an especially crucial role in highly demanding situations, and this is particularly true for preservice teachers (Glock, Kneer, and Kovacs 2013). Preservice teachers feel a higher level of stress than experienced teachers (Yagil 1998), and this may be due to their lack of experience because they have not yet adapted to the demands of working as a teacher (Bradley 2007).

This distinction between implicit and explicit attitudes exists not only on a theoretical level but also with respect to measurement (Hofmann et al. 2005). Implicit measures do not rely on conscious processes but rather tap into automaticity (De Houwer 2006; De Houwer and Moors 2007), which is inherent in implicit attitudes (Petty, Fazio, and Briñol 2009). Thus, the assessment of implicit attitudes provides advantages because implicit measures are less prone to being affected by response biases such as social desirability (De Houwer 2006) and are less susceptible to faking (Steffens 2004).

In summary, both implicit and explicit attitudes may guide behavior and judgments. To our knowledge, there is no research on the influence of explicit and implicit attitudes toward high SES students on judgments, although attitudes have been suggested to be the result of stereotypical expectations (Auwarter and Aruguete 2008). As stereotypical expectations about high SES students have been found to contribute to teachers' and preservice teachers' more favorable judgments of high SES students, the question arises as to whether attitudes might be able to predict judgments. Since high SES students are expected to be higher in intelligence and to exhibit above-average academic performances (Diamond, Randolph, and Spillane 2004; McCombs and Gay 1988), implicit attitudes toward them should be more positive, thus contributing to more favorable judgments of high SES students.

Hence, the aim of our study was to investigate presevice teachers' attitudes toward high SES students and the relation between these attitudes and the teachers' judgments of students. We aimed to close the above-mentioned research gap by assessing implicit as well as explicit attitudes toward students with high SES, measuring preservice teachers' judgments of students' academic achievement and personality, and relating these attitudes to the teachers' judgments. Corresponding to the research findings outlined above, we expected implicit attitudes toward high SES students to be positive. Due to social desirability and social norms, which might suggest that preferring high over low SES students is not appropriate, we expected that explicit attitudes toward high SES students would be neutral. Drawing on the MODE model outlined above, we expected that both implicit and explicit attitudes would predict achievement and personality judgments.

METHOD

Participants

Sixty-five preservice teachers (46 female) from a German university participated in the study. Their mean age was 23.45 years (*SD* = 3.46). Twenty-nine participants had no teaching experience at all, whereas the remaining participants had a mean teaching experience of 11.77 weeks (*SD* = 12.11). Most of the participants (50) were preparing to teach in the highest school track and 12 in the middle school track; 2 participants reported that they were preparing for other school tracks, and one did not answer this question. Forty-eight participants had not received student loans; the remaining participants were eligible for student loans.

Materials

Measuring Implicit Attitudes. To measure implicit attitudes, we used an affective priming task (Fazio, 1986; Fazio et al., 1995). This task is based on the assumption that a prime (the attitude object) is able to activate the corresponding automatic evaluation, which, in turn, facilitates how the valence of subsequently presented words (targets) will be evaluated. We selected 8 colored pictures as primes out of a pool of 100 pictures that had been pretested (see Glock et al., 2013, for a detailed description of the prestudy). The eight pictures displayed only male students, and they were not allowed to differ on the following dimensions: physical attractiveness, intelligence, socioeconomic status, and foreign appearance. The ratings of the different dimensions for the eight pictures were submitted to an 8 x 4 ANOVA with Picture (eight pictures) and Dimension (the four above-mentioned dimensions) as the factors. This ANOVA revealed a significant main effect of Picture, $F(7, 98) = 2.13$, $p < .05$, $\eta^2_p = .13$, indicating that the ratings of the pictures differed independently from the dimension. The ANOVA also revealed a significant main effect of Dimension, $F(3, 98) = 46.37$, $p < .001$, $\eta^2_p = .77$. However and most importantly, the interaction was not significant, $F(21, 294) = 1.15$, $p = .30$, $\eta^2_p = .08$. Hence, the ratings of the pictures did not differ by physical attractiveness, intelligence, socioeconomic status, and foreign appearance. The chosen pictures were all scored as average on physical attractiveness, intelligence, and socioeconomic status and low on foreign appearance. The positive and negative adjectives used as targets were pretested (Glock, Unz, and Kovacs 2012) and were unambiguous in valence (see Glock et al. 2013, for the detailed list of adjectives).

Student Descriptions. We compiled a student description that referred to a No.1 student in class. We added information about the socioeconomic background of the student and described him as the son of a physician. The description was comprised of 16 sentences. The student was described as industrious, with an above-average academic performance, and highly motivated. We additionally compiled a student description of a below-average student and described this student as the son of a factory worker. This student did not perform well in school, did not have much interest in school, and was lazy. This description was also comprised of 16 sentences. Both descriptions referred to male students.

Measuring Explicit Attitudes. Although there are questionnaires for assessing experiences with classism (Thompson and Subich 2013) even in academic settings (Langhout, Rosselli, and Feinstein 2007), we could not rely on existing questionnaires because they were not designed to assess attitudes toward classism but rather assessed a person's own experiences with classism. Therefore, we compiled a questionnaire with 30 statements regarding attitudes toward students from families with high SES (see Table 1 for all of the items from the questionnaire). The statements were chosen to cover different aspects of attitudes toward high SES students including aspects that have been found to be related to stereotypical expectations such as intelligence, academic achievement, and behavior.

To identify the underlying dimensions in the participants' responses to the SES items from the explicit attitudes questionnaire, we performed an exploratory factor analysis using a principal component analysis. We extracted 3 factors underlying 29 items. One item was excluded because it had no loadings on any factor. In the initial solution, the first factor explained 21.2%, the second factor 10.6%, and the third factor 8.3% of the total variance. The item variance jointly explained by the three extracted factors ranged from $R^2 = .13$ to $R^2 = .80$. Because the three factors were supposed to represent different aspects of attitudes toward students with different socioeconomic backgrounds, we did not assume factor orthogonality and allowed for oblique factors by applying an OBLIMIN rotation. Although the rotation allowed for oblique factors, it resulted in nearly orthogonal factors. The factor intercorrelations are displayed in Table 2.

Table 1. Factor Loadings of the Items from the Explicit Attitudes Questionnaire

Statement	Factor 1	Factor 2	Factor 3
S1: Children from low-income families often disrupt instruction even without intending to do so.	**.547**	**-.321**	-.215
S2: Low-income parents expect the school and the teachers to deal with educational tasks.	.189	**-.549**	.123
S3: It is difficult for children from low-income families to find adequate role models in their communities.	**.391**	**-.625**	-.177
S4: Teachers should know and consider their students' social backgrounds when evaluating scholastic achievement.	**.522**	-.064	**-.519**
S5: Incomplete or copied homework can be frequently observed in children from low-income families.	**.718**	**-.411**	-.135
S6: A low-income background often serves as a justification or excuse for scholastic difficulties.	**.539**	**-.723**	.199
S7: During parent-teacher conferences, teachers should adjust their language to the parents' social background.	.244	-.157	-.254
S8: It is good that wealthy parents can obtain professional private tutoring when their children show scholastic weaknesses.	-.147	**-.509**	.078
S9: When children have scholastic difficulties, wealthy parents have less confidence in teachers' competencies than low-income parents.	.024	**-.649**	.009
S10: Low-income parents thwart the scholastic ambitions of their children.	.278	**-.526**	.126
S11: Teachers should encourage children from low-income families to take an interest in material that has practical relevance.	**.422**	-.120	.064
S12: Many differences in conflict resolution behavior stem from the children's social backgrounds.	.245	**-.567**	**.453**
S13: Athletic success is very important for children from low-income families.	.143	**-.334**	**.314**
S14: It is a problem that less-educated parents are not able to support the scholastic tasks of their children.	**.506**	**-.334**	-.267
S15: The existence of tuition-based private schools provides a useful addition to the educational system.	**.514**	**.313**	.090
S16: Wealthy parents are usually more concerned about risks to their children's advancement than parents with low income.	**.360**	.027	**.460**
S17: Children from low-income families face so many problems that their scholastic achievement is affected.	**.695**	**-.323**	-.057
S18: Students from wealthy families are more amenable to purely theoretical and impractical lesson content than students from low-income families.	**.794**	-.139	-.135

Statement	Factor 1	Factor 2	Factor 3
S19: Children from wealthy families score higher in scholastic achievement than children from low-income families.	**.765**	.021	-.066
S20: It is understandable that teachers prefer teaching at schools where the students come from wealthy families.	**.711**	.077	**-.308**
S21: Children with wealthy parents get away with more frequent misbehavior in school without receiving disciplinary measures than children from low-income families.	.161	.005	**-.416**
S22: When a parent has a successful occupational career, this has a positive influence a child's scholastic motivation and ambition.	**.403**	**-.475**	-.276
S23: Wealthy parents do all they can to ensure that their children will achieve at least the same educational level as themselves.	-.062	**-.462**	-.041
S24: Educational success is very important for children from wealthy families.	.079	**-.491**	-.128
S25: In Germany, children with equal abilities have equal chances of educational success.	.063	-.117	**-.731**
S26: Low-income parents are proud if their children receive a higher educational level than themselves.	**.394**	**.360**	.100
S27: Children from families with low income also possess all that is needed to be successful in the educational system.	**.315**	**-.523**	**-.518**
S28: It is a problem that wealthy parents increasingly enroll their children in higher school tracks.	.049	.240	**-.322**
S29: Teachers should avoid requiring additional learning materials if the parents have to purchase them out of pocket.	. 142	.045	**.448**
S30: When planning school trips, teachers should ensure that all parents can afford to pay for the trip.	.157	.052	**-.492**

Table 2. Factor Intercorrelations of the Explicit Attitudes Questionnaire

Component	Factor 1	Factor 2	Factor 3
Factor 1	1.00		
Factor 2	-.136	1.00	
Factor 3	-.093	.049	1.00

To interpret the factors, we assigned each item to the factor on which it had its highest loading. For two items with nearly equal loadings on two factors, we assigned the items to the factor that provided the most consistent interpretation.

On the basis of the rotated solution, we excluded three items from our analysis due to insufficient item-total correlations. A 9-item scale with an internal consistency of Cronbach's $\alpha = .83$ formed Factor 1. An 11-item scale (Cronbach's $\alpha = .79$) formed Factor 2, and a 7-item scale (Cronbach's $\alpha = .62$) formed Factor 3.

The Factor 1 items reflected *Learning and Social Behavior* (see Table 1 for all items and the factor loadings). The Factor 2 items were all concerned with *School Motivation and Ambition*; the Factor 3 items reflected *Egalitarian Beliefs*.

Demographic Variables. In order to assess the participants' demographic variables, we compiled a questionnaire that assessed age, gender, teaching experience, and the school track they prepared for. We additionally asked them whether they were eligible for student loans. As the study was concerned with attitudes toward students from families with high SES, this question was used to control for the SES of the participants.

Procedure

Upon arriving at the lab, participants gave their informed consent. Participants were tested individually. They were seated in front of the computer screen, and the first task was run. In this first task, the student pictures were presented sequentially to the participants. Each picture appeared for 5 seconds on the screen with the student's father's occupation displayed below the picture. Participants were instructed to learn the different pictures and the corresponding fathers' occupations. Four of the fathers' occupations indicated that the family had a low SES (truck driver, facility manager, window cleaner, factory worker), and four indicated a high SES (lawyer, high school teacher, architect, medical doctor).

After the learning phase, a test phase was run. In this phase, a picture appeared on the screen, and the different fathers' occupations were shown one after another. When participants thought that the correct occupation was displayed, they were asked to press the space key. They were provided with feedback on the correctness of their answer. Participants remained in this phase until they gave correct answers for all pictures to ensure that they had successfully learned the associations between the pictures and occupations. The second test phase then began. In this test phase, participants were asked to categorize the pictures according to the fathers' occupation into high vs. low SES categories.

This test was implemented in order to ensure that the fathers' occupations that we had chosen reflected the SES they were intended to reflect and that the participants were aware of each student's socioeconomic status. This phase was adopted from the procedure of the Implicit Association Test (Greenwald, McGhee, and Schwartz 1998). The pictures were displayed without occupation, and the participants' task was to categorize the pictures into the high or the low SES category by pressing either the "E" or the "I" key on the keyboard. This phase consisted of twenty trials; if a participant made more than two errors, the twenty trials were repeated. The repetition of the twenty trials was stopped when participants made fewer than two errors on the categorization task. Then, the affective priming task was run. Participants were informed that they would be presented with a picture followed by a word and that their task was to evaluate the word's valence (positive vs. negative) by pressing either the "E" or the "I" key (see Glock et al. 2013, for the detailed list of words). The picture was shown for 250 ms, and after 50 ms, the word appeared, resulting in a stimulus onset asynchrony (SOA) of 300 ms, which is optimal for affective priming tasks (Hermans et al. 2002). The pictures and the words appeared in the center of the screen, with a picture size of 150 × 300 pixels. Participants were given 10 practice trials followed by 80 critical trials. Response latencies were measured. We included four different trial types: high SES pictures followed by (a) a positive word or (b) a negative word, and low SES pictures followed by (c) a positive word or (d) a negative word. In order to ensure that no picture-occupation effect emerged, one group of participants received four pictures paired with low SES occupations, and the other group received those pictures with high SES occupations. The same switch was realized for the other four pictures. After the affective priming task, participants were presented with the first student description. We randomized whether the description of the high SES student or the low SES student appeared first.

After reading the description, participants were asked to judge the student on eight different dimensions. They were asked to indicate their judgments of the student's German language proficiency, mathematical performance, intelligence, school engagement, information processing, social isolation, emotionality, and assertiveness on a 7-point Likert scale ranging from 1 (*low*) to 7 (*high*).

When participants had finished this task, the next student description appeared with the same instructions. After participants had judged the second student on the same eight judgment dimensions, they were presented with the questionnaire assessing their explicit attitudes. They were asked to indicate their agreement on a 7-point Likert scale ranging from 1 (*no agreement*) to 7 (*high agreement*).

Finally, participants were administered the questionnaire assessing their demographic data, thanked, and debriefed. They were given 5 Euro for their participation.

RESULTS

Implicit Attitudes

First, we screened response latencies for errors and latencies below 250 ms and above 1500 ms (Hermans et al. 2005). These were excluded from further analysis. This resulted in the exclusion of 7.3% of the trials. Three participants were additionally excluded because they had excessive missing data (more than 20%). For one picture, the reliability analyses showed an internal consistency that was too low (Cronbach's alpha .19 to .50); hence, the trials containing this picture were excluded. Cronbach's alpha for the remaining pictures ranged from .42 to .82.

The remaining response latencies were submitted to a 2 (picture: high SES vs. low SES) × 2 (word: positive vs. negative) repeated-measures ANOVA. This ANOVA revealed a significant main effect of picture, $F(1, 64) = 7.48$, $p < .05$, $\eta^2_p = .11$, indicating that participants responded more quickly to high ($M = 719.50$, $SD = 106.75$) than to low SES pictures ($M = 736.11$, $SD = 103.78$).

The main effect of word was significant, $F(1, 64) = 81.77$, $p < .001$, $\eta^2_p = .56$, indicating that participants responded more quickly to positive ($M = 695.84$, $SD = 102.67$) than to negative words ($M = 759.78$, $SD = 109.78$). The two main effects were qualified by a significant interaction, $F(1, 64) = 15.92$, $p < .001$, $\eta^2_p = .20$ (see Figure 1 for all means and standard deviations).

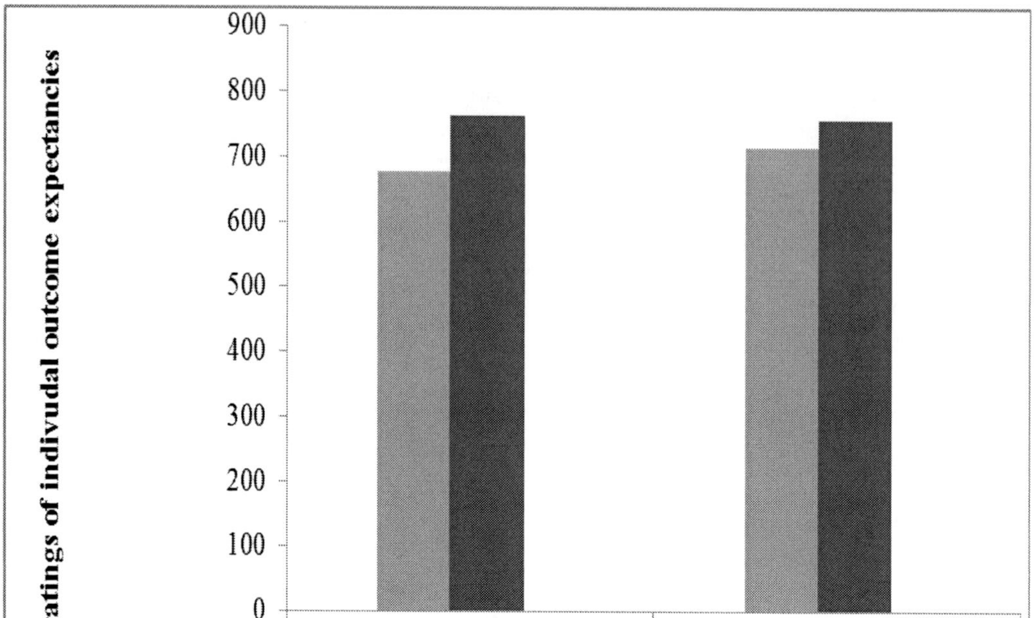

	high SES pictures	low SES pictures
Mean positive words	676.88	714.79
SD positive words	110.33	105.27
Mean negative words	762.11	757.44
SD negative words	114.94	113.88

Figure 1. Response latencies of the affective priming task as a function of picture and word.

Simple effect tests showed that participants responded more quickly to positive words than to negative words that followed high SES pictures, $t(64) = 9.54$, $p < .001$, $d = 1.18$. The same difference was found for the words that followed the low SES pictures, $t(64) = 4.86$, $p < .001$, $d = 0.60$.

However, participants responded more quickly to positive words that followed high SES than low SES pictures, $t(64) = 4.63$, $p < .001$, $d = 0.57$, but this difference was not found for negative words, $t(64) = 0.58$, $p = .56$, $d = 0.07$. Thus, implicit attitudes toward students from high SES families were positive.

Explicit Attitudes

First, we calculated the means for the three subscales that resulted from the factor analysis of the questionnaire. We then tested the means against the middle of the scale (3.5), the value that would indicate neutral attitudes. Preservice teachers' attitudes toward the learning and social behavior of high SES students were positive ($M = 4.30$, $SD = 0.84$), $t(64) = 7.73$, $d = 0.95$, $p < .001$. Their attitudes toward the school motivation and ambition of high SES students were also positive ($M = 4.99$, $SD = 0.61$), $t(64) = 19.72$, $d = 2.44$, $p < .001$, and they showed high egalitarian beliefs ($M = 3.76$, $SD = 0.88$), $t(64) = 2.35$, $d = 0.30$, $p < .05$.

Correlations between Implict and Explicit Attitudes

The response latencies of the implicit attitude measures were merged into a difference score with positive values reflecting positive attitudes toward high SES students. In order to calculate this score, we first subtracted the response latencies for the positive words from those for the negative words that followed the high SES pictures; we did the same for the words that followed the low SES pictures. In a second step, we subtracted the difference score for low SES pictures from the difference score for high SES pictures. Thus, positive values of the resulting difference scores reflected positive attitudes toward high SES students. The implicit attitude score had no significant correlation with the three dimensions of explicit attitudes: learning and social behavior (r = -.09, p = .50), school motivation and ambition (r = -.09, p = .50), and egalitarian beliefs (r = -.09, p = .49). Learning and social behavior was significantly correlated with school motivation and ambition, r = .26, $p < .05$, as well as with egalitarian beliefs, r = .38, $p < .05$. School motivation and ambition was not significantly correlated with egalitarian beliefs, r = .12, p = .34.

Relations between Attitudes and Judgments

To investigate how explicit and implicit attitudes contributed to the judgments, we computed several multiple regression analyses using the means of the three dimensions of the explicit attitudes questionnaire and the implicit attitudes difference score as predictors and the different judgment dimensions as criteria. We will report the multiple regression analysis for the high SES student first (see Table 3).

High SES Student. The judgment of mathematics performance was predicted by implicit attitudes as well as attitudes toward school motivation and ambition. Participants who were implicitly more positive and were more positive about the school motivation and ambition of high SES students judged the mathematics performance of the high SES student more favorably. The same direction of influence was observed for the judgments of information processing. Participants with more positive implicit attitudes and more positive attitudes toward school motivation and ambition rated the high SES student as less socially isolated. Participants with more positive attitudes toward school motivation and ambition judged the high SES student as less emotionally unstable. Regarding assertiveness, participants' ratings were lower when they had more positive implicit attitudes and more positive attitudes toward the learning and social behavior of high SES students. Neither German language proficiency, intelligence, nor school engagement judgments were predicted by implicit or explicit attitudes.

Table 3. Summary of the multiple regression analyses for variables predicting the judgments of the high SES No. 1 student (N = 65)

Variable	B	SE B	β
German language proficiency			
Implicit attitudes	< 0.01	< 0.01	.13
Learning and social behavior	0.07	0.17	.06

Table 3. (Continued)

Variable	B	SE B	β
School motivation and ambition	0.06	0.22	.04
Egalitarian beliefs	-0.07	0.16	-.06
Mathematics performance			
Implicit attitudes	< 0.01	< 0.01	.27*
Learning and social behavior	0.17	0.13	.16
School motivation and ambition	0.39	0.17	.27*
Egalitarian beliefs	-0.17	0.13	-.17
Intelligence			
Implicit attitudes	< 0.01	< 0.01	.13
Learning and social behavior	0.07	0.17	.06
School motivation and ambition	0.06	0.22	.04
Egalitarian beliefs	-0.07	0.16	-.06
Engagement			
Implicit attitudes	< 0.01	< 0.01	.14
Learning and social behavior	0.17	0.16	.14
School motivation and ambition	0.05	0.21	.03
Egalitarian beliefs	-0.29	0.15	-.26
Information processing			
Implicit attitudes	< 0.01	< 0.01	.24*
Learning and social behavior	0.09	0.12	.10
School motivation and ambition	0.55	0.15	.43*
Egalitarian beliefs	-0.01	0.11	.01
Social isolation			
Implicit attitudes	< 0.01	< 0.01	-.24*
Learning and social behavior	0.10	0.18	.06
School motivation and ambition	-0.70	0.23	-.37*
Egalitarian beliefs	0.03	0.17	.02
Emotionality			
Implicit attitudes	< 0.01	< 0.01	-.10
Learning and social behavior	0.05	0.17	.04
School motivation and ambition	-0.70	0.22	-.39*
Egalitarian beliefs	0.09	0.16	.08
Assertiveness			
Implicit attitudes	< 0.01	< 0.01	-.27*
Learning and social behavior	-0.36	0.17	-.28*
School motivation and ambition	0.14	0.22	.08
Egalitarian beliefs	0.11	0.16	.09

Note. R^2 = .02 for German language proficiency, R^2 = .18 for mathematics performance, R^2 = .04 for intelligence, R^2 = .08 for engagement, R^2 = .25 for information processing, R^2 = .17 for social isolation, R^2 = .15 for emotionality, R^2 = .13 for assertiveness.

*$p < .05$.

Low SES Student. Due to a computer error, only half of the participants received the description of the low SES student. However, attitudes predicted the judgments (see Table 4). Participants with more positive attitudes toward the learning and social behavior of high SES students judged the low SES student less favorably in German language proficiency and rated the student as less intelligent. Moreover, participants with more positive implicit attitudes toward high SES students, more positive attitudes toward the learning and social behavior of high SES students, and lower egalitarian beliefs judged the low SES student as more socially isolated. Multiple regression analyses showed that the judgments of mathematics performance, school engagement, information processing, emotionality, and assertiveness of the low SES student were not predicted by any attitude measure.

Table 4. Summary of multiple regression analyses for variables predicting the judgments of the low SES below-average student (N = 33)

Variable	B	SE B	β
German language proficiency			
Implicit attitudes	< 0.01	< 0.01	-.12
Learning and social behavior	-0.64	0.26	-.49*
School motivation and ambition	-0.15	0.33	-.08
Egalitarian beliefs	0.24	0.25	.18
Mathematics performance			
Implicit attitudes	< 0.01	< 0.01	< .01
Learning and social behavior	-0.26	0.22	-.25
School motivation and ambition	0.22	0.28	.14
Egalitarian beliefs	0.08	0.21	-.08
Intelligence			
Implicit attitudes	< 0.01	< 0.01	-.09
Learning and social behavior	-0.67	0.22	-.58*
School motivation and ambition	-0.14	0.28	-.08
Egalitarian beliefs	0.31	0.22	.27
Engagement			
Implicit attitudes	< 0.01	< 0.01	.01
Learning and social behavior	0.03	0.26	.02
School motivation and ambition	-0.21	0.33	-.12
Egalitarian beliefs	-0.03	0.25	-.03
Information processing			
Implicit attitudes	< 0.01	< 0.01	-.03
Learning and social behavior	-0.45	0.25	-.36
School motivation and ambition	-0.03	0.32	-.02
Egalitarian beliefs	0.17	0.25	.14
Social isolation			
Implicit attitudes	0.01	< 0.01	.45*
Learning and social behavior	1.23	0.48	.46*
School motivation and ambition	-0.26	0.61	-.08
Egalitarian beliefs	-1.01	0.47	-.38*

Table 4. (Continued)

Variable	B	SE B	β
Emotionality			
Implicit attitudes	< 0.01	< 0.01	-.05
Learning and social behavior	0.24	0.39	.13
School motivation and ambition	0.84	0.50	-.30
Egalitarian beliefs	0.23	0.38	-.12
Assertiveness			
Implicit attitudes	< 0.01	< 0.01	.09
Learning and social behavior	-0.05	0.26	-.04
School motivation and ambition	-0.37	0.33	.-.20
Egalitarian beliefs	0.35	0.25	.28

Note. R^2 = .19 for German language proficiency, R^2 = .07 for mathematics performance, R^2 = .25 for intelligence, R^2 = .02 for engagement, R^2 = .10 for information processing, R^2 = .33 for social isolation, R^2 = .12 for emotionality, R^2 = .11 for assertiveness.

*$p < .05$.

Discussion

To our knowledge, this study was the first to assess implicit and explicit attitudes toward high SES students and the relations of these attitudes to judgments. We found positive implicit and explicit attitudes toward high SES students, and consequently, those positive attitudes contributed to a more favorable judgment of the high SES student and to a less favorable judgment of the low SES student. However, attitudes were not able to predict each judgment dimension. For the high SES student, we found that more positive attitudes resulted in more favorable judgments of mathematics achievement and information processing. Participants with more positive attitudes toward high SES students rated the high SES student as less socially isolated, less emotional, and less assertive. For the low SES student, we found that more positive attitudes toward high SES students resulted in less favorable judgments of the low SES student's German language proficiency and intelligence and in higher ratings of social isolation. The judgments of school engagement could not be predicted by attitudes. Thus, one might ask which factors drive this judgment dimension. As school engagement has been suggested to be malleable and context-sensitive (Fredricks, Blumenfeld, and Paris 2004), it might be plausible that attitudes do not contribute to the judgment of this construct. In particular, if preservice teachers consider the fact that school engagement might depend strongly on contextual factors and vary from situation to situation, they might rely less on stereotypical expectations and thereby rely less on their attitudes when judging students' school engagement. Since stereotypical expectations are quite accurate (Jussim and Harber 2005), teachers and preservice teachers most likely did not develop expectations about school engagement, particularly if they realized that this dimension does not relate to high or low SES students but rather to different contextual factors. Hence, in order to gain insight into the dimensions that are subject to stereotypical expectations, future research should ask teachers and preservice teachers which attributes they believe high SES students share.

The MODE model suggests that implicit attitudes guide spontaneous behavior and that explicit attitudes elicit more controlled behavior (Fazio 1990). However, our results indicate that most of these processes are mixed (Olson and Fazio 2009) because preservice teachers' implicit and explicit attitudes were able to predict their judgments. Implicit attitudes did not contribute to each judgment; nevertheless, they had predictive value over and above explicit attitudes. Information processing, social isolation, assertiveness ratings, and most importantly, the ratings of mathematics achievement were predicted by implicit attitudes. This seems particularly important because the judgment of mathematics achievement plays a pivotal role in the educational success of the student, and preservice teachers might not necessarily be aware that their implicit attitudes may be coloring their judgments. However, the mathematics achievement judgments in our study did not rely on actual performance on mathematical tests but on a verbal description of the student. Future research should present participants with curriculum-based school work tasks in mathematics in order to investigate whether implicit attitudes influence grading.

Explicit attitudes were derived from a questionnaire developed specifically for this study because existing questionnaires on social class were designed to assess experiences with classism rather than teachers' attitudes. Our questionnaire indicated three different factors that were interpreted as learning and social behavior, school motivation and ambition, and egalitarin beliefs. Learning and social behavior and school motivation were found to be the factors with the highest predictive values. In particular, school motivation and ambition predicted preservice teachers' judgments of the high SES student. As high SES parents hold higher educational standards for their children (de Graaf 1988) and show more involvement (Luster, Rhoades, and Haas 1989), which is linked to student achievement (Spera 2005), it is obvious that preservice teachers' attitudes toward school motivation and ambition contribute to their judgments. The attitudes toward the learning and social behavior of high SES students primarily contributed to the judgment of the low SES student such that participants with more positive attitudes toward high SES students judged the low SES student less favorably. This also makes sense if teachers have differential behavioral expectations for high and low SES students (Diamond, Randolph, and Spillane 2004).

When interpreting the results of our study, some limitations should be kept in mind. First, our questionnaire was developed specifically for the purpose of the current study. The factor analysis indicated three factors, and although the items on each factor showed sufficient-to-good internal consistencies, a replication is necessary to confirm the factor structure and the validity of the scales. The current study already provided some support for the construct validity of the scales by demonstrating the observed attitude-behavior link between judgments and explicit attitudes. Although we investigated the concurrent validity of the questionnaire by comparing the implicit and explicit attitude scores, the association between the measures was low. However, implicit and explicit measures of attitudes often show a low or no relationship even when both measures are significant predictors of the judgment (Fazio et al. 1995). On a theoretical level, they tap into different constructs (Banaji 2001) and therefore might not necessarily be correlated.

Second, we did not vary student gender as we used pictures and descriptions of only boys. Although it might be expected that teachers' and perservice teachers' attitudes toward high SES students might be positive in general, this effect should be more pronounced for boys (Auwarter and Aruguete 2008). Hence, future research should replicate this study with a manipulation of student gender in order to investigate whether gender affects attitudes and whether attitudes contribute differently to judgments according to the gender of the student.

Third, due to a computer error, only 33 participants responded to the low SES student. This might weaken the power of the multiple regression analyses concerning the judgments of the low SES student because we were underpowered for the detection of smaller effects. Hence, these data should be interpreted with caution, and future research should validate the findings using a larger sample.

Although we showed that attitudes contribute to judgments, they are not the only factor underlying judgments as can be seen in the levels of explained variance.

Thus, there are other factors that contribute to student judgments not investigated here. Future research is needed to determine which factors play roles in the judgments besides attitudes. One factor that might be valuable to investigate is efficacy, as highly efficacious teachers were found to rely less on SES information about the student when making special education referrals (Podell and Soodak 1993). Another factor might be the personality traits of teachers and preservice teachers. Research has provided evidence that preservice teachers in particular feel more anxious and more altruistic than their peers who are not preparing to teach (Decker and Rimm-Kaufman 2008). Obviously, the comparison between teachers and preservice teachers might also prove fruitful as experience might influence judgments in that more experienced teachers might judge students more positively (Podell and Tournaki 2007). Thus, future research should consider additional teacher characteristics in order to gain a deeper insight into the factors, besides attitudes, that drive judgments.

Acknowledgment

We would like to thank Stefanie Tekath for her help in collecting the data.

References

Alvidrez, Jennifer, and Rhona Weinstein. 1999. "Early Teacher Perceptions and Later Student Academic Achievement." *Journal of Educational Psychology,* 91: 731–46. doi:10.1037//0022-0663.91.4.731.

Auwarter, A. E., and M. S. Aruguete. 2008. "Effects of Student Gender and Socioeconomic Status on Teacher Perceptions." *The Journal of Educational Research,* 101: 243–46. doi:10.3200/JOER.101.4.243-246.

Babad, E. 1993. "Teachers' Differential Behavior." *Educational Psychology Review,* 5: 347–76. doi:10.1007/BF01320223.

Banaji, M. R. 2001. "Implicit Attitudes Can Be Measured." In The Nature of Remembering: Essays in Honor of Robert G. Crowder, edited by H. L. Roediger, J. S. Nairne, I. Neath, and A. Surprenant, 117–50. Washington, DC: American Psychological Association.

Bassili, J. N., and R. D. Brown. 2005. "Implicit and Explicit Attitudes: Research, Challenges, and Theory." In Handbook of Attitudes and Attitude Change, edited by D. Albarracín, B. T. Johnson, and M. P. Zanna, 543–74. Mahwah, NJ: Erlbaum.

Bradley, G. 2007. "Job Tenure as a Moderator of Stressor-Strain Relations: A Comparison of Experienced and New-Start Teachers." *Work and Stress,* 21: 48–64. doi:10.1080/02678370701264685.

De Boer, H., R. J. Bosker, and M. P. C. van der Werf. 2010. "Sustainability of Teacher Expectation Bias Effects on Long-Term Student Performance." *Journal of Educational Psychology,* 102: 168–79. doi:10.1037/a0017289.

De Graaf, P. M. 1988. "Parents' Financial and Cultural Resources, Grades, and Transition to Secondary School in the Federal Republic of Germany." *European Sociological Review,* 4: 209–21.

De Houwer, J. 2006. "What Are Implicit Measures and Why Are We Using Them?" In Handbook of Implicit Cognition and Addiction, edited by R. W. Wiers and A. W. Stacy, 11–28. Thousand Oaks, CA: Sage Publisher.

De Houwer, J., and A. Moors. 2007. "How to Define and Examine the Implicitness of Implicit Measures." In Implicit Measures of Attitudes: Procedures and Controversies, edited by B. Wittenbrink and N. Schwarz, 179–94. New York, NY: Guilford Press.

Decker, L. E., and S. E. Rimm-Kaufman. 2008. "Personality Characteristics and Teacher Beliefs among Pre-Service Teachers." *Teacher Education Quarterly,* 35: 45–64.

Devine, P. G. 1989. "Stereotypes and Prejudice: Their Automatic and Controlled Components." *Journal of Personality and Social Psychology,* 56: 5–18. doi:10.1037//0022-3514.56.1.5.

Diamond, J. B., A. Randolph, and J. P. Spillane. 2004. "Teachers' Expectations and Sense of Responsibility for Student Learning: The Importance of Race, Class, and Organizational Habitus." *Anthropology and Education Quarterly,* 35 (March): 75–98. doi:10.1525/aeq.2004.35.1.75.

Dovidio, J. F., J. C. Brigham, B. S. Johnson, and S. L. Gaertner. 1996. "Stereotyping, Prejudice, and Discrimination: Another Look." In Foundations of Stereotypes and Stereotyping, edited by C. N. Macrae, M. Hewstone, and C. Stangor, 276–319. New York: Guilford Press.

Fazio, R. H. 1986. "How Do Attitudes Guide Behavior?" In The Handbook of Motivation and Cognition: Foundations of Social Behavior, edited by R. M. Sorrentino and E. T. Higgins, 204–43. New York, NY: Guilford Press.

———. 1990. "Multiple Processes by Which Attitudes Guide Behavior: The MODE Model as an Integrative Framework." In Advances in Experimental Social Psychology, edited by M. P. Zanna, 75–109, Vol. 23. New York, NY: Academic Press.

———. 2007. "Attitudes as Object-Evaluation Associations of Varying Strength." *Social Cognition,* 25: 664–703. doi:10.1521/soco.2007.25.5.603.

Fazio, R. H., J. R. Jackson, B. C. Dunton, and C. J. Williams. 1995. "Variability in Automatic Activation as an Unobtrusive Measure of Racial Attitudes: A Bona Fide Pipeline?" *Journal of Personality and Social Psychology,* 69: 1013–27. doi:10.1037/0022-3514.69.6.1013.

Fazio, R. H., and D. R. Roskos-Ewoldsen. 2005. "Acting as We Feel: When and How Attitudes Guide Behavior." In *Persuasion:* Psychological Insights and Perspectives, edited by T. C. Brock and M. C. Green, 2nd ed., 41–62. Thousand Oaks, CA: Sage Publications.

Fazio, R. H., D. M. Sanbonmatsu, M. C. Powell, and F. R. Kardes. 1986. "On the Automatic Activation of Attitudes." *Journal of Personality and Social Psychology,* 50 (February): 229–38. doi:10.1037//0022-3514.50.2.229.

Fazio, R. H., and T. Towles-Schwen. 1999. "The MODE Model of Attitude-Behavior Processes." In Dual Process Theories in Social Psychology, edited by S. Chaiken and Y. Trope, 97–116. New York, NY: Guilford Press.

Fredricks, J. A., P. C. Blumenfeld, and A. H. Paris. 2004. "School Engagement: Potential of the Concept, State of the Evidence." *Review of Educational Research,* 74: 59–109. doi:10.3102%2F00346543074001059.

Frey, A. 2002. "Predictors of Placement Recommendations for Children with Behavioral or Emotional Disorders." *Behavioral Disorders,* 27: 126–36.

Gawronski, B., and G. V. Bodenhausen. 2006. "Associative and Propositional Processes in Evaluation: An Integrative Review of Implicit and Explicit Attitude Change." *Psychological Bulletin,* 132 (September): 692–731. doi:10.1037/0033-2909.132.5.692 http://www.ncbi.nlm.nih.gov/pubmed/16910748.

Glock, S., J. Kneer, and C. Kovacs. 2013. "Preservice Teachers' Implicit Attitudes toward Students with and without Immigration Background: A Pilot Study." *Studies in Educational Evaluation,* 39: 204–10. doi:10.1016/j.stueduc.2013.09.003.

Glock, S., D. Unz, and C. Kovacs. 2012. "Beyond Fear Appeals: Contradicting Positive Smoking Outcome Expectancies to Influence Smokers' Implicit Attitudes, Perception, and Behavior." *Addictive Behaviors,* 37 (April): 548–51. doi:10.1016/j.addbeh.2011.11.032.

Greenwald, A. G., D. E. McGhee, and J. K. L. Schwartz. 1998. "Measuring Individual Differences in Implicit Cognition: The Implicit Association Test." *Journal of Personality and Social Psychology,* 74: 1464–80. doi:10.1037/0022-3514.74.6.1464.

Harvey, D. G., and G. T. Slatin. 1975. "The Relationship between Child's SES and Teacher Expectations: A Test of the Middle-Class Bias Hypothesis." *Social Forces,* 54: 140–59. doi:10.1093/sf/54.1.140.

Hermans, D., F. Baeyens, S. Lamote, A. Spruyt, and P. Eelen. 2005. "Affective Priming as an Indirect Measure of Food Preferences Acquired through Odor Conditioning." *Experimental Psychology,* 52: 180–86. doi:10.1027/1618-3169.52.3.180.

Hermans, D., D. Vansteenwegen, G. Crombet, F. Baeyens, and P. Eelen. 2002. "Expectancy-Learning and Evaluate Learning in Human Classical Conditioning: Affective Priming as an Indirect and Unobtrusive Measure of Conditioned Stimulus Valence." *Behaviour Research and Therapy,* 40: 217–34. doi:10.1016/S0005-7967(01)00006-7.

Hofmann, W., T. Gschwendner, L. Castelli, and M. Schmitt. 2008. "Implicit and Explicit Attitudes and Interracial Interaction: The Moderating Role of Situationally Available Control Resources." *Group Processes and Intergroup Relations,* 11: 69–87. doi:10.1177/1368430207084847.

Hofmann, W., T. Gschwendner, B. A. Nosek, and M. Schmitt. 2005. "What Moderates Implicit—explicit Consistency?" *European Review of Social Psychology,* 16 (January): 335–90. doi:10.1080/10463280500443228 http://www.tandfonline.com/doi/abs/10.1080/10463280500443228.

Jussim, Lee, and Kent D. Harber. 2005. "Teacher Expectations and Self-Fulfilling Prophecies: Knowns and Unknowns, Resolved and Unresolved Controversies."

Personality and Social Psychology Review, 9: 131–55. doi:10.1207/s15327957 pspr0902_3.

Langhout, R. D., F. Rosselli, and J. Feinstein. 2007. "Assessing Classism in Academic Settings." *The Review of Higher Education,* 30: 145–84. doi:10.1353/rhe.2006.0073 http://muse.jhu.edu/content/crossref/journals/review_of_higher_education/v030/30.2lang hout.html.

Luster, T., K. Rhoades, and B. Haas. 1989. "The Relation between Parental Values and Parenting Behavior: A Test of the Kohn Hypothesis." *Journal of Marriage and Family,* 51: 139–47. doi:10.2307%2F352375.

McCombs, Regina C., and Judith Gay. 1988. "Effects of Race, Class, and IQ Information on Judgments of Parochial Grade School Teachers." *The Journal of Social Psychology,* 128: 647–52. doi:10.1080/00224545.1988.9922918.

Neumann, Roland, Katharina Hülsenbeck, and Beate Seibt. 2004. "Attitudes towards People with AIDS and Avoidance Behavior: Automatic and Reflective Bases of Behavior." *Journal of Experimental Social Psychology,* 40 (July): 543–50. doi:10.1016/j.jesp.2003.10.006 http://linkinghub.elsevier.com/retrieve/pii/S00221031 03001677.

Olson, M. A., and R. H. Fazio. 2009. "Implicit and Explicit Measures of Attitudes: The Perspective of the MODE Model." In Attitudes: Insights from the New Implicit Measures, edited by R. E. Petty, R. H. Fazio, and P. Briñol, 19–63. New York, NY: Psychology Press.

Petty, R. E., R. H. Fazio, and P. Briñol. 2009. "The New Implicit Measures: An Overview." In Attitudes: Insights from the New Implicit Measures, edited by R. E. Petty, R. H. Fazio, and P. Briñol, 3–18. New York, NY: Psychology Press.

Podell, D. M., and L. C. Soodak. 1993. "Teacher Efficacy and Bias in Special Education Referrals." *The Journal of Educational Research,* 86: 247–53. doi:10.1080/ 00220671.1993.9941836.

Podell, D. M., and N. Tournaki. 2007. "General and Special Educators' Predictions of Student Success as a Function of Learner Characteristics and Teacher Experience." *Teacher Education and Special Education: The Journal of the Teacher Education Division of the Council for Exceptional Children,* 30 (4): 249–63. doi:10.1177/088840640703000405. http://tes.sagepub.com/cgi/doi/10.1177/088840640703000405.

Rudman, L. A. 2004. "Sources of Implicit Attitudes." *Current Directions in Psychological Science,* 13 (April): 79–82. doi:10.1111/j.0963-7214.2004.00279.x. http:// cdp.sagepub.com/lookup/doi/10.1111/j.0963-7214.2004.00279.x.

Sanbonmatsu, D. M., and R. H. Fazio. 1990. "The Role of Attitudes in Memory-Based Decision Making." *Journal of Personality and Social Psychology,* 59: 614–22. doi:10.1037//0022-3514.59.4.614.

Santavirta, N., S. Solovieva, and T. Theorell. 2007. "The Association between Job Strain and Emotional Exhaustion in a Cohort of 1.028 Finnish Teachers." *British Journal of Educational Psychology,* 77: 213–28. doi:10.1348/000709905X92045.

Schwarz, N., and G. Bohner. 2001. "The Construction of Attitudes." In Blackwell Handbook of Social Psychology: Intraindividuel Processes, edited by A. Tesser and N. Schwarz, 436–57. Malden, MA: Blackwell.

Spera, C. 2005. "A Review of the Relationship among Parenting Practices, Parenting Styles, and Adolescent School Achievement." *Educational Psychology Review,* 17 (June): 125–

46. doi:10.1007/s10648-005-3950-1. http://link.springer.com/10.1007/s10648-005-3950-1.

Steffens, M. C. 2004. "Is the Implicit Association Test Immune to Faking?" *Experimental Psychology (formerly "Zeitschrift Für Experimentelle Psychologie"),* 51 (June): 165–79. doi:10.1027/1618-3169.51.3.165 http://psycontent.metapress.com/openurl.asp?genre=article&id=doi:10.1027/1618-3169.51.3.165.

Strack, F., and R. Deutsch. 2004. "Reflective and Impulsive Determinants of Social Behavior." *Personality and Social Psychology Review,* 8 (January): 220–47. doi:10.1207/s15327957pspr0803_1.

Thompson, M. N., and L. M. Subich. 2013. "Development and Exploration of the Experiences with Classism Scale." *Journal of Career Assessment,* 21 (June): 139–58. doi:10.1177/1069072712450494. http://jca.sagepub.com/cgi/doi/10.1177/1069072712450494.

Yagil, D. 1998. "If Anything Can Go Wrong It Will: Occupational Stress among Inexperienced Teachers." *International Journal of Stress Management,* 5: 179–88.

In: Stereotypes and Stereotyping
Editor: Claude Fields
ISBN: 978-1-63484-510-6

Chapter 2

STEREOTYPES OF DISADVANTAGED STUDENTS PERPETUATE EDUCATIONAL DISPARITIES

Bettina J. Casad[1] and Abdiel J. Flores[2]
[1]University of Missouri-St. Louis, St. Louis, MO, US
[2]Columbia University, New York, NY, US

ABSTRACT

This review documents trends in educational disparities related to students' gender, race, social class, and college generational status. More women earn four-year degrees than men, yet they are underrepresented in science, technology, engineering, and mathematics fields. The racial gap in standardized testing still remains and continues to grow. The gap between high-and low-income students' educational attainment is widening. A related phenomenon is the underrepresentation of first generation college students in higher education, particularly in elite universities, compared to their continuing generation counterparts. How do researchers account for these demographic disparities in higher education? Research from social psychology and related fields reports that social and cultural factors are largely responsible for creating and maintaining these educational disparities, thus social interventions can remedy this social problem. The chapter concludes by reviewing empirical work documenting the successful implementation of interventions to reduce achievement gaps.

Keywords: educational disparities, achievement gap, race, gender, social class

Education is an important social institution that serves to prepare children and young adults to thrive in modern society and contribute to economic development. In hierarchical, capitalistic societies such as the US, education is thought to be the great equalizer to allow all children, no matter their demographic background, to obtain the education and training they need to obtain fruitful employment. However, as the education achievement gap between the rich and poor widens (Reardon, 2011) it is evident that education is not fully serving its equalizing purpose (Bailey and Dynarski, 2011). This chapter reviews current national trends and interdisciplinary research in psychology, sociology, and education documenting educational disparities related to students' gender, race and ethnicity, social class, and college generational status. The chapter concludes with suggestions for interventions to reduce achievement gaps.

EDUCATIONAL DISPARITIES

Gender

Although small gender differences in reading (favoring girls) and math performance (favoring boys) persist, the gender gap in educational achievement has disappeared in the last 40 years, to the point where some critics argue that boys are being left behind (AAUW, 2008). Nationally, more women earn bachelor and master degrees than men, yet the fields in which they earn their degrees and obtain employment indicate a persistent gender gap (AAUW, 2008; 2010).

Women now approach equal representation in degrees in formerly male-dominated professions such as medicine (49%) and law (46%; Snyder and Dillow, 2011), yet women still remain underrepresented in some sciences such as physics (20%), computer sciences (18%), and engineering (18%; National Science Foundation, 2011). Disparities in degree attainment lead to disparities in the workplace, with women constituting only 25% of the science, technology, engineering, and mathematics (STEM) workforce (US Department of Commerce, 2011). This is particularly disconcerting as STEM careers are expected to grow 20% over the next 10 years, and women in STEM earn one-third more than people in non-STEM jobs (US Department of Commerce, 2011).

Race and Ethnicity

The racial gap in standardized testing still remains, indicating black, Latino, and Native American students score lower on standardized tests compared to their Euro American and Asian American counterparts. Out of all the students who took the Scholastic Aptitude Test in 2010, Hispanic students scored an average of 267 points lower than whites, and black students scored an average of 352 points lower than whites (The College Board, 2011).

Racial minorities are also underrepresented in higher education and are less likely to pursue graduate degrees compared to their white counterparts. White students represented 62% of college students enrolled in 4-year degree granting institutions in 2010-2011 whereas black students represented 15% and Hispanic students represented only 14% of students (National Center for Education Statistics [NCES], 2012). Similarly, racial minorities are less likely to enroll in post-baccalaureate education. In 2010-2011, black students represented only 14% of all students enrolled in master or doctoral programs and Hispanic students represented only 8%, compared to 69% of white students (NCES, 2012).

Racial minorities are also less likely to complete their degrees. In 2005, only 47% of black and 61% of Hispanic students completed a bachelor degree compared to 63% of white students (NCES, 2010).

Social Class

Research has shown that the achievement gap between high-and low-income students has widened by 40% in the past four decades and is now nearly twice as large as the racial gap (Reardon, 2011), reflecting the same shrinkage of the middle class seen in the US economy. In fact, parental income has long been a predictor of other important academic outcomes. For instance, Ostrove and Long (2007) found that students from lower socioeconomic backgrounds reported lower academic adjustment, sense of belonging in academia, quality of experience in higher education, and academic performance. Research has shown that students from low-income families tend to develop language skills at a slower rate and are at risk for greater reading difficulties (Aikens and Barbarin, 2008), as well as having more problems with math (Coley, 2002). Although the mechanisms through which this relationship exists have been widely discussed—whether it is access to resources, school quality, parent educational attainment, or neighborhood conditions—the insurmountable work in this area clearly shows that students from low-income families achieve less academically compared to their affluent counterparts.

First Generation College Students

Academia has a legacy of educating privileged students who have the social and economic status to obtain a higher education, which is particularly true of private and Ivy League colleges and universities (Bernstein, 1974; Bourdieu and Passeron, 1990; Bourdieu and Wacquant, 1992). Students whose parents and grandparents have attended college typically have advantages such as preferential admission, alumni networks, parental role models, and greater parental financial investment (Kornrich and Furstenberg, 2013). Students who are the first in their family to obtain a college degree, or first generation college students, typically do not have these advantages and lack parental role models to help them navigate the path to a degree (Housel and Harvey, 2009; McCarron and Inkelas, 2006). First-generation college students often have lower grades and have higher dropout rates and are less likely to pursue graduate school compared to students whose parents earned a college degree (Housel and Harvey, 2009; Pascarella, Pierson, Wolniak and Terenzini, 2004; Pike and Kuh, 2005). First generation college students may also experience stigma and feel excluded and ostracized from the prestigious ivory tower that they have breached (Casad and Flores, 2015; Francis and Miller, 2008; Johnson, Richeson and Finkel, 2011).

Social and Cultural Factors in Educational Disparities

How do researchers account for these demographic disparities in higher education? Research from social psychology, sociology, and related fields reports that social and cultural factors are largely responsible for creating and maintaining these educational disparities. Prominent research in the areas of stereotype threat, person-environment fit, and educational bias is reviewed to explain these disparities. Given that social and cultural factors are a major cause of achievement gaps, social interventions can remedy this social problem. This chapter concludes by reviewing empirical work documenting the successful implementation of interventions to reduce achievement gaps, for example, by eliminating stereotype threat through self-affirmation, reframing lay theories of intelligence, and fostering a sense of identity and belonging.

Stereotype Threat

Popular and lay theories that explain these disparities are often based on stereotypes, characterizing those with lower achievement as intellectually inferior compared to their high achieving counterparts. Stereotypes linking racial minorities, low-income students, and women to intellectual inferiority are prevalent in our culture (Steele, 2010). Yet, research in social psychology has shown that the achievement gap between high- and low-status group members is due, at least in part, to a phenomenon known as stereotype threat (Steele and Aronson, 1995).

Stereotype threat is the concern that stigmatized group members experience when their behavior can potentially be judged as stereotypical. The threat of confirming negative stereotypes triggers a variety of mechanisms that work together to impair performance on evaluative tasks, such as standardized exams (Schmader, Johns and Forbes, 2008). Low status group members may experience this in situations where negative stereotypes about their intellectual ability can be attributed to their performance, such as in standardized testing environments. Although how individuals respond is contingent on context, research has shown that environmental cues can increase the likelihood that minority group members will experience stereotype threat. For example, situations that make a stigmatized identity salient are more likely to produce stereotype threat effects (Inzlicht, Aronson and Mendoza-Denton, 2009). Field experiments have shown that demographic questions (e.g., race and gender) that students answer before taking a standardized exam are enough to impair minority group members' performance (Stricker and Ward, 2004). Further, by simply moving those questions to the end of the test, research has shown that women and racial minorities perform better on standardized exams, such as the Advanced Placement Calculus Exam (Stricker and Ward, 2004).

More recently, research shows that stereotype threat not only affects performance, but also extends to other areas, such as students' self-perceptions, academic goals, and even impairs learning (Rydell, Rydell and Boucher, 2010; Schmader, Johns and Barquissau, 2008). It has been hypothesized that stereotype threat may also contribute to the high dropout rate among racial minorities and other underrepresented groups in higher education. Research has shown that racial minorities may disengage from domains in which they are stereotyped to cope with this threat in an effort to protect their self-esteem (Major, Spencer, Schmader, Wolfe and Crocker, 1998). Chronic disengagement can lead students to completely disidentify with academia and subsequently drop out of school (Inzlicht et al., 2009; Major and Schmader, 1998).

Bias in Education

Another source from which students may encounter bias is their professors. Although educators may have students' best interests at heart, there is evidence that teachers' own personal biases seep into the classroom, which can have a profound impact on students' quality of educational experiences (AAUW, 2008; Kozol, 1991). Research has shown that in general, instructors tend to expect lower performance from Latino and black students compared to white students, lower expectations for girls than boys in math and science, are less likely to give positive feedback to these students, and are less likely to be encouraging (AAUW, 2010; Tenenbaum and Ruck, 2007). However, researchers found that expectations of minority students are driven by instructors' implicit bias (van den Bergh, Denessen, Hornstra, Voeten and Holland, 2010). Specifically, instructors with implicit racial bias were more likely to evaluate minority students as less intelligent and having less potential for success in the future. Further, the racial achievement gap was greater in classes with instructors with high implicit racial biases (van den Bergh et al., 2010).

Similarly, instructors' beliefs about intelligence (i.e., entity vs. incremental theories of intelligence) also influence students in the classroom. For instance, researchers found that instructors who held fixed (entity) views of intelligence were more likely to judge students as having lower mathematical ability than instructors with an incremental view of intelligence (Rattan, Good and Dweck, 2012). Students with teachers holding an entity view also reported lower motivation and lower expectations for their own performance. In contrast, instructors with an incremental view of intelligence were more likely to use comforting strategies with struggling students, such as assigning less homework.

Person-Environment Fit

Several social psychological theories have examined factors related to how well a particular person (e.g., women, racial minorities, lower income students) fits into particular contexts (e.g., male-dominated domains, predominately white universities), such as social role theory (Eagly and Steffen, 1984), role congruity theory (Eagly and Karau, 2002), and person-organization fit (Heilman, 1983). Perceptions of fit are beliefs regarding how well one's personal characteristics align with those of the environment (Franco-Zamudio, 2009). Positive outcomes, such as benefits to psychological well-being (Schneider, Smith and Goldstein, 2000), are related to having person-environment fit, whereas negative outcomes, such as disengagement from academics (Jansen and Kristof-Brown, 2006), are associated with lack of person-environment fit. Women, racial minorities, lower income students, and first generation college students are all at risk of experiencing a lack of person-environment fit in higher education (Dovidio, Gaertner, Niemann and Snider, 2001).

Each of us has multiple social identities, such as belonging to a certain gender, racial or ethnic group, social class, or occupation. However, people vary in the importance they place on each of their social identities (Tajfel and Turner, 1979; 1986) and the emphasis on one identity over another can vary by context (Inzlicht, Aronson, Good and McKay, 2006; Inzlicht and Ben-Zeev, 2000). The importance and emphasis we place on each of our social identities can influence our perceptions of fit with a given social environment (Dovidio et al., 2001). For example, a black student may feel a lack of fit while attending a predominantly white university, particularly when his/her racial identity is emphasized more so that his/her identity as a college student (Inzlicht et al., 2006; Walton and Carr, 2011). The identities we consciously or unconsciously choose to identity with in a given context have important implications for academic performance. For example, one's identification as a college student is a better predictor of academic performance and degree attainment than identification with one's racial or ethnic identity (Bonous-Hammarth, 2000; Osborne and Walker, 2006). Also, certain social identities are more highly valued in academia, such as white or Asian racial identities, higher social class, and continuing generation college students (those whose parents hold a college degree; Dovidio et al., 2001; Ostrove and Long, 2007; Steele and Aronson, 1995). Stereotypes of racial minorities, the working class, and first generation college students are related to lower academic expectations (Lott, 2002; Steele and Aronson, 1995; Terenzini, Springer, Yaeger, Pascarella and Nora, 1996), which often predicts lower academic performance (Tenenbaum and Ruck, 2007). Perceptions of lack of fit in academia and lower academic performance can lead to disengagement from academics and dropping out of college altogether (Inzlicht et al., 2009; Major and Schmader, 1998).

Research suggests that individuals' social identity also relates to the academic majors and occupations they pursue, based in part on perceptions of fit (Diekman, Brown, Johnston and Clark, 2010; Inzlicht et al., 2009). For example women may avoid STEM disciplines because they do not see their personal life goals as congruent with the expected quality of life of a STEM student or scientist (Diekman et al., 2010). Many women have communal goals, or an orientation to nurture others. Consistent with social role theory, women more than men endorse communal goals (Diekman et al., 2010). Women also report that STEM careers are incompatible with communal goals (Diekman et al., 2010), which is one possible reason why fewer women than men seek STEM careers. Societal stereotypes of STEM disciplines suggest that scientists, mathematicians, and engineers are typically male, work in isolation in a laboratory, value competitiveness, and have little time for family (Barbercheck, 2001; Steele, 2002). Stereotypes of scientists make STEM unappealing fields of study or work for many women (Cheryan, 2012; Cheryan et al., 2009), particularly those with communal goals (Diekman et al., 2010).

Sense of Belonging

The mechanism that explains the relationship between perceptions of fit and academic outcomes is sense of belonging. When individuals perceive a lack of fit within a particular context, they may feel isolated, marginalized, or otherwise feel they do not belong in that particular environment (Contreras and Gandara, 2006; Gloria and Castellanos, 2006). Having a sense of belonging to a group is a fundamental motivation of human behavior (Baumeister and Leary, 1995) and provides a sense of being valued and accepted by members within that group (Good, Rattan and Dweck, 2012).

Recent research by Good et al. (2012) found that rather than a general need to belong specific types of belonging in specific environments can determine outcomes. They examined the role of sense of belonging in academics, but further specified the construct as belonging in the math domain, and this math belonging predicted motivation and academic achievement over time. Specifically, women who perceived that their academic context (e.g., math professors, peers, and greater academic community) endorsed fixed beliefs of math intelligence and endorsed stereotypes about women's math ability reported lower motivation to pursue future math education and had lower math grades. This relationship was fully mediated by women's sense of belonging in math. Thus, sense of belonging, in this case to math, is the mechanism through which negative perceptions of fit (e.g., women do not belong in math classes due to low ability) lead to negative academic outcomes such as reduced achievement motivation and lower performance (Good et al., 2012).

Research by Walton et al. (2007; 2011) documented the role of sense of belonging in racial minority youths' academic achievement (Walton and Carr, 2011; Walton and Cohen, 2007). Negative stereotypes about non-Asian racial minorities' academic intelligence can undermine their performance, as reviewed previously in the section on stereotype threat. These negative stereotypes affect minorities' sense of belonging in academic environments and can lower their achievement motivation and pursuit of a college degree (Walton and Carr, 2011). In one experiment, black students who experienced belonging uncertainty in computer science evaluated their chance for success in the field lower than black students who experienced a sense of belonging (Walton and Cohen, 2007). Further, black students who felt belonging uncertainly in computer science generalized their potential lack of future success to their racial group and discouraged black (but not white) peers from pursuing advising in computer science (Walton and Cohen, 2007).

Sense of belonging in academics is also important for students from lower social class backgrounds (Ostrove and Long, 2007). Beyond affordability, the desire to belong has influenced students' choices regarding where to attend college, for example Ivy League or state schools (Ostrove and Long, 2007). Many working-class students choose to attend technical colleges instead of four year universities because of the need to belong (Read, Archer, and Leathwood, 2003). Research indicates a positive correlation between both objective and subjective social class and sense of belonging in academics (Ostrove and Long, 2007). More importantly, sense of belonging is a mediator between social class and academic and social adjustment in college. That is, the positive relationship between social class and academic and social adjustment in college depends on sense of belonging. In order for lower class students to adjust to the academic and social demands of college life, a sense of belonging is necessary.

Since gender, race and ethnicity, and social class often intersect, it is not surprising that sense of belonging also affects first generation college students' academic outcomes. First generation college students are more likely to be racial minorities and/or have lower incomes (NCES, 2005; Terenzini et al., 1996); therefore intersectionality (Cole, 2009) may compound the importance of having a sense of belonging to succeed in higher education. A recent study found that first generation college students may perceive a lack of fit, and therefore have lower belonging, between their personal and cultural values and the values of traditional universities (Stephens, Fryberg, Markus, Johnson and Covarrubias, 2012). University culture, as with US culture, tends to focus on independence and individualism (Markus and Kitayama, 2003), which creates a "cultural mismatch" for first generation college students who typically prefer a collaborative approach to learning (Stephens et al., 2012). This lack of fit between first generation college students and independence-focused universities predicts lower academic performance (Stephens et al., 2012).

Social Change through Interventions

Basic research has uncovered factors that negatively impact the educational success of women in STEM, racial and ethnic minorities, low income, and first generation college students in higher education, contributing to achievement gaps. Basic and applied research has documented successful interventions, often simple to implement, that can reduce these achievement gaps.

Reducing Stereotype Threat

Researchers have been working toward bridging educational gaps. Research on social identity threat has shown that when cues in the environment suggests that an identity can be devalued, such as describing a task as intellectually diagnostic, performance on these tasks is hindered. However, by explicitly nullifying the diagnosticity of a test or simply describing that test as a problem-solving task can reduce and completely eliminate the effects of stereotype threat on performance (Good, Aronson and Harder, 2008; Steele and Aronson, 1995). In addition, research on self-affirmation has shown that a brief self-affirmation exercise that encourages students to focus on their important characteristics, skills, or values can close the performance gap between black and white students (Cohen, Garcia, Apfel and Master, 2006). For example, when women are encouraged to self-affirm important aspects of their self, values, or roles, performance on math tests improves (Martens, Johns, Greenberg and Schimel, 2006). Furthermore, research has found that informing students about the possibility of succumbing to stereotype threat can be powerful in reducing its effects (Johns, Schmader and Martens, 2005).

Research also shows that perceptions of intelligence are an important predictor of students' academic engagement. Studies have found that students who believe that intelligence is a malleable part of the self were more likely to believe that effort led to more positive outcomes, report learning as a source of motivation, engage in positive academic strategies (i.e., spend more time studying), and were less likely to attribute failure to helplessness compared to students who believed that intelligence was a fixed trait (Blackwell, Trzesniewski and Dweck, 2007). Interventions in this area have shown that by encouraging an incremental view of intelligence (or that intelligence can be improved with effort), students are more likely to report valuing education and receive better grades (Aronson, Fried and Good, 2002). In addition, these interventions reduce stereotype threat effects and close the gender gap in math (Good, Aronson and Inzlicht, 2003).

Promoting Equal Education by Improving Fit and Belonging

Person-environment fit and sense of belonging are important factors in students' success in higher education, therefore interventions targeted at factors that increase fit and belonging may be effective. Work by Diekman et al. (2010) finds that women who value communal goals see a lack of fit between their personal values and the values promoted in STEM. This can be remedied by promoting the communal aspects of STEM fields (Diekman et al., 2010). For example, girls who connect science with values of altruism show more interest in science careers (Weisgram and Bigler, 2006). Diekman et al. (2011) found that framing scientific work as collaborative rather than independent increased women's positivity toward science careers. This relationship was mediated by goal affordances such that only women who reported the collaborative approach to science meets communal goals reported positive attitudes toward science. Thus, STEM courses, and their catalog descriptions, should include accounts of science as collaborative and how STEM is used to help people and solve social problems. This focus on communality will attract more women to STEM (Diekman et al., 2010; 2011).

As described previously, first generation college students can perceive a "cultural mismatch" between their collaborative learning orientation with universities' independence orientation (Stephens et al., 2011). Stephens et al. (2011) implemented a brief intervention to reframe universities' values as fostering interdependence and test the effects on first generation college students' performance. During orientation, new students were randomly assigned a welcome letter from the University president that described the university's promotion of independent or interdependent learning norms. First generation college students who received the interdependent letter had higher performance on an academic task. Further, the type of letter received affected first generation college students' perceptions of task difficulty, linking a cultural mismatch to greater perceived difficulty and a cultural match to less difficulty. For first generation college students, those who received an interdependent letter and perceived the academic task as less difficult had better performance compared to first generation students receiving an independence letter (Stephens et al., 2011).

Research has shown that changing subtle cues in academic environments, such as a President's welcome letter encouraging collaborative learning and teamwork, can increase students' sense of belonging. Research by Cheryan et al. (2009) found that physical cues in academic environments can encourage or discourage women from pursuing computer science. When environments such as an office have décor stereotypic of computer science (e.g., Star Trek posters, soda cans), women reported less interest in computer science. However, when office décor was neutral (e.g., nature posters, water bottles), women reported more interest in computer science. Follow-up studies found that perceived masculinity explained this relationship, thus women who perceived stereotypic computer science environments to be more masculine and therefore felt less belonging and reported less interest in computer science. Thus, STEM departments should ensure that physical environments (e.g., classrooms, labs, offices) do not communicate stereotypes about the field or promote masculinity.

As described previously, sense of belonging is an important predictor of academic success. Because minority group members often feel marginalized and are often the numeric minority, they may have a difficult time seeing themselves as belonging in higher education. Interventions to improve minority group members' sense of belonging are effective in not only improving their sense of belonging in the long run, but also in reducing the racial achievement gap (Walton and Cohen, 2011).

In an intervention developed by Walton and Cohen (2011), a group of incoming freshmen were encouraged to view future social adversity as temporary and as improving over time and to attribute such adversity to external rather than to internal sources. Students were tracked over three years and results showed that black students who were exposed to the intervention showed the most positive outcomes with increases in GPA over the three years, and in effect narrowing the achievement gap.

A final cue that signals belonging is numeric representation. In many academic contexts racial minorities find themselves in the numeric minority (e.g., predominantly white universities) as do women (e.g., in most STEM majors). This mere numeric minority status can trigger stereotype threat and cause performance decrements (Inzlicht and Ben-Zeev, 2000; Murphy, Steele and Gross, 2007). One study examined how women STEM majors responded to varying gender representation in a video of conference attendees. Women who saw a video showing more men than women performed poorly on cognitive tasks, had heighted physiological reactivity, had lower belonging, and reported less interest in attending the conference compared to women who saw a gender balanced video.

Numeric representation of same race and gender groups highlights the importance of having role models. A vast research literature has documented the critical function of role models, including peers, professors, and famous people, in increasing students' sense of belonging and success in higher education (Dasgupta and Asgari, 2004; Lockwood, 2006; Marx and Roman, 2002; Stout, Dasgupta, Hunsinger and McManus, 2011). Stout et al. (2011) found that when working with female engineering peers, female engineering students performed better on an engineering task, had more participation, and reported more interest in a STEM career than females working with male peers. The mechanism shown to explain this relationship is greater subjective identification with the peers and a sense of belonging to the STEM domain.

Other research has documented the importance of female role models as professors or experts. Dasgupta and Asgari (2004) found that women attending an all-women's college had less implicit gender stereotypes about men as leaders and women as followers compared to women at a co-educational college. This relationship was mediated by number of female faculty such that having more female professors reduced implicit stereotyping. Further, the more math and science classes female students took, the greater the role proportion of female faculty played in reducing students' implicit gender biases.

In another longitudinal field study, Stout et al. (2011) found that women STEM majors who had a female calculus professor had more positive implicit attitudes toward STEM, greater implicit identification with STEM, higher self-efficacy, more participation, and higher grade expectations compared to women who had male calculus professors. Because increasing the number of female peers and faculty in STEM may not be feasible in the short-term, exposure to female STEM experts can be just as effective (Stout et al., 2011). Women exposed to a female STEM expert, as opposed to a male or control condition, had more positive implicit attitudes toward STEM, identified with the engineering expert, had higher self-efficacy, and reported greater STEM career intentions.

CONCLUSION

The US education system was designed to prepare children and young adults to thrive in modern society and contribute to economic development. However, this chapter reviewed several gaps in educational achievement among women, racial and ethnic minorities, low income students, and first generation college students that indicates the US educational system is not serving its intended equalizing purpose (Bailey and Dynarski, 2011). Further, the research reviewed herein indicates that social and cultural factors are largely to blame for achievement gaps rather than individual shortcomings.

Since social and cultural factors play a major role in educational disparities, interventions can be implemented to enact social change. Through conducting interdisciplinary research in psychology, sociology, and education, researchers have demonstrated the effectiveness of brief interventions in reducing achievement gaps and helping to level the playing field for all students regardless of their demographic backgrounds. By implementing brief interventions on self-affirmation, theories of intelligence, and sense of belonging, educators can work toward achieving educational equity. Implementing interventions, along with institutional level and policy changes, can help alleviate educational disparities and restore the original mission of the US education system.

AUTHOR NOTE

Bettina J. Casad, Department of Psychological Sciences, University of Missouri-St. Louis; Abdiel J. Flores, Department of Psychology, Columbia University.

Preparation of this manuscript was supported by NIH grant GM094536. Any opinions, findings, and conclusions or recommendations expressed in this paper are those of the authors and do not necessarily reflect the views of the National Institutes of Health.

Correspondence concerning this chapter should be addressed to Bettina J. Casad, University of Missouri-St. Louis, Department of Psychological Sciences, 325 Stadler Hall, One University Blvd. St. Louis, MO 63121. E-mail: casadbj@umsl.edu.

REFERENCES

AAUW. (2008). *Where the girls are: The facts about gender equity in education.* C. Corbett, C. Hill and A. St. Rose. Washington, DC: Author.

AAUW. (2010). *Why so few? Women in science, technology, engineering, and mathematics.* C. Hill, C. Corbett and A. St. Rose. Washington, DC: Author.

Aikens, N. L. and Barbarin, O. (2008). Socioeconomic differences in reading trajectories: The contribution of family, neighborhood, and school contexts. *Journal of Educational Psychology, 100*, 235-251.

Aronson, J., Fried, C. B. and Good, C. (2002). Reducing the effects of stereotype threat on African American college students by shaping theories of intelligence. *Journal of Experimental Social Psychology, 38*, 113-125.

Bailey, M. J. and Dynarski, S. M. (2011). Gains and gaps: Changing inequality in U.S. college entry and completion. National Bureau of Economic Research Working Paper No. 17633.

Barbercheck, M. (2001). Mixed messages: Men and women in advertisements in science. In M. Wyer, D. Giesman, M. Barbercheck, H. Ozturk and M. Wayne (Eds.) *Women, science, and technology: A reader in feminist science studies* (pp. 117-132). Routledge Publishing.

Baumeister, R. F. and Leary, M. R. (1995). The need to belong: Desire for interpersonal attachments as a fundamental human motivation. *Psychological Bulletin, 117*, 497-529.

Bernstein, B. (1974). *Class codes and control: Theoretical studies towards a sociology of language* (2nd ed.). New York, NY: Schocken Books.

Blackwell, L. S., Trzesniewski, K. H. and Dweck. C. S. (2007). Implicit theories of intelligence predict achievement across an adolescent transition: A longitudinal study and intervention. *Child Development, 78,* 246-263.

Bonous-Hammarth, M. (2000). Pathways to success: Affirming opportunities for science, mathematics, and engineering majors. *Journal of Negro Education, 69*, 92-111.

Bourdieu, P. and Passeron, J. C. (1990). *Reproduction in education, society and culture.* London, England: Sage.

Bourdieu, P. and Wacquant, L. J. D. (1992). *An invitation to reflexive sociology.* Chicago, IL: University of Chicago Press.

Casad, B. J. and Flores, A. J. (2015). Academic (*under*)achievement: How stereotype threat impairs first generation college students' test performance. Manuscript in preparation. University of Missouri-St. Louis.

Cheryan, S. (2012). Understanding the paradox in math-related fields: Why do some gender gaps remain while others do not? *Sex Roles*, *66*(3-4), 184-190.

Cheryan, S., Plaut, V. C., Davies, P. G. and Steele, C. M. (2009) Ambient belonging: How stereotypical cues impact gender participation in computer science. *Journal of Personality and Social Psychology, 97*, 1045-1060.

Cohen, G. L., Garcia, J., Apfel, N. and Master, A. (2006). Reducing the racial achievement gap: A social-psychological intervention. *Science, 313*, 1307-1310.

Cole, E. R. (2009). Intersectionality and research in psychology. *American Psychologist, 64*, 170-180.

Coley, R. J. (2002). *An uneven start: Indicators of inequality in school readiness.* Princeton, NJ: Educational Testing Service.

Contreras, F. E. and Gandara, P. (2006). The Latina/o Ph. D. pipeline: A case of historical and contemporary under-representation. In J. Castellanos, A. M. Gloria, and M. Kamimura (Eds.), *The Latina/o pathway to the Ph. D.: Abriendo caminos* (pp. 91-112). Sterling, VA: Stylus.

Dasgupta, N. and Asgari, S. (2004). Seeing is believing: Exposure to counterstereotypic women leaders and its effect on the malleability of automatic gender stereotyping. *Journal of Experimental Social Psychology, 40,* 642–658.

Diekman, A. B., Brown, E. R., Johnston, A. M. and Clark, E. K. (2010). Seeking congruity between goals and roles: A new look at why women opt out of science, technology, engineering, and mathematics careers. *Psychological Science, 21*, 1051-1057.

Diekman, A. B., Clark, E. K., Johnston, A. M., Brown, E. R. and Steinberg, M. (2011). Malleability in communal goals and beliefs influences attraction to stem careers: Evidence for a goal congruity perspective. *Journal of Personality and Social Psychology, 101*, 902-918.

Dovidio, J. F., Gaertner, S. L., Niemann, Y. F. and Snider, K. (2001). Racial, ethnic, and cultural differences in responding to distinctiveness and discrimination on campus: Stigma and common group identity. *Journal of Social Issues, 57,* 167–188.

Eagly, A. H. and Karau, S. J. (2002). Role congruity theory of prejudice toward female. leaders. *Psychological Review*, *109*(3), 573-598.

Eagly, A. H. and Steffen, V. J. (1984). Gender stereotypes stem from the distribution of women and men into social roles. *Journal of Personality and Social Psychology, 46*, 735-754.

Francis, T. A. and Miller, M. T. (2008). Communication apprehension: Levels of first-generation college students at a 2-year institution. *Community College Journal of Research and Practice, 32*, 38-55.

Franco-Zamudio, J. L. (2009). *Graduate student persistence: The effect of perceptions of person-environment fit.* Dissertation Abstracts International: Section B: The Sciences and Engineering, 70(7-B), 4534.

Gloria, A. M. and Castellanos, J. (2006). Sustaining Latina/o doctoral students: A psychosociocultural approach for faculty. In J. Castellanos, A. M. Gloria, and M. Kamimura (Eds.), *The Latina/o pathway to the Ph. D.: Abriendo caminos* (pp. 169-190). Sterling, VA: Stylus.

Good, C., Aronson, J. and Harder, J. A. (2008). Problem in the pipeline: Stereotype threat and women's achievement in high-level math courses. *Journal of Applied Developmental psychology, 29,* 17-28.

Good, C., Aronson, J. and Inzlicht, M. (2003). Improving adolescents' standardized test performance: An intervention to reduce the effects of stereotype threat. *Journal of Applied Developmental Psychology, 24*, 645-662.

Good, C., Rattan, A. and Dweck, C. S. (2012). Why do women opt out? Sense of belonging and women's representation in mathematics. *Journal of Personality and Social Psychology*, *102*(4), 700-717.

Heilman, M. E. (1983). Sex bias in work settings: The Lack of Fit model. *Research in Organizational Behavior, 5*, 269-298.

Housel, T. H. and Harvey, V. L. (2009). *The invisibility factor: Administrators and faculty reach out to first-generation college students.* Boca Raton, FL: Brown Walker Press.

Inzlicht, M., Aronson, J. and Mendoza-Denton, R. (2009). On being the target of prejudice: Educational implications. In F. Butera and J. Levine (Eds.), *Coping with minority status: Responses to exclusion and inclusion* (pp. 13-36). Cambridge, UK: Cambridge University Press.

Inzlicht, M. and Ben-Zeev, T. (2000). A threatening intellectual environment: Why females are susceptible to experiencing problem-solving deficits in the presence of males. *Psychological Science, 11,* 365–371.

Jansen, K. J. and Kristof-Brown, A. (2006). Toward a multidimensional theory of person-environment fit. *Journal of Managerial issues*, 193-212.

Johns, M., Schmader, T. and Martens, A. (2005). Knowing is half the battle: Teaching stereotype threat as a means of improving women's math performance. *Psychological Science, 16*, 175-179.

Johnson, S. E., Richeson, J. A. and Finkel, E. J. (2011). Middle class and marginal? Socioeconomic status, stigma, and self-regulation at an elite university. *Journal of Personality and Social Psychology, 100*(5), 838-852.

Kornrich, S. and Furstenberg, F. (2013). Investing in children: Changes in spending on children, 1972 to 2007. *Demography*, *50*, 1-23.

Kozol, J. (1991). *Savage inequalities: Children in America's schools.* New York, NY: Crown Publishers.

Lockwood, P. (2006). "Someone like me can be successful": Do college students need same-gender role models? *Psychology of Women Quarterly*, *30*(1), 36-46.

Lott, B. (2002). Cognitive and behavioral distancing from the poor. *American Psychologist, 57*(2), 100-110.

Major, B., Spencer, S. J., Schmader, T., Wolfe, C. and Crocker, J. (1998). Coping with negative stereotypes about intellectual performance: The role of psychological disengagement. *Personality and Social Psychology Bulletin, 24*, 34-50.

Markus, H. R. and Kitayama, S. (2003). Models of agency: Sociocultural diversity in the construction of action. In V. Murphy-Berman and J. J. Berman (Eds.), *Nebraska symposium on motivation: Vol. 49. Crosscultural differences in perspectives on self* (pp. 1–57). Lincoln, NE: University of Nebraska Press.

Martens, A., Johns, M., Greenberg, J. and Schimel, J. (2006). Combating stereotype threat: The effect of self-affirmation on women's intellectual performance. *Journal of Experimental Social Psychology, 42,* 236-243.

Marx, D. M. and Roman, J. S. (2002). Female role models: Protecting women's math test performance. *Personality and Social Psychology Bulletin, 28*(9), 1183-1193.

McCarron, G. P. and Inkelas, K. K. (2006). The gap between educational aspirations and attainment for first-generation college students and the role of parental involvement. *Journal of College Student Development, 47*, 534-549.

Murphy, M. C., Steele, C. M. and Gross, J. J. (2007). Signaling threat: How situational cues affect women in math, science, and engineering settings. *Psychological Science, 18*, 879-885.

National Center for Education Statistics, U.S. Department of Education (2011). *The condition of education 2012*. Retrieved June 10, 2012, from the National Center for Education Statistics Web site: http://nces.ed.gov/pubs2012/2012045_2.pdf.

National Science Foundation, National Center for Science and Engineering Statistics. (2011). *Science and Engineering Degrees: 1966–2008.* Detailed Statistical Tables NSF 11-316. Arlington, VA. Available at http://www.nsf.gov/statistics/nsf11316/.

Osborne, J. W. and Walker, C. (2006). Stereotype threat, identification with academics, and withdrawal from school: Why the most successful students of colour might be most likely to withdraw. *Educational Pscyhology: An International Journal of Experimental Educational Psychology, 26*(4), 563-577.

Ostrove, J. M. and Long, S. M. (2007). Social class and belonging: Implications for college adjustment. *The Review of Higher Education, 30,* 363–389.

Pascarella, E., Pierson, C., Wolniak, G. and Terenzini, P. (2004). First generation college students: Additional evidence on college experiences and outcomes. *Journal of Higher Education, 75,* 249–284.

Pike, G. R. and Kuh, G. D. (2005). First- and second-generation college students: A comparison of their engagement and intellectual development. *Journal of Higher Education, 76*, 276-300.

Rattan, A., Good, C. and Dweck, C. S., (2012). "It's ok—not everyone can be good at math:" Instructors with an entity theory comfort (and demotivate) students. *Journal of Experimental Social Psychology, 48*(3), 731-737.

Read, B., Archer, L. and Leathwood, C. (2003). Challenging cultures? Student conceptions of "belonging" and "isolation" at a post–1992 university. *Studies in Higher Education, 28,* 261–277.

Reardon, S.F. (2011). The widening academic achievement gap between the rich and the poor: New evidence and possible explanations. In R. Murnane and G. Duncan (Eds.), *Whither opportunity? Rising inequality and the uncertain life chances of low-income children* (pp. 91-115). New York: Russell Sage Foundation Press.

Rydell, R. J., Rydell, M. T., Boucher, K. L. (2010). The effect of negative performance stereotypes on learning. *Journal of Personality and Social Psychology, 99,* 883-896.

Schmader, T., Johns, M. and Barquissau, M. (2004). The costs of accepting gender differences: The role of stereotype endorsement in women's experience in the math domain. *Sex Roles, 50*, 835-850.

Schmader, T., Johns, M. and Forbes, C. (2008). An integrated process model of stereotype threat effects on performance. *Psychological Review, 115,* 336-356.

Schneider, B., Smith, D. B. and Goldstein, H. W. (2000). Attraction–selection–attrition: Toward a person–environment psychology of organizations. In H. W. Walsh, W. Bruce, K. H. Craik, and R. H. Prince (Eds.), *Person–environment psychology: New directions and perspectives* (2nd ed.; pp. 61-85). Mahwah, NJ: Lawrence Erlbaum.

Snyder, T. D. and Dillow, S. A. (2011). *Digest of Education Statistics 2010 (NCES 2011-015).* Washington, DC: National Center for Education Statistics, Institute of Education Sciences, U.S. Department of Education.

Steele, C. M. (2010). *Whistling Vivaldi and other clues to how stereotypes affect us.* New York, NY: W. W. Norton and Company.

Steele, C. M. and Aronson, J. (1995). Stereotype threat and the intellectual test performance of African-Americans. *Journal of Personality and Social Psychology, 62,* 26-37.

Steele, C. M., Spencer, S. J. and Aronson, J. (2002). Contending with images of one's group: the psychology of stereotype and social identity threat. *Advances in Experimental Social Psychology, 34*, 379-440.

Stephens, N. M., Fryberg, S. A., Markus, H. R., Johnson, C. S. and Covarrubias, R. (2012). Unseen disadvantage: How American universities' focus on independence undermines the academic performance of first-generation college students. *Journal of Personality and Social Psychology, 102*, 1178-1197.

Stout, J. G., Dasgupta, N., Hunsinger, M. and McManus, M. (2011). STEMing the tide: Using ingroup experts to inoculate women's self-concept and professional goals in science, technology, engineering, and mathematics (STEM). *Journal of Personality and Social Psychology, 100*, 255–270.

Stricker, L. J. and Ward, W. C. (2004). Stereotype threat, inquiring about test takers' ethnicity and gender, and standardized test performance. *Journal of Applied and Social Psychology, 34*, 665-693.

Tajfel, H. and Turner, J. C. (1979). An integrative theory of intergroup conflict. In W. G. Austin and S. Worchel (Eds), *The social psychology of intergroup relations* (pp. 33-47). Monterey, CA: Brooks/Cole.

Tajfel, H. and Turner, J. C. (1986). The social identity theory of intergroup behavior. In S. Worchel and W. G. Austin (Eds.), *Psychology of intergroup relations* (pp. 7-24). Chicago, IL: Nelson-Hall.

Tenenbaum, H. R. and Ruck, M. D. (2007). Are teachers' expectations different for racial minority than for European American Students? A meta-analysis. *Journal of Educational Psychology, 99,* 253-273.

Terenzini, P. T., Springer, L., Yaeger, P. M., Pascarella, E. T. and Nora, A. (1996). First-generation college students: Characteristics, experiences, and cognitive development. *Research in Higher Education, 37*, 1-22.

The College Board (2011). 2011 College-Bound Seniors. Total Group Profile Report. Retrieved from: http://professionals.collegeboard.com/profdownload/cbs2011_total_group_report.pdf.

U.S. Department of Commerce. (2011). *Women in STEM: A Gender Gap in Innovation.* U.S. Department of Commerce, Economics and Statistics Administration, ESA Issue Brief 04-11.

U.S. Department of Education, National Center for Education Statistics (2012). 2001-02 to 2008-09 Integrated Postsecondary Education Data System, Fall 2001, and Spring 2002 through Spring 2009. Retrieved June 10, 2012, from the National Center for Education Statistics Web site: http://nces.ed.gov/programs/digest/d10/tables/dt10_341.asp.

Van den Berg, L., Denessen, E., Hornstra, L., Voeten, M. and Holland, R. (2010). The implicit prejudiced attitudes of teachers: Relations to teacher expectations and the ethnic achievement gap. *American Educational Research Journal, 41*, 497-527.

Walton, G. M. and Carr, P. B. (2011). Do I belong? How negative intellectual stereotypes undermine people's sense of social belonging in school and how to fix it. In M. Inzlicht and T. Schmader (Eds.) *Stereotype threat: Theory, processes, and application* (pp. 129-150). New York, NY: Oxford University Press.

Walton, G. M. and Cohen, G. L. (2007). A question of belonging: Race, social fit, and achievement. *Journal of Personality and Social Psychology, 92*, 82-96.

Walton, G., M. and Cohen, G. L. (2011). A brief social-belonging intervention improves academic and health outcomes of minority students. *Science, 331*, 1447-1451.

Weisgram, E. S. and Bigler, R. S. (2006). Girls and science careers: The role of altruistic values and attitudes about scientific tasks. *Journal of Applied Developental Psychology, 27*(4), 326-348.

In: Stereotypes and Stereotyping
Editor: Claude Fields

ISBN: 978-1-63484-510-6

Chapter 3

Stereotypes about People with AIDS among College Students: A Comparative Study in Two Cohorts

Yolanda Pastor* and Vanesa Pérez
Rey Juan Carlos University, Madrid, Spain

Abstract

People with AIDS remain in today's society as a stigmatized group. However, the content and expression of stereotypes in Europe may be changing thanks to the progress made regarding knowledge about the disease, its treatment and its prevention (Labra, 2015). The main objective of this paper is to describe and compare stereotypes in regard to people with AIDS in two cohorts of Spanish university students: 2004 (n = 230, M_{age} = 19.77; SD = 1.71; 72.6% girls) and 2012 (n = 264; M_{age} = 19.47; SD = 1.73; 73.5% girls). Stereotypes were evaluated using two scales, one of which was addressed to assess the cognitive dimension (personal characteristics attributed to people with AIDS), and the other one, to evaluate the emotional dimension (emotions aroused). Both adopted the format of the semantic differential, with opposite poles of adjectives like: wise-reckless rating with a 7-point scale from + 3 to - 3. The reliability of the scales (Cronbach's alpha) in both groups took values between 0.71 and 0.84. Descriptive statistics (M, SD, Percentages, Crosstabs) and MANOVA (gender x cohort) were performed. Our results showed that people with AIDS are perceived by university students in both cohorts as reckless, drug users, promiscuous, unfaithful, careless, sick, and prone to prostitution and vice. The emotions aroused with greater intensity in both groups were: grief, concern, compassion, surprise, displeasure and fear. Our data show significant differences by cohort as regards stereotypes-in both dimensions, cognitive (Willks = .91, F = 1.87, df = 22, p = .010) and emotional (Willks = .89, F = 3.29, df = 16, p = .000). Students in Cohort 1 indicated they perceive people with AIDS as less attractive, more marginalized and less abnormal and dirty than students in cohort 2. Cohort 2 showed more negative emotions toward people with AIDS. Most students in both cohorts did not know anyone with AIDS (89.5% versus 88.6% respectively), have never been tested for it (98.2% versus 95.8) and also made it clear they would not mind working or studying with a

* Corresponding author: Yolanda Pastor. E-mail: yolanda.pastor@urjc.es.

positive zero (89.8% versus 87.1%). No significant differences were found in these latter variables between both groups. These results indicate that stereotypes of Spanish college students concerning people with AIDS may be increasing over the years. Students show inconsistent views concerning what they think, what they feel and what they say they would do. Our results allow us to delve into these inconsistencies and to take them into account to plan an intervention with this group.

INTRODUCTION

In recent years, with the effectiveness of antiviral therapies, the reduction of HIV (Human Immunodeficiency Virus) infected people and the awareness campaigns on AIDS (Acquired Immune Deficiency Syndrome) have raised expectations that prejudice, stereotypes or stigma in connection with this disease may decrease (Lekas 2006, 1180). However, there has been a growing interest in studying the stigma against AIDS, since it is acknowledged that a negative social response to the pandemic remains. In this respect, some studies on social representation of AIDS showed that a negative social response to certain groups, such as prostitutes or drug addicts, has been strengthened over time. For example, research in Central and Eastern Europe showed that various professional groups, like business people and health professionals, associated the disease with substance abuse (for example, sharing needles) as well as sexual risk behavior (i.e., prostitution or occasional sexual encounters without protection) (Goodwin et al. 2004, 677). Therefore, HIV transmission remained linked to the characteristic behaviors of some social groups such as gay men, drug users or prostitutes (Parker and Aggleton 2003, 13) and "at the same time, the risk of contracting HIV through one's own sexual behavior is minimized" (Pittam and Gallois 2000, 26).

This is related to the AIDS risk reduction model that explains sexual risk behavior through an individual perspective. This model states that the individual needs, in the first place, to identify and label that behavior as risky; then he has to make a commitment to make the behavioral change and, finally, he could take the behavioral steps involved to achieve the change. This model suggests that stereotyped beliefs about the kind of person who is likely to contract the disease may affect the labeling stage. In this way, if a person believes that the disease only affects drug users, prostitutes or homosexuals and perceives that he does not belong to that social group, then this will not identify their own behavior as risky and, consequently, will not prompt preventive behavioral measures (Catania, Coates and Kegeles 1994, 551). Because "the stigma serves to emphasize and enhance the differences between those doing the stigmatizing and those being stigmatized" (Riley and Baah-Odoom 2010, 605) the people who stigmatize social groups in HIV/AIDS may perceive a distance and difference between themselves and those with the disease. "This enhanced sense of difference may underlie their perceptions of being less vulnerable to the disease" (Riley and Baah-Odoom 2010, 605). Specifically these cognitive manifestations of AIDS stigma (stereotypes), represent a heuristic that people can use to define who is at risk to acquire this disease and moreover evaluate their own risk (Earnshaw et al. 2012, 575). Furthermore, the stigmatization model (Corrigan et al. 2003, 162) explains that individuals make attributions about the cause and controllability of a particular characteristic like being homosexual or a prostitute-that lead to inferences about responsibility-and these attributions trigger emotional reactions that influence behavior.

This is especially pertinent in young people, considering that in 2012 it was estimated that there were around 2.1 million adolescents living with AIDS (United Nations Fund for Children UNICEF, 2013) and every day 2,500 young people between 15 and 24 years old were infected (World Health Organization WHO, 2013). Youth and adolescents are a vulnerable group for transmission of the disease and it is highly relevant to study the vision or stereotypes that they have as regards those people with AIDS. If we add the characteristics of the development of this period such as the formation of identity, the search for new sensations and experiences, onset of sexual life, first romantic relationships and frequent partner changes, we can consider the youth to be a high-risk group as to contracting the disease.

In Spain, research carried out with university students showed that they perceived a person with AIDS as reckless, a drug user, dangerous, promiscuous, unfaithful, careless, sick, a prostitute, dirty and prone to vice. There was an association of disease and stereotypes that make up the social representation of AIDS. Most of them also perceived themselves as less vulnerable than other people to contracting the disease (Rojas-Murcia, Pastor and Esteban-Hernández 2015, 36). A study in Canada 2009 with young university students-between 18 to 25 years of age-based on discourse analysis about HIV/AIDS showed that it was defined as "huge, terrible, horrible, sad, and a big deal. These used terms denoted the relevance of the problem for interviewees and its emotional connotation (mainly negative feelings)" (Graffigna and Olson 2009, 792). In this study, respondents also circumscribed the HIV/AIDS risk to a specific population such as gay or drug user. Although they did not perceive themselves as being at risk, "the link between HIV/AIDS and death stood out, and this provoked fear and refusal to think about the problem" (Graffigna and Olson 2009, 799).

In the same way, research in South Africa with young people revealed that knowledge of HIV/AIDS was sufficient and clear for them. However, few participants said that they discussed HIV/AIDS with their partner or know people with HIV/AIDS, and they associated the disease with a risk group and, therefore, they were taking away the potential personal risk (Levine and Ross 2002, 101). In México, a study with adolescents dealing with social representation of HIV/AIDS showed the association between HIV/AIDS and old people. The image of the disease corresponded to an evil that only affected older people and therefore they were not a risk population. Moreover, only 18% of participants knew someone with HIV/AIDS, which could be related to feeling free of the disease (García 2006, 19).

Research in Japan, where there are national school programs on sexually transmitted diseases including HIV/AIDS, revealed that the young got their information about it from the mass media. Therefore, they showed having very little communication with their parents or teachers about HIV/AIDS. In spite of this, most of the student participants in the said research demonstrated good knowledge of HIV/AIDS but half of them responded that "they would not live in the same house with a person with HIV/AIDS without worrying" (Maswanya et al. 2000, 9).

A study with a representative sample of 6,137 Portuguese adolescents used a focus group to explore stigma and attitudes toward AIDS. Although the majority of young people believed that HIV-infected people experienced stigma, discrimination and social exclusion and the feeling of more than 50 percent of the students was compassion, their attitude about HIV-infected was ambivalent. Some of them reported that they felt fear when they were near a person with AIDS due to the possibility of becoming infected. The authors point out "these feelings of discomfort might well translate into avoidance or discrimination in some real-world interactions" (Dias, Matos and Golcalves 2006, 213).

In the current paper, we explored what came to mind when a given social concept like AIDS was activated in a group of university students. The main aim of this paper was to describe stereotypes in relation to people with AIDS in two cohorts of Spanish students, to detect any changes in them over time. We assumed that adopting a multidimensional perspective of stigma (cognitive, emotional and behavioral) would allow us to identify inconsistencies in the studied population.

METHOD

Design and Participants

A cross-sectional design with two cohorts was used. The sample was selected using a convenience sampling method for both cohorts, choosing those courses whose teachers agreed to pass the questionnaire round during their teaching hours in the second semester.

Since it was a large study, sample size determination was made based on the prevalence of illusion of invulnerability (76%) reported in previous studies (Ubillos et al. 2003, 261) with an accuracy of 5% and confidence level of 95%. This involved using a sample of 289 subjects.

The sample consisted of two groups of Spanish university students with similar characteristics (age, gender, enrolled in degree courses, semester courses, schools to which they belong) from two different cohorts. In Cohort 1 (2004), we found 230 students aged between 17 and 24 (M_{age} = 19.77; SD = 1.71; 72.6% girls). In Cohort 2 (2012), 264 students, whose age ranged between 18 and 24 (M_{age} = 19.47; SD = 1.73; 73.5% girls) participated.

Variables and Instruments

The variables considered in this study were sociodemographic characteristics (age, gender), stereotypes with respect to AIDS (cognitive dimension and emotional dimension) and related behaviors such as knowing or not knowing people who have the disease, whether they have ever had the diagnostic test done, whether they usually asked their partner to have their diagnostic test done and their views on whether they would mind working or studying with people with AIDS.

The questionnaire on stereotypes concerning AIDS was developed from a review of literature on this subject. A questionnaire with all reagents associated with these stereotypes in previous studies was designed. It began with a list of 40 opposing pairs of different adjectives and nouns-to assess the cognitive dimension of the stereotype-and another list of 32 opposing pairs of emotions-to measure the emotional dimension of the stereotype. These lists were subject to an assessment of three independent judges, all of them experts in Social Psychology, who weighed the extent they were useful to assess the stereotypes levelled against people with AIDS.

Finally, those items that were chosen by at least two judges, as very suitable for this purpose, were selected. The final scales consisted of the presentation of 22 concepts (cognitive dimension) and 16 emotions (emotional dimension) related to stereotypes about people with AIDS. Following the procedure of semantic differential, each conceptual unit that evaluates people with AIDS was presented by two opposing poles-such as homosexual-heterosexual, young-old, (see the complete list in Table 1)-in which subjects had to describe a person with AIDS by means of a 7-point scale, from - 3 to + 3 (cognitive dimension), frequently used in the study of stereotypes (Schneider, 2005, 41); and two opposite emotions, such as sadness-joy, with the same scale format (see the complete list in Table 2), in which respondents had to describe emotions that a person with AIDS causes them to feel (emotional dimension).

To avoid acquiescence, some pairs of terms were reversed in both scales in the opposite direction from the stereotype traditionally shown towards this group. Cronbach's alpha coefficients for these scales were 0.72 and 0.79 for the cognitive dimension scale in cohorts 1 and 2 respectively, and 0.71 and 0.84 for the emotional dimension scale.

The rest of the variables considered were evaluated with closed answer questions developed ad hoc for this study.

Procedure

The questionnaires were administered during lecture periods. Prior to the administration, students were informed of the anonymity of responses and voluntary nature of participation. The respondents signed informed consent documents. A researcher was present at the time of administration, which was introduced by each class teacher who left the classroom afterwards. The average time of questionnaire administration ranged from approximately 25 to 35 minutes. The response rate was 72.3% in cohort 1 and 74.7% in cohort 2.

Data Analysis

To describe stereotypes, crosstabs with the items of both scales of stereotypes were performed by cohort. Chi-squared test was calculated to observe the dependence versus independence of the different items by cohort.

Additionally, to study statistically significant mean differences, two MANOVAs (gender x cohort) were performed, one with items of each stereotype dimension (cognitive and emotional). It was considered important to perform a multivariate analysis of variance as it was a more robust statistic and consequently not sensitive to slight deviations from the parametric assumptions, mainly of multivariate normality and homoscedasticity (Bisquerra, 1989, 142) and to reduce the Type I error. To perform MANOVA, the scores of different items of each scale of stereotypes were recoded to 1-7 and some items were inverted, so that the higher the score the greater the degree of the stereotype.

To describe the remaining variables, crosstabs were used by cohort in the same way. T-test was calculated to analyze mean differences in these variables.

RESULTS

With regard to the characteristics that college students attributed to people with AIDS, our data showed that over 80% in both cohorts considered they were imprudent and careless or even prostitutes. About 70% of university students thought they were drug users, promiscuous, unfaithful and prone to vice. Around 50% in both cohorts deemed them older, homosexual, dangerous, sick and dirty. About 40% of respondents believed that people with AIDS were guilty, men, introverts and marginalized. Between 20 and 30% of students considered them unattractive, sedentary, abnormal, failed and poor. Our results indicated a statistical dependence with the cohort of the following reagents of the cognitive dimension of stereotype: heterosexual versus homosexual, attractive versus unattractive and integrated versus marginalized (See table 1).

Regarding the emotions a person with AIDS aroused in them, close to or over 80% of students felt that they caused them grief, concern and compassion. About 70% considered they felt surprise, displeasure and fear. Around 50% of respondents reported rage, frustration, impotence and nervousness. Between 30 and 40% highlighted modesty, hopelessness and distrust. The chi-square test indicated statistical dependence with the cohort of the following terms related with the emotional dimension of the stereotype: interest versus disinterest, indifference versus surprise, attraction versus disgust, security versus fear, esteem versus contempt, and confidence versus distrust (See table 2).

The MANOVA (gender x cohort) performed on the cognitive dimension of the stereotype detected the existence of significant main effects for the cohort (Wilks = .91; F = 1.878; df = 22, p = .010; Eta^2 = .084) but not for gender (Wilks = .93; F = 1.494; df = 22, p = .071; Eta^2 = .068), nor for interaction gender x cohort (Wilks = .96; F = 0.783; df = 22, p = .748; Eta^2 = .037). However, the value of the eta squared -the cohort only explained 8% of variability- and a detailed analysis of the univariate effects revealed that differences between the two cohorts were small. Students in cohort 1 considered people with AIDS less normal (F = 4.150; df = 1; p = .042) and dirtier (F = 6.751; df = 1; p = .010) than students in cohort 2; whereas students in cohort 2 perceived them as less attractive (F = 5.838; df = 1; p = .016) and more marginalized than students in cohort 1 (F = 20.022; df = 1; p = .000).

In relation to the emotional dimension of the stereotype, MANOVA (gender x cohort) results also showed significant main effects for the cohort (Wilks = .89; F = 3.293; df = 16, p = .000; Eta^2 = .103), but no significant effects in the case of gender (Wilks = .95; F = 1.572; df = 16, p = .072; Eta^2 = .052) nor in that of the interaction gender x cohort (Wilks = .98; F = .726; df = 16, p = .768; Eta^2 = .025). Cohort only explained 10% of the variables' variability. Concerning univariate effects, students in cohort 2 expressed more negative emotions toward people with AIDS than students in cohort 1. Those students (cohort 2) expressed feeling more disinterest (F = 14.936; df = 1; p = .000), disgust (F = 23.414; df = 1; p = .000), fear (F = 13.796; df = 1; p = .000), contempt (F = 17.381; df = 1; p = .000) and mistrust (F = 13.804; df = 1; p = .000).

In both cohorts there were few college students who personally knew someone with AIDS, 10.5% and 11.4% in cohort 1 and 2 respectively. Also, most of the students said they would not mind working or studying with a partner who suffered from the AIDS disease (89.8% and 87.1% respectively). Only 4.8% in cohort 1 and 7.8% in cohort 2 have ever been tested for the AIDS virus. Consistently, about half of respondents stated that they would never ask their sex partner to get tested for AIDS (50.4% and 47.7% respectively), 45% would inquire sometimes and, only 4.4% in cohort 1 and 6.5% in cohort 2 would usually or always ask. Significant differences were not detected by cohort in these variables (see table 3).

Table 1. Percentage of students in each response item (cognitive dimension of stereotypes toward people with aids)

	Response item																
	- 3		- 2		**- 1**		0		**1**		2		**3**			Chi^2	p
	C1	**C2**	C1	C2	**C1**	**C2**	C1	C2	**C1**	**C2**	C1	C2	**C1**	**C2**			
Young	**0.4**	**1.1**	8	6.1	**14.2**	**11.7**	31.4	31.1	**18.1**	**20.5**	21.7	21.2	**6.2**	**8.3**	Old	3.01	.806
Heterosexual	**3.1**	**0.8**	4.0	4.9	**1.8**	**5.3**	38.9	41.3	**28.8**	**19.7**	16.8	20.5	**6.6**	**7.6**	Homosexual	13.37	.037
Attractive	**0.9**	**0**	2.2	1.5	**8.4**	**4.5**	69.3	62.5	**12.4**	**18.2**	4.0	10.6	**2.7**	**2.7**	Unattractive	16.03	.014
Prudent	**0.9**	**1.1**	0.9	2.3	**3.6**	**2.3**	10.8	8.0	**12.6**	**16.3**	35	29.5	**36.3**	**40.5**	Imprudent	6.04	.419
Innocent	**4.9**	**2.7**	5.3	7.2	**8.9**	**8.3**	50.7	44.3	**13.3**	**15.5**	10.7	11.7	**6.2**	**10.2**	Guilty	6.25	.396
Not drug user	**1.3**	**1.5**	3.5	1.5	**4**	**3.4**	20.8	22.3	**25.7**	**31.1**	30.5	25.8	**14.2**	**14.4**	Drug user	4.55	.603
Dependable	**1.3**	**0.8**	0.4	0.8	**4.9**	**3.0**	46.0	44.3	**19.5**	**21.6**	18.1	22.7	**9.7**	**6.8**	Dangerous	4.49	.609
Woman	**0.4**	**0.4**	1.3	1.5	**2.2**	**4.5**	58	51.9	**18.6**	**18.6**	13.7	18.2	**5.8**	**4.9**	Man	4.43	.618
Not promiscuous	**1.3**	**0**	1.8	0.8	**1.8**	**3**	20.5	26.9	**28.1**	**23.9**	30.8	25.4	**15.6**	**20.1**	Promiscuous	10.84	.093
Faithful	**0.4**	**1.5**	0.9	1.5	**6.2**	**2.3**	28.9	26.9	**19.6**	**22.7**	31.6	28.8	**12.4**	**16.3**	Unfaithful	8.67	.193
Careful	**0.9**	**2.3**	0.9	2.3	**3.5**	**1.9**	9.3	5.7	**18.6**	**18.9**	36.7	35.6	**30.1**	**33.3**	Careless	6.72	.347
Friend	**2.2**	**4.5**	2.7	2.3	**3.1**	**5.3**	81.4	78.8	**6.2**	**3.8**	2.7	3.8	**1.8**	**1.5**	Enemy	5.43	.489
Athlete	**0.4**	**1.5**	0.4	2.3	**5.3**	**6.1**	69.8	67	**13.8**	**10.2**	5.3	7.6	**4.9**	**5.3**	Sedentary	6.70	.349
Normal	**5.3**	**2.7**	5.3	7.2	**3.6**	**4.5**	68	62.5	**11.1**	**9.5**	4.4	8.3	**2.2**	**5.3**	Abnormal	9.86	.130
Healthy	**1.3**	**1.5**	3.5	1.9	**4.9**	**4.2**	32.7	34.5	**19.5**	**15.9**	16.8	20.8	**21.2**	**21.2**	Sick	3.43	.753
Extrovert	**0.9**	**0.4**	2.7	4.2	**4.9**	**4.2**	52.7	42.4	**20.8**	**21.2**	12.8	20.8	**5.3**	**6.8**	Introvert	9.15	.165
Entrepreneur	**1.3**	**1.1**	2.2	5.3	**6.2**	**6.4**	65	67.8	**15**	**11**	8.4	6.4	**1.8**	**1.9**	Failed	5.39	.494
Integrated	**1.3**	**3.4**	6.7	11	**7.1**	**9.8**	37.8	48.9	**23.6**	**16.7**	16.9	7.2	**6.7**	**3**	Outcast	25.23	.000
Not prostitute	**1.3**	**2.7**	0.9	1.9	**6.2**	**1.5**	15	11.4	**17.3**	**16.7**	26.5	25.8	**32.7**	**40.2**	Prostitute	12.30	.055
Clean	**1.8**	**2.7**	2.7	3	**5.3**	**3.8**	47.1	34.5	**18.7**	**20.1**	15.1	22	**9.3**	**14**	Dirty	11.33	.078
Rich	**0.4**	**1.5**	2.7	1.9	**5.3**	**4.9**	62.4	68.6	**13.7**	**11**	11.9	8.3	**3.5**	**3.8**	Poor	4.78	.572
Respectable	**0.4**	**0.8**	1.3	0.4	**1.3**	**1.9**	27.6	24.2	**29.8**	**22**	21.8	28.4	**17.8**	**22.3**	Prone to vice	8.55	.200

C1 = cohort 1 (2004); C2 = cohort 2 (2012).

Table 2. Percentage of students in each response item (emotional dimension of stereotypes toward people with aids)

	Response item																
	- 3		- 2		**- 1**		0		**1**		2		**3**				
	C1	**C2**	C1	C2	**C1**	**C2**	C1	C2	**C1**	**C2**	C1	C2	**C1**	**C2**		Chi^2	p
Interest	**5.8**	**2.7**	11.2	10.3	**21**	**16.8**	47.3	39.3	**7.6**	**9.9**	3.1	11.1	**4**	**9.9**	Disinterest	22.77	.001
Indifference	**0.4**	**0.8**	0	2.7	**4.5**	**5.3**	28.1	20.2	**37.1**	**33.8**	22.8	25.9	**7.1**	**11.4**	Surprise	12.71	.048
Happiness	**0**	**0.8**	2.7	1.5	**0.9**	**1.5**	12.1	17.2	**28.6**	**25.6**	30.8	29	**25**	**24.4**	Sadness	5.56	.473
Pride	**0.9**	**0.4**	0.9	0	**1.8**	**1.9**	66.4	65.5	**10.3**	**14.4**	9.4	10.6	**10.3**	**7.2**	Modesty	6.05	.417
Calm	**0.9**	**0.4**	1.8	0.8	**3.1**	**4.5**	43.3	52.3	**27.7**	**24.2**	14.3	11.4	**8.9**	**6.4**	Rage	6.57	.362
Hope	**3.6**	**3**	8	6.1	**19.2**	**16.3**	33.9	31.1	**18.3**	**23.1**	12.1	14	**4.9**	**6.4**	Hopelessness	3.86	.695
Pleasantness	**0.9**	**0**	1.3	1.5	**0.9**	**1.5**	30	23.1	**25.6**	**29.9**	22.4	21.2	**18.8**	**22.7**	Dislike	6.76	.343
Attraction	**2.7**	**1.1**	3.1	0.8	**5.8**	**3**	74.1	64.4	**12.1**	**20.8**	1.3	5.7	**0.9**	**4.2**	Disgust	25.7	.000
Satisfaction	**0**	**0.8**	0.9	0.4	**1.3**	**1.1**	45.5	43.3	**32.1**	**31.6**	12.9	16	**7.1**	**6.8**	Frustration	3.17	.786
Security	**0.9**	**0.4**	2.2	0.4	**4.0**	**1.1**	30.8	29.7	**39.3**	**28.9**	14.3	24.7	**8.5**	**14.8**	Fear	22.57	.001
Esteem	**3.6**	**1.9**	7.1	3.8	**17.4**	**12.5**	63.8	63.3	**6.7**	**11**	0.9	6.4	**0.4**	**1.1**	Contempt	18.57	.005
Unconcern	**0**	**0.8**	0	1.9	**0.4**	**1.9**	10.8	11.4	**39**	**35.4**	29.6	27.4	**20.2**	**21.3**	Concern	8.75	.188
Harshness	**0**	**0.4**	0.4	0.8	**1.3**	**1.5**	22.4	23.5	**35.4**	**35.6**	26	23.5	**14.3**	**14.8**	Compassion	1.44	.963
Capacity	**0.4**	**0.4**	0.9	0.8	**1.3**	**3**	36.2	44.3	**27.7**	**22**	14.3	15.9	**19.2**	**13.6**	Impotence	7.69	.261
Confidence	**1.8**	**1.9**	3.1	3.8	**12.9**	**12.1**	59.8	42.4	**14.3**	**21.6**	6.3	13.6	**1.8**	**4.5**	Distrust	20.31	.002
Tranquility	**1.8**	**1.5**	2.7	1.9	**1.3**	**4.2**	48.7	40.2	**27.2**	**29.5**	13.4	14.8	**4.9**	**8**	Nervousness	7.85	.249

C1 = cohort 1 (2004); C2 = cohort 2 (2012).

Table 3. Mean and t test for differences by cohort in different variables

	Mean		t	df	p
	Cohort 1	Cohort 2			
Know someone with AIDS	1.89	1.89	.296	490	.768
Working or studing with someone with AIDS	1.10	1.13	- .929	488	.353
Have ever been tested for the AIDS	1.95	1.92	1.568	484	.117
Ask your sex partner get tested for AIDS	1.55	1.60	- .942	486	.347

Discussion

Far from reducing the stereotypes towards AIDS nowadays, our data has indicated that college students held a stereotypical view of people with AIDS and that vision is fairly stable over time, in accordance with previous research (Lekas 2006; Parker and Aggleton 2003).

The approach to the study of stereotypes from a multidimensional perspective (cognitive versus emotional dimension) has proved useful to knowing and describing stereotypes in greater depth. In this paper, we evaluated two aspects or dimensions of stereotypes (cognitive and emotional), as well as some related behaviors, in two cohorts of college students 8 years apart (2004-2012). The cognitive dimension referred to beliefs about the characteristics attributed to people with AIDS, which is linked to the classic definition of stereotype. The emotional dimension included the emotions that were aroused by a person with AIDS, which is linked to the definition of prejudice, since prejudice is assumed to be about largely negative emotions. At behavioral level, we evaluated the intention to establish a relationship with a person with AIDS, the intention to ask their partner to perform the diagnostic test and whether they had ever performed the test.

Our results have shown that a person with AIDS was perceived by most college students (over 50%) in both cohorts as imprudent, careless, a prostitute, a drug user, promiscuous, unfaithful and prone to vice. Additionally, around 50% of them considered such a person as older, homosexual, dangerous, sick and dirty. These findings were similar to some previous research with young people in different countries like Canada or Spain (Graffigna and Olson 2009; Rojas-Murcia et al. 2015). Although our data showed significant differences in the cognitive dimension by cohort, these were small (8% of explained variance) and not consistent-that is, it favored either cohort interchangeably. In line with previous research (Graffigna and Olson 2009; Parker and Aggleton 2003; Rojas-Murcia et al. 2015), AIDS perception remained linked to some social groups such as homosexual, drug users or prostitutes and the supposed characteristics associated with them. As Labra (2015, 245) reported, changes in the social representation of AIDS in recent years only affected their peripheral elements but not the central structure of it.

The emotional response of students to a person with AIDS has proved ambivalent. On the one hand, most students (over 50%) in both cohorts said they experienceed grief, concern, compassion or surprise. On the other hand, they reported feeling displeasure, fear, rage, frustration, impotence and nervousness. These results were similar to those reported by Dias, Matos and Goncalves (2006) in Portugal where young people showed ambivalence between compassion and fear. This type of response could be explained by the stigmatization model described by Corrigan and colleagues (2003), where as the individuals attributed the cause of

AIDS to being homosexual or a prostitute, and linked AIDS to death, this triggers an emotional reaction of fear and rejection that moreover can influence their own behavior. However, students were also aware that people with AIDS are stigmatized, for which they showed compassion. Labra (2015, 245) reported that recent changes in the social representations of AIDS were precisely related to a more humane and empathetic vision toward those suffering from the disease, since it has increased awareness of their social exclusion.

In addition, although the differences between cohorts were small regarding this emotional dimension in our study (10% of explained variance), these showed that students in the later cohort (2012) further expressed a more intense emotional response toward people with AIDS. This could be an indication of a slight increase in prejudice against this group over time. Given that this disease is considered as more clinically manageable nowadays, it is worth wondering if the preventive efforts are being reduced.

In contrast to this emotional response, when students were asked directly if they cared to study or work with a person with AIDS, they mostly expressed that they did not mind at all. We believe that the answer to this question is a reflection of the emotional ambivalence manifested and, fundamentally, is the result of social desirability. College students are an educated part of the population who are aware that holding and expressing prejudice against particular social groups could be considered inappropriate.

When asked upon what they based their ideas of this, it was found that about 90% of the students did not have direct contact with people suffering from this disease, as far as they knew. This indicates that their knowledge of the disease does not derive from direct experience with it. Moreover, very few of them have been tested for AIDS once and also few would usually ask their partner to have the test done. As previous research pointed out (Graffigna and Olson 2009; Levine and Ross 2002; Rojas-Murcia et al. 2015), these behaviours may indicate that students do not feel susceptible to AIDS.

Attempts to generalize from the present findings should be tempered by the methodological limitations inherent in the study design. Firstly, the use of a non-probability sampling method implies that the generalization of the results to the general population should be made with caution. Moreover, since data collection was cross-sectional in two cohorts with a difference of only 8 years, inferences about the effects of time on stereotypes should also be considered carefully.

In conclusion, our study seems to support the theory (Catania et al. 1994; Graffigna and Olson 2009; Levine and Ross 2002, Riley and Baah-Odoom 2010) that college students perceive AIDS as a disease linked to certain risk groups, helping them to distance themselves from such groups and consequently, not feeling susceptible to the disease. These findings highlight the importance of recognizing that prevention efforts with young people should not stop and should be addressed to change stereotypes so that AIDS is decoupled from the usual risk groups and to increase perceptions of susceptibility to HIV.

References

Bisquerra, Rafael. 1989. *Introducción conceptual al análisis multivariante. Un enfoque informático con los paquetes SPSS-X, BMDP, LISREL y SPAD*. Barcelona: P.P.U.

Catania, Joseph; Coates, Thomas and Kegeles, Susan. 1994. A test of the AIDS risk reduction model: psychosocial correlates of condom use in the AMEN cohort survey. *Health Psychology* 13: 548-555.

Dias, Sonia; Matos, Margarida and Goncalves, Aldina. 2006. "AIDS-related stigma and attitudes towards AIDS-infected people among adolescents." *AIDS Care* 18(3): 208-214.

Earnshaw, Valerie; Smith, Laramie; Chaudoir, Sthephenie; Lee, I-Ching and Copenhaver, Michael. 2012. "Stereotypes about people living with HIV: implications for perceptions of HIV risk and testing frequency among at-risk populations." AIDS *Education and Prevention* 24(6): 574-581.

Fondo de las Naciones Unidas para la Infancia (UNICEF). 2013. "Hacia una generación libre de SIDA. La infancia y el SIDA: Sexto inventario de la situación 2013." Nueva York: UNICEF Accessed October 18, 2015 from http://www.childrenandaids.org/files/str6_full_report_basic_sp.pdf.

García, Janet. 2006. Interacción social y comunicación para la salud. Las representaciones sociales de los jóvenes poblanos sobre sexualidad y VIH/Sida como fundamento para la implementación de programas institucionales de mejoramiento de la salud pública. *UNIrevista* 3(1): 17-25. Accessed October 24, 2015 from http://www.unirevista.unisinos.br/_pdf/UNIrev_Gonzalez.PDF.

Goodwin, Robin; Kwiatkowska, Anna; Realo, Anu; Kozlova, Alexandra; Nguyen Lan Anh and Nizharadze, George. 2004. "Social representations of HIV/AIDS in five Central European and Eastern European countries: a multidimensional analysis." *AIDS CARE* 16 (6): 669-680.

Graffigna Guendalina and Kärin Olson. 2009. "The Ineffable Disease: Exploring Young People's Discourses about HIV/AIDS in Alberta, Canada." *Qualitative Health Research* 19(6): 790-801. Accessed September 20, 2015. doi: 10.1177/1049732309335393.

Labra, Oscar. 2015. Social representations of HIV/AIDS in mass media: some important lessons for caregivers. *International Social Work* 58(2): 238-248.

Lekas, Helen-Maria. 2006. "Continuities and Discontinuities in the Experiences of Felt and Enacted Stigma Among Women With HIV/AIDS." *Qualitative Health Research* 16(9): 1165-1190.

Levine, Susan and Ross, Fiona. 2002. "Perceptions of and attitudes to HIV/AIDS among young adults in Cape Town". *Social Dynamic* 28(1): 89-108.

Maswanya, E., Moji, K., Aoyagi, K., Yahata, Y., Kusano, Y., Nagata, K., Izumi, T. and Takemoto, T. 2000. "Knowledge and attitudes toward AIDS among female college students in Nagasaki, Japan." *Health Education Research* 15(1): 5-11.

Pittam, Jeffery and Cynthia Gallois. 2000. "Malevolence, stigma, and social distance: maximizing intergroup differences in HIV/AIDS discourse." *Journal of Applied Communication Research* 28(1): 24-43.

Richard Parker and Peter Aggleton. 2003. "HIV and AIDS-related stigma and discrimination: a conceptual framework and implications for action," *Social Science and Medicine* 57(1) 13-24.

Riley, Gerard and Dinah Baah-Odoom. 2010. "Do stigma, blame and stereotyping contribute to unsafe sexual behaviour? A test of claims about the spread of HIV/AIDS arising from social representation theory and the AIDS risk reduction model." *Social Science and Medicine* 71: 600-607. Accessed September 28, 2015. doi:10.1016/j.socscimed.2010.04.026.

Rojas-Murcia, Carolina; Pastor, Yolanda and Esteban-Hernández, Jesús. 2015. "Ilusión de invulnerabilidad, estereotipos y percepción de control del SIDA en universitarios." *Revista Iberoamericana de Psicología y Salud* 6: 28-38.

Schneider, David J. 2005. "The psychology of stereotyping". London: The Guilford Press.

Ubillos, Silvia, Páez, Darío, Mayordomo, Sonia, and Sánchez, Flor. 2003. "Sesgos cognitivos y explicaciones asociadas como factores determinantes de las conductas sexuales de riesgo." *Revista de Psicología Social, 18:* 261-279. doi: 10.1177/1049732309335393.

World Health Organization (WHO) 2013. "HIV and adolescents: Guidance for HIV testing and counselling and care for adolescents living with HIV". Ginebra, Suiza. World Health Organization. Accesed October 20, 2015 from http://apps.who.int/iris/bitstream/10665/94334/1/9789241506168_eng.pdf.

Biographical Sketch

Name: Yolanda Pastor

Affiliation: Rey Juan Carlos University

Date of Birth: 18/02/1971

Education: PhD in Psychology

Address: Yolanda Pastor, Universidad Rey Juan Carlos, Departamento de Psicología, Despacho 2037. Avda. Atenas, s/n, 28922. Alcorcón, Madrid, Spain. E-mail:yolanda.pastor@urjc.es

Research and Professional Experience:

Yolanda Pastor has completed her PhD at the age of 27 years from University of Valencia (Valencia, Spain). She is professor in Social Psychology at Rey Juan Carlos University (Madrid, Spain). Her research is focused on the study of psychosocial factors that surround adolescence and youth. She has published more than 20 papers in reputed journals and has presented over 75 papers in national and international conferences on these topics.

Professional Appointments:

2nd International Conference on Retroviruses and Novel Drugs

XIII National Congress of Social Psychology

I International Congress of Clinical and Health Psychology with Children and Adolescents

4th International Congress of Educational Sciences and Development

Honors: Extraordinary Doctoral Award. University of Valencia. 18/04/2000

Publications Last 3 Years:

Fernández, J. J. and Pastor, Y. (2014). *Social psychology of tourism*. Madrid, OMM Editorial.

Martínez, F., Benavides, G., Ato, M., Solanes, A., Martín, B., Fernández, J. and Pastor, Y. (2014). Predictors of distress in hospital physicians: protective and vulnerability factors. *Anales de psicología*, 30(2), 579-587. doi: 10.6018/analesps.30.2.161421.

Pastor, Y., Quiles, Y. and Pamies, L. (2012). Social support in adolescence: psychometric properties of "Social Support Scale for Children." *Revista de Psicología Social*, 27(1), 39-54.

Rojas, C., Pastor, Y., Esteban, J. (2015) Illusion of invulnerability, stereotypes and perception of control to AIDS in undergraduate students. *Revista Iberoamericana de psicología y salud*, 6, 28-38.

Troyano, Y. and Pastor, Y. (2014). La comunicación mediada: de la masa a la audiencia. En: T. Núñez (coord.), Competencias *psicosociales para profesionales de los medios* (pp. 149-162). Madrid: Pirámide.

***Name*:** Vanesa Pérez

***Affiliation*:** Rey Juan Carlos University

***Date of Birth*:** 04/27/73

***Education*:** PhD in Psychology

***Address*:** Vanesa Pérez, Universidad Rey Juan Carlos, Departamento de Psicología, Despacho 2046. Avda. Atenas, s/n, 28922. Alcorcón, Madrid, Spain. E-mail:vanesa.perez@urjc.es

***Research and Professional Experience*:**

Vanesa Pérez has completed her PhD in Psychology at the Rey Juan Carlos University (Madrid, Spain). She is professor in Rey Juan Carlos University and her research activity is focused on the areas of social psychology, learning and developmental psychology. She is also coordinator of the subject of psychology of motivation and emotion and thesis director in master degree.

***Professional Appointments*:**

2nd International Conference on Retroviruses and Novel Drugs

XIII National Congress of Social Psychology

***Publications Last 3 Years*:**

Pérez, V. (2015) Afrontamiento y regulación emocional en personas en situación de desempleo (Coping and emotional regulation in unemployment), *Revista de Trabajo y Seguridad Social*, (383), 236-256.

Pérez, V., Alcover, C. M. and Chambel, M. J. (2015). Job attitudes in workers with disabilities: the importance of family support in addition to organizational support. *WORK, A Journal of Prevention, Assessment and Rehabilitation*, 51(4), 817-836. doi 10. 3233/WOR-141905.

Pérez, V., Alcover, C. M. (2013). Job Attitudes in Workers with Disabilities: The Importance of Family Support in Addition to Organizational Support. *Paper presented at 16th Congress of the European Association of Work and Organizational Psychology (EAWOP) in Münster, Germany, May 22-25th*. URN: http://nbn-resolving.de/urn:nbn:de: hbz:6-66399491491.

In: Stereotypes and Stereotyping
Editor: Claude Fields

ISBN: 978-1-63484-510-6

Chapter 4

SOCIAL MEDIA'S RELATIONSHIP TO COLLEGE WOMEN'S TIME ALLOCATIONS TO PHYSICAL AND ACADEMIC BEHAVIORS

Melinda C. R. Burgess*
Southwestern Oklahoma State University, Oklahoma, US

ABSTRACT

In an era of unprecedented and relentless social comparison made possible by the numerous social media platforms, young women today face unique pressures to demonstrate their achievements be those academic, physical, social (i.e., relationships), or even in more mundane domains such as cooking or home decoration. Previous research has firmly established a link between media consumption and young women's heightened concern over bodily appearance and conformity to social norms regarding bodily appearance; more recent work has illustrated how the pressure to be attractive is often synonymous with being 'hot' or sexy. This work has been expanded to include some of the newer forms of social media such as Pinterest and Tumblr. However, little work has examined the relationship between social media usage and perceptions of how to balance the time-consuming demands for physical appearance and the academic rigor necessary to train for a successful career. This investigation has two goals examining the relationship between social media usage and achievement in both academic and physical domains. First, we examine if college women's social media usage predicts how they budget their time regarding physical appearance and academic work while in school. Second, we examine if college women's social media usage predicts their perceptions of the relative importance of appearance related behaviors and domain specific skills for their future careers.

Keywords: academic performance, social media, physical attractiveness

* Correspondence concerning this chapter should be addressed to Dr. Melinda C.R. Burgess, Southwestern Oklahoma State University, 100 Campus Dr., Weatherford, OK, 73096 or via email at melinda.burgess@swosu.edu.

Introduction

"To get ahead a woman either has to be a total bitch, or really hot; I'm choosing hot."
----*anonymous undergraduate female, discussing how to achieve success, 2015.*

"If you feel your value lies in being merely decorative, I fear that someday you might find yourself believing that's all that you really are. Time erodes all such beauty. But what it cannot diminish is the wonderful workings of your mind..."
---- *Louisa May Alcott, Little Women, (Marmee, to her daughters Meg and Jo) 1880.*

Although these quotes are separated by over 100 years, it is striking how little has changed since Marmee advised Meg and Jo to focus on developing their minds over their appearances. Her admonition was not simply because "time erodes all such beauty," thus making it an ultimately futile endeavor, but rather because the mind was so much more valuable, and rewarding for the woman herself, as well as those who know her. How else could a woman leave the world a better place than she found it, for herself, for her family and for her community?

Today, with the modern media depicting an unrelenting array of ever increasing physical perfection, young women still face this dichotomy. While Alcott and her contemporaries were presented with various magazine and newspaper advertisements extolling the latest fashions and products to achieve the newest beauty fad, today's young women are bombarded with media messages nearly every moment of everyday as they carry a cell phone delivering the latest Instagram and Twitter feeds, the latest Facebook update or the latest how-to pins on Pinterest. How is this onslaught of media perfection related to women's relative value of their bodies and minds? That is the question this chapter seeks to explore.

Media Content

How Are Women Presented in the Media?

The many investigations in psychology and communication exploring the ways that women are portrayed in the media have strikingly similar conclusions: women tend to be underrepresented generally, and when present, portrayed as unusually thin and almost always sexualized (see Scharrer, 2013 for a review). Harrison (2003) perhaps gives the best description of this combination in her term "curvaceously thin" (p. 256) emphasizing anatomically, incongruently large breasts considering the overall thinness of the body. This portrayal is nearly universal, regardless of the type of media presenting it, although the sexualization takes myriad forms (e.g., position of the body, the body type, the clothing, or lack thereof, and accessories adorning the body).

In terms of roles and opportunities, in nearly every genre on prime-time television, women are less likely to be present than men (Signorelli, 2013). Video games, one of the most ubiquitous types of entertainment enjoyed by young adults, both male and female, have faced some of the most scrutinous evaluation in terms of gender portrayal, and rightly so. Burgess, Stermer and Burgess (2007) and Dill and Thill (2007) examined both video game covers and advertisements, respectively, and found that males were more than three times more common as characters than females. The one exception to this was the category of "eye candy," where a character seems to bring little to the situation beyond her ability to arouse the viewer (Burgess et al., 2007, p. 426); 38.5% of the female characters met this definition while only 1.1% of the male characters did. This pattern does not improve inside the games either; a comprehensive investigation of actual game content found that over 85% of the characters one meets are men (Williams, Martins, Colsalvo and Ivory, 2009).

How Does Media Influence Women's Attitudes and Behaviors in Regard to Their Bodies?

Given that the most common female body type presented by modern media is one that is nearly impossible to achieve naturally, it should come as no surprise that exposure to this type of media is related to a variety of negative reactions regarding the body. Grabe, Ward and Hyde (2008) conducted one of the most extensive meta-analyses in the area. As predicted, examining both experimental manipulations and correlational work examining the relationship between media consumption and outcome variables, exposure to these types of portrayals is consistently related to body dissatisfaction, body self-consciousness, internalization of the thin ideal and disordered eating behaviors including caloric restriction and purging through mechanisms such as excessive exercise and laxative abuse.

With the advent of social media such as Facebook, Pinterest and Instagram has come a new form of media promotion of the thin ideal. This new trend is known as "fitspiration" and it, allegedly, is designed to inspire women to focus on fitness as opposed to weight or other more body-focused goals. Fitspiration followed, and was alleged to be a healthful alternative, to what was known as "thinspiration" which was designed to help inspire women to varying thinness goals, up to and including anorexic behaviors. Fitspiration, in contrast, is supposed to promote healthy eating and fitness. In spite of its more noble aims, Fitspiration has been found to have similarly negative impacts on women following even short term exposure (Tiggemann and Zaccardo, 2015). Undergraduate women who viewed fitspiration images, as compared to travel images, experienced decreased mood, increased body dissatisfaction and lowered appearance based self-esteem.

Frederickson and Roberts (1997) first proposed objectification theory to explain how the experience of sexual objectification of women was incorporated into women's views of themselves and how that psychological experience related to the numerous negative mental health events that are seen in women, ranging from depression and anxiety, to eating disorders, to sexual dysfunction. This experience of sexual objectification, which is a normal part of gender socialization for women in the United States, occurs when an over-emphasis is given to a woman's sexual anatomy and/or function when considering her value, sometimes to the extent that her physical being is deemed the only valuable aspect of her being. This is amply illustrated in media representations of women with their over-emphasis on sexuality, generally, and their obsession with the 'curvaceously thin' body type. But it is also evident in how the body is filmed or photographed, often with what has been termed the "objectifying gaze" (Kilbourne, 2013) and even the "pornographic gaze" (Jhally, 2007). Fredrickson and Roberts (1997) argue that this way of being looked at is one of the most central aspects of sexualization that women and girls take from the culture and incorporate into their social identity, learning to treat *themselves* as sexual objects, and to evaluate *themselves* primarily based on their physical appearance; this way of defining the self is self-objectification. Self-objectification can be assessed to varying degrees in samples of women (Noll and Fredrickson, 1998) as a pre-existing tendency, or it can be manipulated through experimental exposure to objectified experiences (Fredrickson, Noll, Quinn and Twenge, 1998).

The now classic 'swimsuit study' (Fredrickson et al., 1998) assessed this experimental heightening of self-objectification and its impact on academic behavior. Fredrickson and her colleagues (1998) asked women to try on either a sweater or a swimsuit for 15 minutes, ostensibly as part of a study investigating consumer behaviors, and had them complete a math task while they were waiting for the time to pass. The women, but not the men, wearing the swimsuit, as compared to the sweater, showed significantly impaired math performance. The sex difference in this work is important in that it illustrates just how different the experience of sexualization is for men and women. For women, but not for men, this experience of being reduced to the body (which was illustrated by heightened self-objectification scores in the swimsuit condition, in addition to the impaired math performance), is a real possibility, with real consequences. Certainly, swimsuits are not standard clothing for academic settings, nor are women typically asked to take a math task at the local pool, but this work illustrates that when the body, and specifically sexuality, is made paramount to a woman's awareness that awareness can interfere with normal, productive cognitive ability.

Given that self-objectification can interfere with academic behaviors, Gervais, Vescio and Allen (2011) investigated how an objectifying gaze would influence math ability in both male and female college students. When the students arrived at the lab they were assigned to a 'partner' (actually a confederate) of the opposite sex with whom they were to complete some word problems in an experiment investigating team work. Before beginning the team work portion, the confederate interviewed the subject (for example, asking the subject to describe a situation in which they had been successful). In the objectification condition, when the subject entered the room the confederate made a sweeping motion with their eyes from the subjects head to their waist, and back up to the head. Additionally, during the third of five interview questions, the confederate stared briefly at the subject's chest. Finally, the confederate also gave the subject written feedback explaining that it was her looks that impressed him. As predicted, women in the objectified gaze condition performed significantly worse on the math task than did the women in the control condition, or the men in either condition. In other words, the objectifying gaze of the partner disrupted women's math performance, but did not disrupt the men's math performance.

Perhaps even more intriguing were the results regarding whether the women would like to spend more time with this man who had previously objectified them (Gervais, et al., 2011). And yes, in spite of the confederate's previous emphasis on their looks over their abilities, the women reported increased interest in spending time with this man, than the women in the control condition. Why would this be? There are a variety of hypotheses that can explain a woman's desire to spend time with an objectifying partner. Given that all the women reported at least some levels of body dissatisfaction, body shame, and body surveillance, it is possible that his objectifying gaze was seen as complimentary. However, when we understand that while the women in both conditions experienced negative attitudes about their bodies, but it was only the women in the objectifying condition, with their subsequently impaired math performance, who wanted to spend more time with the confederate, we are left with the very real possibility that when women feel threatened in their cognitive identity/ability, it is reassuring to know that at least they are valued for their bodies. Considering that most women experience their first brush with objectification in early adolescence (Collins et al., 2007), by the time they are in college women will have had years of being subtly taught that their value lies in their appearance as opposed to their cognitive capabilities.

Just as the opening quote has Marmee encouraging her daughters to live beyond the physical limitations in which society was willing to wrap women over 100 years ago, it is reasonable to ask whether the paramount value society still places on women's bodies holds them back from work for their own betterment. Is it possible that objectification, be it inflicted on a woman by someone else, or embraced on her own, influences her willingness to work to improve her own opportunities, be they academic, financial or legal? Calogero (2013) investigated the relationship between both pre-existing self-objectification as well as experimentally heightened self-objectification and women's engagement in social activism. She found that women who have higher pre-existing levels of self-objectification are more likely to endorse what is known as systems justification (e.g., endorsing the notion that the treatment of men and women is fair today), and this in turn is related to decreased social activism. When asked specifically to write about their experiences with self-objectification (as compared to writing about how they would spend the gift card they could win in exchange for participation), this same relationship emerged. In other words, both engaging in self-objectification and experiencing objectification leads to women who are less likely to pursue gender related social justice. The implications of this are fairly troubling when one considers how pervasive the message is to women today that their primary value lies in their sexual attractiveness.

How Does Media Influence Women's Attitudes and Behaviors?

In today's electronic environment society has an ever more extensive reach in terms of providing material with which to compare oneself, or information about what is valued in your particular social group. How does all this self-comparison influence people? In one of the first investigations of social media and its relationship to how individuals feel about themselves, Vogel and her colleagues (Vogel, Rose, Roberts and Eckles, 2014) conducted both correlational and experimental investigations. They first measured the relationship between social media use (specifically Facebook) and looked to see if increased social media use was related to self-esteem. Indeed, people who had higher levels of Facebook use had lower self-esteem; however, this was mediated by the more frequent upward social comparisons available on social media. In other words, the more upward social comparisons (comparing to someone who is better off) one engages in on Facebook, the lower the self-esteem. This was confirmed to be a causal relationship in a second, experimental study.

While there is no work, of which we are aware, that explicitly examines the social comparison issue with Facebook use and academics, there is some interesting work that shows social networking use is negatively related to academic performance (Paul, Baker and Cochran, 2012). Although this work was largely investigating how online social media use impacted academic performance through things like attention span and time management skills, the suggestion is there that perhaps the very nature of the material likely to be found on social media is deleterious to academic success. Vogel et al. (2014) have demonstrated that it is specifically upward social comparisons in Facebook use that lead to decreased self-esteem, and Tiggemann and Zaccardo (2015) have shown that even brief exposure to things like

'Fitspiration' imagery common to social media are damaging to women's feelings about their bodies. Is it possible that these types of sexualized and objectified media can interfere with women's academic behaviors?

When the phenomenon of stereotype threat was first described (Steele and Aronson, 1995), it could induce, and explain, the relative gap in academic performance between African-American and European American college students. It was quickly extended to the 'math gap' seen in women's academic performance relative to men's (Shih, Pittinsky and Ambady, 1999). However, it quickly became clear that stereotyped media images were related to other outcomes in women. Davies, Spencer, Quinn and Gerhardstein (2002) exposed both male and female college students to stereotypic television commercials. These commercials aired on major networks and featured women acting as what can best be described as bimbos in a state of unrestrained excitement over either a brownie mix or a new acne product.

Across three different experiments, exposure to these commercials, as compared to neutral commercials without people in them, led to three distinct outcomes in the women. First, women who saw the stereotyped commercials performed more poorly on a math test (study 1). Second, when given a test that contained both quantitative and verbal items, the women who were exposed to the stereotyped commercials consistently avoided the math items in favor of the verbal items (study 2). Finally, and most relevant from an occupational perspective, women in the stereotyped commercial condition rated careers in math and science as significantly less appealing than careers in highly verbal areas such as communication or creative writing. It is critical to note that these women were not people for whom mathematics was a drudge. The women in the first experiment were in Calculus 2, and had received a B or better in the previous calculus class they had completed; additionally, the women in all three studies indicated that they felt they were strong in mathematics, and that they enjoyed mathematics. This work demonstrates just how insidious the effect of these kind of stereotyped portrayals can be. When mathematically skilled women can be induced to underperform, to avoid problems and devalue math based careers by the briefest of exposures to these kinds of stereotypes, is it any wonder that young women might consider their value lying in appearance as opposed to intellect? This is precisely the possibility that the work on self-objectification has examined.

Current Investigation

The purpose of this study was to conduct an exploratory investigation between women's social media use and their prioritizing of academic and body-related behaviors. Specifically, how did their dedicated time to studying, and career-related behaviors relate to the amount of time they devoted to physical fitness, and did this comparison relate to their social media use? Given that we all face a limited number of hours in any day, how we choose to spend them can be used as a proxy measure for how much we value certain activities. What are young women's motivations for both academic behaviors and physical fitness behaviors, and do these motivations relate to social media use? In order to answer these questions, I surveyed a large sample of young adult women in a university setting. Ideally, women enrolled in a university understand their personal value lies at least as much in their minds as in their physiques, so this was an appropriate sample to in which to investigate how social media relates to the value they place on learning and the behaviors necessary to obtain the career-related skills associated with the degree.

METHODS

Participants. 132 young women (average age = 20.01, s_{age} = 4.16) from a medium sized university in the southwestern United States participated in exchange for either partial completion of a course requirement or extra credit. Of those who reported race, 78% identified as Caucasian, 5.3% as Other, 6.1% as Native American, 6.8% as Hispanic and 3.0% as African American. Of those indicating a major, the most frequently listed was Nursing (33.3%), followed by Education (11.1%), Psychology (9.9%), and Pharmacy (8.6%).

Materials. The students completed a series of surveys. The first was created for this investigation and simply asked them to indicate how much time they engaged in the following activities each *day* of the week: engaged in cardio-vascular exercise/strength training/abdominal exercise/flexibility training/other exercise, working on their course outside of class, interacting with social media (Facebook, Instagram, Twitter, Tumblr, Pinterest, and Snapchat). They were also asked how much time they spent each *week* engaged in the following career preparation activities: attending workshops, guest speakers, reading non-text materials (e.g., journal articles), searching for internships, other. They also evaluated how much they felt each of the following contributed to their chosen career path (on a scale of 1 - not at all important - to 10 - extremely important): good grades, good connections, physical attractiveness/sexiness, outgoing personality, religion, higher education, internships, clothing and physical fitness. Finally, they completed the Perceived Instrumentality and Academics Scale (Miller, DeBacker and Greene, 1999) and the Motives for Physical Activities Measures - Revised (MPAM-R) (Ryan, Frederick, Lepes, Rubio and Sheldon, 1997). Two questions were added to the MPAM-R: "Because I want to make my body 'sexy'" and "Because I find it relaxing, like a form of meditation."

RESULTS AND DISCUSSION

Question 1: How Much Time Do College Women Spend Interacting with Social Media?

The participants indicated how much time (in minutes) they spent per day on each of the following six social media platforms: Facebook, Instagram, Twitter, Tumblr, Pinterest and Snapchat. Pinterest was the most frequently used ($M_{Pinterest}$ = 66.8 min, $s_{Pinterest}$ = 108.4 min; Median = 30 min; about 1/3 of the sample spent no time, with another 1/3 spending between 60 and 120 min), with Facebook next ($M_{Facebook}$ = 60.9 min, $s_{Facebook}$ = 99.4 min; Media = 30; approximately 25% of the sample never used it and approximately 37% using it between 30 and 60 minutes per day). Instagram was the third most frequently used ($M_{Instagram}$ = 46.3 min, $s_{Instagram}$ = 112.4 min; Median = 10 min)). Twitter was the least frequently used ($M_{Twitter}$ = 12.9 min, $s_{Twitter}$ = 43.4 min; Median = 0 min; 80% of the sample reported no use) with Snapchat and Tumblr just above that ($M_{Snapchat}$ = 26.8 min, $s_{Snapchat}$ = 97.7 min; M_{Tumblr} = 25.8

min, s_{Tumblr} = 48.8 min; both of these also had Medians of 0 with 76% and 61%, respectively, of the sample reporting no use of either). Total social media use (adding the various platforms together) varied dramatically from no use to 2400 minutes/day (one has to assume that this individual is using multiple platforms at one time as opposed to having a longer day than the rest of us), with an average of 239. 7 minutes each day ($s_{socialmediadaily}$ = 335.1 min).

It is important to note that social media use does not include texting. The rationale for that was that texting has become an essential means for conversation among young adults, as opposed to a mechanism for comparison such as Facebook or Instagram offers. It is likely that the estimates for social media would have been dramatically higher had texting been included.

Question 2: How Much Time Do College Women Spend Studying and Exercising Per Week?

As with social media, the range of total time studying per week was quite broad, from 0 min/week to 2580 min per week with an average study time of 678.4 minutes each week ($s_{weeklystudytime}$ = 469.5 min; Median = 600 min). Exercise was similarly variable with a range from 0 min/week to 4200 minutes per week with an average of 527.1 minutes each day ($s_{weeklyexercisetime}$ = 623.6 min; Median = 360 min).

Because the amount of exercise reported was so high in this sample overall, restriction of range was a statistical concern (only 23% of the sample indicated that they exercised at or less than the recommended minimum of four 30 minute sessions per week, and only 32% of the sample indicated that they exercised at or below a regimen of 30 minutes every day). As such, in order to assess the relative amount of time spent exercising and studying, I chose to examine what percentage of the sample was meeting various guidelines regarding both health (exercise) and academic success (studying). The general recommendation for exercise for optimal health is to exercise for 30 minutes a day for a minimum of four days a week (120 min) and possibly every day (210 minutes). For academics, the rule of thumb is that for every hour in a class, a student should study outside of class for 2-3 hours per week. Thus, for a 12 credit hour load (as is typical for this sample), students should be studying between 24 and 36 hours, or 1440 and 2160 minutes each week.

In comparing the difference between the proportion of students who met the minimum exercise goal (120 min) and the proportion who met the minimum study goal (1440 min), we can see a huge difference: 94/120 (77.1%) students met the minimum exercise goal, while only 10/128 (7.8%) met the minimum study goal, $z = 11.102$, $p < .01$. This is also true at the maximum goal (210 minutes of exercise vs. 2160 minutes of studying), with 80/122 (65.6%) students exercising at the maximum, as compared to only 2/128 (1.6%) studying at the maximum goal, $z = 10.7758$, $p < .05$.

Question 3: Is There a Relationship Between Social Media Use and the Relative Amount of Time Spent Studying Versus Exercising?

In order to assess the relationship between social media use and time spent studying relative to the time spent exercising weekly study time total was divided by weekly exercise time. A ratio of 1.0 indicated an equal amount of time devoted to both studying and exercising, ratios under 1.0 indicated more time exercising than studying and ratios over 1.0 indicated more time studying than exercising. There was no relationship between social media use and this ratio ($r_{socialmediause\ x\ study/exerciseratio} = -.098$, $p > .05$); daily social media use was marginally related to weekly exercise time ($r = .242$, $p = .054$) but it was not related to weekly study time ($r = -.099$, $p > .4$)

Question 4: What Are the Motivations for Academic Work and Exercising?

In general, this sample reported relatively high intrinsic ($M_{intrinisc} = 4.35$, $s_{intrinsic} = 1.02$) and learning ($M_{learning} = 4.63$, $s_{learning} = 1.14$) motivations for academic behavior. The equivalent measures to Intrinsic and Learning motivations on the reasons to exercise scale are Interest and Enjoyment ($M_{interstenjoy} = 3.89$, $s_{interestenjoy} = 1.40$) and Competence ($M_{competence} = 3.94$, $s_{competence} = 1.47$). When comparing the proportions of women who indicated a 4 or over (representing agree to strongly agree on the scales) for Intrinsic motivation for learning (83/121) versus Interest and Enjoyment for physical activity (63/121), we see that more women seem to be motivated by the academic work than the physical, $z = 2.628$, $p < .01$. The same pattern emerges for comparing both the Learning motivation (92/121) and the corresponding Competence motivation for physical activity (64/121), $z = 3.761$, $p < .01$. Both of these comparisons suggest that the women in this sample reported higher intrinsic motivation and greater desire to learn in academic settings, relative to their lower interest/enjoyment and competence motivations for physical exercise. In spite of this psychological engagement with learning it did not necessarily translate into increased academic behavior in the form of studying.

Question 5: Are High Exercisers Different Than Low Exercisers in Their Social Media Use and Their Study Time?

Time spent on any one activity can be used as a proxy measure of how much value that activity has to one's life; in this case, spending greater amounts of time exercising can be seen as putting more of a priority on health and fitness as compared to less time exercising. On the other hand, studying can be seen as valuing if not the intellect, then certainly what intellectual achievement can help one accomplish. Given that the media routinely emphasizes the importance of a woman's body as opposed to her mind, it seems reasonable that some women will incorporate this body value into their daily lives (that is certainly borne out in measures like internalization of the thin ideal (e.g., Hawkins, Richards, Granley and Stein, 2004). Therefore, this question seeks to address whether high exercisers (clearly valuing the body) use social media differently, and whether they value the intellect less. To address this I divided weekly exercise time into three equal groups. The low group was 0-210 minutes per week (corresponding just at or below the recommended 30 minutes per day), the intermediate group was 211-539 minutes per week and the high group was 540+ minutes per week. There was a clear difference between the three groups in their social media use (F (2, 121) = 3.506, $p < .05$); the high exercisers ($M_{HighExercise} = 345.56$, $s_{HighExercise} = 471.13$) spending significantly more time on social media than the low exercisers ($M_{LowExercise}$ = 149.12, $s_{LowExercise}$ = 147.43), but neither low nor high exercisers differing from the moderate exercisers ($M_{ModerateExercise}$ = 237.66, $s_{ModerateExercise}$ = 317.71). Interestingly, weekly study time did not differ by exercise group ($F < 1$).

Question 6: Does Outside-of-class Career Preparation Differ by Exercising Group? Is There a Difference Between the Relative Amount of Time Spent on Extra-Curricular Career Preparation and Social Media?

Outside of class career preparation (searching for internships, attending workshops, reading journal articles) was generally low in this sample (as might be expected in a group of general education students; in fact 78 of the 132 women indicated either 0 minutes per week, or left the items blank), with an average of 78.33 minutes per week (s = 133. 10). This did not differ by exercising group (F (2, 98) = 1.022, $p > .05$), nor was it related to social media use ($r_{socialmediause\ x\ outsidecareerpreptime} = -.053, p > .05$).

Question 7: Do High Exercisers Rate the Relative Importance of Physical and Intellectual Attributes to Their Career Higher Than Moderate or Low Exercisers?

Similarly to question 3, I created a ratio from the questions asking the students to rate the relative importance of intellectual and physical skills (i.e., attractiveness) to their future careers dividing the physical attributes average by the intellectual attributes average. A ratio greater than 1.0 indicated more relative importance to the physical while a ratio under 1.0 indicated more relative importance to the intellectual. The physical items were sexiness and fitness, while the intellectual items were grades, higher education and internships. The difference between the three exercising groups was not significant (F (2, 160) = 2.136, $p > .05$); however there was a clear trend for the high exercisers ($M_{highexercisers}$ = .736, $s_{higexercisers}$ = .27) to rate the physical attributes as more important than the low exercisers ($M_{highexercisers}$ = .618, $s_{higexercisers}$ = .39).

General Discussion

This study sought to explore questions about college women's exercise and study habits and motivations, in relation to social media useage as well as address their beliefs about what was important to their future careers. In general, the women engaged in quite a bit of exercise. In fact, 77.1% of the women were meeting the recommended minimums in terms of exercise per week. Yet only 7.8% of the women were meeting the recommended minimums for studying. This is the most interesting finding, albeit a bit discouraging on a college campus, suggesting, perhaps, that women do recognize the increased value society emphasizes on their bodies over their minds, and as such are much more diligent in taking care of their physical selves. However, the women were reluctant to admit that they themselves placed more emphasis on physical attributes when considering career success, when compared to intellectual skills (e.g., grades were rated on average as an 8.95 (s = 2.51) out of 10 while sexiness and fitness were rated on average as 4.75 (2.24) and 6.19 (5.0) out of 10, respectively).

Perhaps the most discouraging component to all these data was the finding that although the women reported more intrinsic motivation and a greater desire to learn in an academic setting, these motivations did not translate into a corresponding likelihood to work as hard on their academics as they reported working on their bodies. What is most disheartening about this is that the women reported significantly lower interest and enjoyment in physical activities as compared to intrinsic and learning motivations for academics, yet they were surprisingly diligent in meeting the recommended minimums for daily exercise.

It is entirely possible that this sample of women simply did not have to work that hard academically to succeed, and that ease of success drove the relatively low amount of time spent studying. However, the demographics of the university where these data were collected suggest that this is unlikely as a significant number of first year students receive a D, F, or W in the classes from which these data were collected. Future research needs to explore the reasons why women might be so much more likely to engage in what they reported as the less desirable physical activity as compared to the more enjoyable academic activity. As it stands, these data suggest that even though they don't subjectively agree based on the self-reported values, women are dividing up their time in a way that is consistent with what the media tells them: physical attractiveness, while difficult to achieve the standards as promoted, is more valuable than intellectual strength, and is worth a significant investment of their limited time.

Perhaps the most surprising results came from the finding that daily social media use was not related to the women's self-reported study time. The average time per day that this sample spent on social media was 239.73 min (s = 335.1; Median = 150), and the high exercisers in this sample did spend significantly more time on social media than the low exercisers (but not the moderate exercisers). However, it is unclear how exercise and social media use are related. Are high exercisers posting about their exercise time (e.g., posting selfies of their improved fitness, updating their status to note that they exercised on a given day, etc.)? Are they looking for recommended exercise programs and tips (e.g., looking at 'fitspiration' images)? Are they connecting with other exercisers to make plans to socialize in an exercise setting? This is clearly something that needs to be explored in future research. And while the high exercisers differed significantly from the other groups in their motivations to exercise (but not their motivations to study), reporting more enjoyment, increased sense of competence, social connections, greater relaxation and more desire to exercise to achieve appearance, fitness and sexiness goals, social media use was not related to any of these.

In the end, this study offers some tantalizing hints that women *behave* as if they understand their bodies are more valuable than their intellectual skills, even though they are loathe to admit it. This investigation provides more questions than answers but it does suggest the importance of future research exploring this area.

References

Alcott, L. M. (2004). *Little women*. New York: Signet Classic.

Burgess, M. C., Stermer, S. P. and Burgess, S. R. (2007). Sex, lies, and video games: The portrayal of male and female characters on video game covers. *Sex Roles, 57(5-6)*, 419-433.

Calogero, R. M. (2013). Objects Don't Object: Evidence That Self-Objectification Disrupts Women's Social Activism. *Psychological Science*, *24*(3), 312–318.

Collins, R. L. R., Lamb, S., Roberts, T.-A., Tolman, D. L., Ward, L. M., Blake, J. and Zurbriggen, E. (2007). Report of the APA Task Force on the Sexualization of Girls APA Task Force on the Sexualization of Girls. *American Psychological Association*, 1–72.

Davies, P. G., Spencer, S. J., Quinn, D. M. and Gerhardstein, R. (2002). Consuming images: How television commercials that elicit stereotype threat can restrain women academically and professionally. *Personality and Social Psychology Bulletin*, *28*(12), 1615-1628.

Dill, K. E. and Thill, K. P. (2007). Video game characters and the socialization of gender roles: Young people's perceptions mirror sexist media depictions. *Sex roles*, *57*(11-12), 851-864.

Fredrickson, B. L., Roberts, T. A., Noll, S. M., Quinn, D. M. and Twenge, J. M. (1998). That swimsuit becomes you: sex differences in self-objectification, restrained eating, and math performance. *Journal of personality and social psychology*, *75*(1), 269.

Fredrickson, B. L. and Roberts, T. A. (1997). Objectification theory. *Psychology of women quarterly, 21(2)*, 173-206.

Gervais, S. J., Vescio, T. K. and Allen, J. (2011). When What You See Is What You Get: The Consequences of the Objectifying Gaze for Women and Men. *Psychology of Women Quarterly*, *35*(1), 5–17.

Grabe, S., Ward, L. M. and Hyde, J. S. (2008). The role of the media in body image concerns among women: a meta-analysis of experimental and correlational studies. *Psychological bulletin, 134(3)*, 460.

Hawkins, N., Richards, P. S., Granley, H. M. and Stein, D. M. (2004). The impact of exposure to the thin-ideal media image on women. *Eating disorders, 12(1)*, 35-50.

Harrison, K. (2003). Television viewers' ideal body proportions: The case of the curvaceously thin woman. *Sex Roles, 48(5-6)*, 255-264.

Jhally, S. (2007). *Dreamworlds 3*. DVD.

Kilbourne, J. (2013). Killing Us Softly 3: Advertising's Images of Women.

Miller, R. B., DeBacker, T. K. and Greene, B. A. (1999). Perceived instrumentality and academics: The link to task valuing. *Journal of Instructional Psychology*, 26(4), 250-260.

Noll, S. M. and Fredrickson, B. L. (1998). A mediational model linking self-objectification, body shame, and disordered eating. *Psychology of Women Quarterly, 22(4)*, 623-636.

Paul, J. A., Baker, H. M. and Cochran, J. D. (2012). Effect of online social networking on student academic performance. *Computers in Human Behavior*, *28*(6), 2117–2127.

Ryan, R. M., Frederick, C. M., Lepes, D., Rubio, N. and Sheldon, K. M. (1997). Intrinsic motivation and exercise adherence. *International Journal of Sport Psychology*, 28, 335-354.

Scharrer, E. (2013). Representations of gender in the media. In Oxford Handbook of Media Psychology, Karen Dill (editor). New York: Oxford University Press.

Signorielli, N. (2013). Gender role socialization in the 21st century. In Scharrer, E. (Vol. Ed.), Media Effects/Media Psychology and A. Valdivia (Gen. Ed.) The International Encyclopedia of Media Studies. Boston: Wiley Blackwell.

Shih, M., Pittinsky, T. L. and Ambady, N. (1999). Stereotype susceptibility: Identity salience and shifts in quantitative performance. *Psychological Science*, *10*(1), 80–83.

Steele, C. M. and Aronson, J. (1995). Stereotype threat and the intellectual test performance of African Americans. *Journal of Personality and Social Psychology*, *69*(5), 797–811.

Tiggemann, M. and Zaccardo, M. (2015). "Exercise to be fit, not skinny": The effect of fitspiration imagery on women's body image. *Body Image*, *15*, 61–67.

Vogel, E. a., Rose, J. P., Roberts, L. R. and Eckles, K. (2014). Social comparison, social media, and self-esteem. *Psychology of Popular Media Culture*, *3*(4), 206–222.

Williams, D., Martins, N., Consalvo, M. and Ivory, J. D. (2009). The virtual census: Representations of gender, race and age in video games. *New Media and Society*, *11*(5), 815-834.

In: Stereotypes and Stereotyping
Editor: Claude Fields

ISBN: 978-1-63484-510-6

Chapter 5

DEMOGRAPHIC DIFFERENCES IN THE LEVEL OF INTERCULTURAL SENSITIVITY, EFL INTERESTS, AND ETHNOCENTRISM AMONG COLLEGE STUDENTS IN TAIWAN

Ya-Chen Su
Professor, Department of Applied English,
Southern Taiwan University of Science and Technology, Tainan, Taiwan

ABSTRACT

The world has increasingly become a global village in the 21st century, as people from different cultures and countries have more opportunities for close contact and interaction with each other. The purpose of this study was to develop an understanding of (1) whether the degree of intercultural sensitivity (including its subcomponents), English as a Foreign Language (EFL) interests, and ethnocentrism differ according to students' demographic characteristics, including students' academic majors, duration of learning English, frequency of traveling to other countries, and gender; and (2) the significant predictors affecting development of intercultural sensitivity. A total of 1191 college-aged students (558 males, 633 females) participated in this study. Participants filled out a battery of questionnaires, including the Intercultural Sensitivity Scale (ISS), Interest in Foreign Language Scale (IFLS), and General Ethnocentrism Scale (GES). Results found that the degree of intercultural sensitivity (including its four subcomponents), EFL interests, and ethnocentrism differ according to certain demographic characteristics. Demographic characteristics, EFL interests, and ethnocentrism are significantly positive or negative predictors in intercultural sensitivity development.

INTRODUCTION

As the world has become a global village in the 21st century, it is increasingly interconnected in economics, politics, education, and technology. People from different cultures and countries have more opportunities of close contact, interaction, and communication with one another. Globalization has increased awareness of the importance of foreign language (FL) education. Some of the main purposes of FL instruction are to develop students' intercultural competence, which involves the development of the learner's ability to interact with members of other cultures, and to be aware of differences and similarities while preventing overemphasis on foreignness or stereotyping (Kramsch, 1993). Bennett, Bennett, and Allen (2003) and Bhawuk and Brislin (1992) indicate that in order to be an optimally functional communicator in a pluralistic society, individuals need to overcome the ethnocentrism regarding their own culture, be interested in other cultures, and develop intercultural competence and sensitivity. Individuals also need to modify their behavior to show respect for people of other cultures, as they live in increasingly pluralistic and diverse environments.

The emphasis on intercultural learning in EFL study leads to a question of whether Taiwanese students develop an sensitivity toward or an intercultural awareness and appreciation of diversity after having studied English for many years. It is thus significant to determine factors (including demographic background, EFL learning interests, and ethnocentrism) contributing to their development of intercultural sensitivity as well as significant similarities and differences of the ISS and the factors (EFL interests and ethnocentrism) among demographic backgrounds.

THEORETICAL FRAMEWORK

Intercultural Competence and Intercultural Sensitivity

The terms *intercultural competence* and *intercultural learning* have been widely discussed in the field of intercultural communication. While there is no agreement on its definition, there seems to be a "general agreement among the supporters of intercultural learning as to its key underlying goals and their consequences for language instruction" (O'Dowd, 2003, p. 119). According to Sercu (2006; 2002), the objective of the communication approach is to develop students' target-based communicative competence, which refers to a person's ability to act in an FL in linguistically, socio-linguistically, and pragmatically appropriate ways. But this approach is not sufficient to meet the needs of economic globalization. To become competent speakers of an FL, learners need to acquire the necessary linguistic, pragmatic, and discourse competence to be able to communicate successfully in intercultural contact situations (Council of Europe, 2001). Sercu (2006) prefers to use the term *intercultural competence* to over *intercultural communicative competence* because it incorporates *communicative competence* with intercultural dimensions. *Intercultural competence* is defined as "the ability of a person to behave adequately in a flexible manner when confronted with actions, attitudes, and expectations of representatives of foreign cultures" (Meyer, 1991, p. 138). In Bennett's words, intercultural competence refers to "the ability to transcend ethnocentrism, appreciate other cultures, and generate appropriate behavior in one or more different cultures" (Bennett, Bennett and Allen, 2003, p. 237). Bennett (1993) treats intercultural sensitivity as interactants' ability to transform themselves not only affectively but also cognitively and behaviorally from the denial stage to the integration stage in the development process of intercultural communication. In order words, interculturally sensitive persons are able to reach the level of dual identity and enjoy cultural differences by gradually overcoming the problems of denying or concealing the existence of ethnocentrism.

Although intercultural sensitivity is an important concept in intercultural studies, its definition has been confused and overlapped with intercultural awareness and intercultural adroitness, which make it difficult to measure (Chen and Staroshta, 1996, 2000). Chen and Staroshta (1996; 2000) clarify that these three concepts are interdependent, but they are separate in that each refers to different aspects of the communication process. Intercultural communication competence is an umbrella concept that subsumes intercultural awareness, intercultural sensitivity, and intercultural adroitness. Furthermore, Chen and Starosta (1996) indicate that in order to develop valid and reliable measures to assess the development of intercultural communicative competence, the clarification of these three concepts is needed. Chen and Starosta conceptualize intercultural sensitivity as the affective aspect of intercultural communication in order to distinguish it from intercultural awareness (the cognitive aspect of intercultural communication) and intercultural adroitness (the behavioral aspect of intercultural communication). Intercultural awareness (cognitive) is the foundation of intercultural sensitivity (affective), which, in turn, leads to intercultural competence (behavior) (Chen and Starosta, 1997). Intercultural sensitivity refers to the "subjects'" active desire to motivate themselves. The cognitive aspect of intercultural communication competence refers to the understanding of cultural contentions that affect how we think and behave. The behavioral aspect of intercultural competence refers to the ability to get the job done and attain communication goals in intercultural interactions. Building on this conceptualization, Chen and Starosta (2000) developed an Intercultural Sensitivity Scale (ISS) consisting of several dimensions: intercultural engagement, respect for cultural differences, interaction confidence, and intercultural engagement. These concepts incorporate six affective elements that are supposed to affect an individual's intercultural sensitivity, including self-esteem, self-monitoring, open-mindedness, empathy, and interaction involvement. A study conducted by Fritz, Mollenberg, and Chen (2002) confirms that the Intercultural Sensitivity Scale has a high level of reliability and validity.

The above studies have highlighted the significance of intercultural sensitivity in the dimension of intercultural communication competence. Intercultural sensitivity is viewed as a crucial predictor of successful intercultural encounters (Bhawuk and Brislin, 1992).

The Relation of Intercultural Sensitivity with EFL Interests, Ethnocentrism, and Demographic Characteristics

Recently, many studies have discussed the relative contributions of intergroup and intercultural situations. As discussed above, learners themselves and their attitudes are two of the key factors affecting intercultural sensitivity and tolerance. What is termed *attitude* refers to affect and is an evaluative, emotional reaction (i.e., the degree of like or dislike associated with the attitudinal object). For example, the degree to which a student likes or dislikes speakers of the language being studied is the expression of attitude toward those people (Mantle-Bromley, 1995). "Attitude" allows us to understand many different behaviors as well as values and self-concept variables. It is also known to directly complement human behavior and enable researchers to understand and predict a variety of human behavior (Ajzen and Fishbein, 1980).

Regarding intercultural issues, communication with those of a different culture is frequently associated with adverse emotional responses. Because of communication obstacles, individuals might feel awkward and anxious when interacting with others of a different culture, which might prevent positive intergroup/intercultural interaction and understanding. Thus learners' attitudes might influence their perception toward target language learning and speakers. Gardner (1985), and Gardner and MacIntyre (1993) demonstrate that certain attitudes and beliefs have a notable impact on the learner's affective state and that this affective disposition plays a central role in Second Language Acquisition (SLA). In his study, Gardner (1985) found that more positive attitudes toward the object of study, the language, and its speakers and cultures lead to higher learning achievement. This phenomenon is statistically significant in relation to attitudes toward language learning, and affective statuses are interrelated factors influencing learning outcomes and rates of acquisition. Besides learners' EFL interests and attitudes, ethnocentrism is viewed as one of the key factors in developing intercultural sensitivity and understanding intergroup relation and intercultural communication. According to LeVine and Campbell (1972), ethnocentrism refers to people's tendencies to view their own group as the center of everything and to judge other groups based on its standards, and it reflects the effects of social and psychological factors operating concomitantly. Neuliep and McCroskey (1997) argue that everyone is ethnocentric to some degree, and, while it may be possible and preferable to have a lower degree of ethnocentrism, to be nonethnocentric is impossible. In intercultural interaction, high levels of ethnocentrism can result in misperceptions of people from different cultures and misinterpretations of their behaviors (Gudykunst and Kim, 1997). Lukens (1978) looked at the level of ethnocentrism and its impact on the way people speak to others and demonstrated that different levels of ethnocentrism create different distances between communicators and different cultural groups. Neuliep and McCroskey (1997) developed the Generalized Ethnocentrism Scale (GENE), measuring the level of ethnocentrism among outgroup attitudes. Using the GENE scale, Neuliep et al. (2001) found that Japanese students have significantly higher scores than American students in ethnocentrism. The result suggests that ethnocentric attitudes might affect intercultural sensitivity. Individual variables such as nationality, gender, and the frequency of intercultural interaction contributed to a higher or lower degree of ethnocentrism.

Paige et al. (2003) have also demonstrated that demographic factors influence levels of intercultural sensitivity. For example, prior intercultural experiences, language and cultural experience, and language and cultural study in high school and college students are positively associated with increased intercultural sensitivity. In their studies, Engle and Engle (2004), Kitsanta (2004), and Kisantas and Meyers (2001) found that the effect of study abroad programs on students' intercultural awareness and sensitivity, which included developing positive emotion, emotional resilience, flexibility, openness, and global understanding (Kitsantas, 2004; Kisantas and Meyers, 2001). Although these studies repeatedly suggest that diverse individuals' variables (e.g., learners' attitudes toward language study, perceptions of target language speakers, and ethnocentrism) might shape their intercultural development, few studies provide empirical evidence actually demonstrating these results. Most studies focus on the effects of study abroad programs on intercultural awareness and sensitivity (e.g., Engle and Engle, 2004; Kitsantas, 2004; Kisantas and Meyres, 2001). Results found positive effects of short-term study programs on FL interests and intercultural sensitivity. Students became more willing to accept cultural differences and reduce their ethnocentric tendencies. However, the research focus is specifically on study abroad programs. Few studies focus on those learners who learn FL or EFL for long times but have little contact with intercultural speakers in their home countries or have no intercultural experiences as research subjects to determine whether their EFL interests, intercultural sensitivity, and ethnocentrism differ according to certain demographic characteristics. Most studies also do not discuss which factors—among students' demographic characteristics, EFL interests, attitudes toward native English speakers, and ethnocentrism—significantly affect intercultural sensitivity development.

THE PURPOSE OF THE STUDY

The purpose of the study was to assess (1) the degree of Taiwanese college students' intercultural sensitivities, EFL learning interests, and ethnocentrism; (2) whether these variables (including intercultural sensitivity subcomponents) differ according to students' demographic characteristics, including students' academic majors, duration of learning English, frequency of traveling other countries, and gender; and (3) the significant predictors affecting the development of intercultural sensitivity.

Three research questions were posed:

1) What are the levels of college students' intercultural sensitivity (including its subcomponents), EFL interests, and ethnocentrism?
2) Does the level of intercultural sensitivity, EFL interests, and ethnocentrism differ according to (due to) academic majors, the duration of time spent learning English, the frequency of traveling to FL countries, and gender?
3) Which variables (selected demographic characteristics, EFL interests or ethnocentrism) are predictors that significantly affect intercultural sensitivity?

METHODOLOGY

Respondents

The subjects were 1191 college-aged, non-English major students (558 males, 633 females) from three academic divisions: 17.6% (n = 210) from the College of Humanities and Social Science (e.g., early childhood education, Japanese as a foreign language), 44.8% (n = 533) from the College of Business (e.g., business administration, finance, information management, international business, hospitality management, marketing), and 37.6% (n = 448) from the College of Engineering (e.g., chemical and materials engineering, computer science and information science, electrical engineering, mechanical engineering), at a medium-sized private university located in Southern Taiwan. 1191 respondents enrolled in the required EFL course, “Freshmen English,” which emphasizes reading and listening. The average age was 20 years. Less than 18.6% reported having lived abroad or having visited foreign countries for a very short time. Table 1 shows the demographic characteristics of the students in the samples.

The Instruments

The questionnaire used in this study took approximately 20 minutes to complete. It was conducted to collect information on intercultural sensitivity, EFL interests, and attitudes toward NES. The questionnaire was comprised of the following sections: (1) students' intercultural sensitivity; (2) EFL interests and attitudes toward NES, (3) ethnocentrism; and (4) biographical information, including questions about students' background information (e.g., gender, length of time spent learning English, academic major, prior travel experiences to other countries). In the first two sections, the subjects were asked to read a statement and respond according to a 5-item Likert Scale ranking from *strongly disagree* (1) to *strongly agree* (5).

Table 1. Demographics of the sample

Variables		Number	Percentage
Academic divisions	Humanities	210	17.6
	Business	533	44.8
	Engineering	448	37.6
Gender	Male	558	46.9
	Female	633	53.1
Years of learning English	+ 10 years	144	12.1
	7-9 years	511	42.9
	4-6 years	387	32.8
	- 4 years	125	10.5
	Missing	22	1.8
Frequency of traveling to other countries	None	1036	87.0
	1-3 times	134	11.3
	4-6 times	14	1.2
	+ 7 times	7	0.6
	Total	1191	100

Three scales were modified to be used in this study: the “Intercultrual Sensitivity Scale” (ISS) developed by Chen and Starosta (2000), a “General Ethnocentrism Scale” (GENE) developed by Neuliep and McCroskey (1997), and the “Attitudes and Motivation Test Battery” (AMTB) developed by Gardner, Smythe, and Clement (1974). These measures were used because of several studies which provide evidence for the reliability of these measures based on strong internal consistency (e.g., Chen and Starosta, 2000; Neuliep, 2002; Gardner, 1985; Gardner and MacIntyre, 1993).

Intercultural Sensitivity Scale

The Intercultural Sensitivity Scale (ISS) developed by Chen and Starosta (2000) was used to measure students' different dimensions of intercultural sensitivity. The ISS was modified into four subscales. First, the scale for *Interaction Engagement* (ISS1) was divided into 5 items in order to measure respondents' feelings of participation in intercultural communication. The subscale for *Respect for Cultural Differences* (ISS2) was divided into 5 items in order to measure how respondents orient to or tolerate their counterparts' cultures and opinions. The subscale for *Interaction Confidence* (ISS3) was comprised of 3 items, which were used to measure how confident respondents are in intercultural settings. The subscale for Interaction Enjoyment (ISS4) consisted of three items, which were used to measure respondents' positive or negative reactions towards communicating with people from different cultures.

Interests in Foreign Language

Mantle-Bromley's (1995) "Interest in Foreign Language Scale" (IFLS), adopted from Gardner, Smythe, and Clement (1974), was used to assess foreign language interests. The scale consists of five statements related to "Interests in English as a Foreign Language Scale" (IEFLS). Each item was modified to be language-general by replacing the original "French" or "Spanish" with "an English language" and "French-speaking people" or "Spanish-speaking people" with "native English speakers."

Ethnocentric Attitudes

"The General Ethnocentrism Scale" (GENE) consisted of 6 items developed by Neuliep and NcCroskey (1997). It was used to assess respondents' ethnocentric attitudes. High scores on this measure reflect the view that one's own culture is superior to others and should be used as the standard by which other cultures are judged.

Data Collection and Analysis

The data analysis involved several statistical procedures. First, descriptive statistics—including frequencies, means, and standard deviations of the data—were computed to summarize students' responses according to each scale. The mean of each scale (including the four ISS subscales) was used to determine respondents' actual intercultural sensitivity, attitude, and interest level. The frequency of 3.5 and above is taken to indicate high positivity or frequency, 2.5 to 3.4 is taken as medium, and less than 2.5 is taken as low, as suggested by Oxford and Burry-Stock (1995).

Second, a *t*-test was conducted to examine whether there are significantly different responses according to the gender of respondents. One-way analyses of variances (ANOVAs) were conducted to determine whether there were any significantly different responses among respondents' academic divisions, the length of time spent learning English, and the frequency of traveling to foreign countries. If there were significantly different responses, the post-hoc *Scheffé* test was used for comparing across the groups. Finally, multiple regression analyses were used to determine predictable variables. The overall ISS and each of the ISS subcomponents were indicated as "dependent variables," and demographic characteristics (including gender, the length of learning English, and frequency of traveling to other countries), EFL interests, and ethnocentrism were indicated as "predicators" in order to determine which predictors might significantly contribute to the development of intercultural sensitivity.

RESULTS

Research Question 1

What are the levels of college students' intercultural sensitivity, EFL learning interests, and ethnocentrism?

Scale mean, reliabilities, and scale inter-correlations were computed for the ISS scores for the total of 1191 non-English major students (Table 2). The reliability of all scales resulted in Cronbach's alphas meeting or exceeding Nunnally's (1978) recommended minimum of 0.7. Each mean score of scales was slightly above the midpoint (= 3) of the scale. In particular, the ISS2 and IEFLS have higher scores (3.8258 and 3.7578) while the mean score for ISS3 and GENE have lower scores (3.0234 and 3.0595 respectively) than others. This suggests that students have a general tendency to be interculturally sensitive. They have high FL learning interests, positive emotions with respect to cultural differences, and moderate ethnocentric attitudes, but they have less confidence when interacting with people from other cultures.

Table 2. Means, Standard Deviations and Reliabilities of Each Scale

Scale (Variables)	*Midpoint*	*M*	*SD*	α
Intercultural Sensitivity Scale (ISS)	3.0	3.2881	.38254	0.871
1. Intercation engagement (ISS1)	3.0	3.6117	.51827	0.745
2. Respect for cultural differences (ISS2)	3.0	3.8258	.55625	0.751
3. Interaction confidence (ISS3)	3.0	3.0234	.60412	0.723
4 Interaction enjoyment (ISS4)	3.0	3.2432	.70047	0.732
Interests in EFL Scale (IEFLS)	3.0	3.7578	.54528	0.717
7. Ethnocentrism (GENE)	3.0	3.0595	.53336	0.726

Research Question 2

Does the level of intercultural sensitivity, EFL interests, and ethnocentrism differ according to academic majors, the duration of time spent learning English, the frequency of traveling to FL countries, and gender?

In order to compare and determine the multiple demographic differences among students, an ANOVA analysis and Scheffé post-hoc test or t-test were used. Tables 3, 4, and 5 showed the result of means, standard deviations, one-way between-groups ANOVA, and the Scheffé test for the comparisons of intercultural sensitivity, EFL interest, and ethnocentrism across demographics (academic majors, length of time spent learning English, and frequency of traveling to foreign countries). The results found that the mean scores of the overall ISS for subjects in Humanities and Business were higher than those for subjects in Engineering. Regarding four ISS subcomponents and other scales, except for the ISS3 and GENE, the mean in the Humanities and Business had higher scores for the ISS1, ISS2, and IEFLS than did the subjects in Engineering. The scale means of the ISS3 and GENE in three academic divisions were all near the frequency of 3.0 (see Table 3). An ANOVA result also revealed that only the mean scores for the ISS3 did not differ among students from three academic divisions, but a significant main effect ($p < 0.05$) was obtained from other scale scores, including (1) ISS (2, 1157) = 5.023, (2) ISS1, F (2, 1177) = 3.333, (3) ISS2, F (2, 1176) = 6.573, (4) ISS4, F (2, 1182) = 4.851, (5) IEFLS, F (2, 925) = 7.927, and (6) GENE, $F(2, 1181) = 4.615$ (see Table 3). The post hoc comparison showed that significant negative or positive differences were found between students in Engineering and Business in the overall ISS (MD engineering-business = -0.07732, $p < 0.05$), ISS1 (MD engineering-business = -0.8338, $p < 0.05$), ISS2 (MD engineering-business = 0.12448, $p < 0.05$), and ISS3 (MD engineer-business = 0.12448, $p < 0.05$), where significant positive differences were found between these two groups of students in the GENE (MD engineering-business = -0.10361 $p < 0.05$). No significant differences were found between subjects in the Humanities and Business (MD humanities-business = -0.1977, -0.6286, -0.01548, -0.01647, 0.03747, $p > 0.05$, respectively) or between those in the Humanities and Engineering (MD humanities-engineering = 0.05755, 0.02052, 0.10900, 0.08842, -0.6614 $p > 0.05$, respectively). In ISS4 and IEFLS, significant differences were found between students in the Humanities and Business and in Engineering (MD humanities-engineer = 0.16139, MD business-engineering = 0.11073, $p < 0.05$; MD humanities-engineering = 0.13647, MD business-engineering = 0.14915, respectively, $p < 0.05$). No significant differences were found between students in the Humanities and Business (MD humanities-business = 0.5066, -0.0268, respectively, $p > 0.05$). The results suggest that Engineering-major students have significantly lower levels of overall intercultural sensitivity (including interaction engagement, respect for cultural differences, and interaction enjoyment) and EFL interests, but higher ethnocentrism, than Business-major students. Students in all three academic divisions have moderate degrees of interaction confidence.

Table 4 illustrates the result of comparing the mean score of each scale across students' duration of time spent learning English. The results found that only the scale mean of the overall ISS and its three subcomponents, ISS1, ISS2 and ISS4, increase by length of time. An ANOVA result showed that the mean scores for the overall ISS, F (3, 1137) = 3.411, ISS2, F (3, 1154) = 4.292, and ISS4, F (3, 1160) = 3.478, have a significant effect ($p < 0.05$; see Table 4). The *post hoc* comparison showed that significant differences were found between learning English for more than 10 years and less than 4 years in the scales for the overall ISS (MD 10 years above-4 years below = 0.14339, $p < 0.05$) and ISS4 (MD 10 years above-4 years below = 0.27113, $p < 0.05$), and between learning English 7-9 years and less than 4 years in the scale for the ISS2 (MD 7-9 years -4 years below = 0.18680, $p < 0.05$). This finding indicates that those who learn English for more than 10 years have a higher degree of overall intercultural sensitivity and interaction enjoyment than those who learn English for less than 4 years. Those who learn English between 7-9 years have a more significantly positive attitude of respect for cultural differences than those who learn English for less than 4 years.

Table 3. Means, standard deviations, *F*-radio, the *post hoc* comparison for academic divisions

	Humanities		Business		Engineering			
	M	*SD*	*M*	*SD*	*M*	*SD*	*F*	*Post hoc* test
ISS	3.3010	0.39504	3.3208	0.37049	3.2435	0.38716	5.023**	BN > EE
ISS1	3.5913	0.55714	3.6542	0.48961	3.5708	0.52979	3.333*	BN > EE
ISS2	3.8599	0.51604	3.8574	0.55457	3.7509	0.56921	6.573**	BN > EE
ISS3	2.9729	0.61569	3.0151	0.59510	3.0571	0.60865	1.470	
ISS4	3.3266	0.64450	3.2759	0.66066	3.1652	0.76300	4.851**	BN, HM > EE
IEFLS	3.8037	0.50904	3.8164	0.54420	3.6672	0.55202	7.927***	BN, HM > EE
GENE	3.0514	0.49265	3.0140	0.52423	3.1176	0.55020	4.615**	BN > EE

Note: HM = Humanities; BN = Business; EE = Engineering
* < 0.05; **0.01; ***0.000

Table 4. Means, standard deviations, *F*-radio, the *post hoc* comparison for the length of learning English

	4 years below		4-6 years		7-9 years		10 years			*Post hoc*
Scale	*M*	*SD*	*M*	*SD*	*M*	*SD*	*M*	*SD*	*F*	test
ISS	3.2077	.41852	3.2757	.38985	3.3025	.33031	3.3450	.47810	3.411*	4 > 1
ISS1	3.5236	.58982	3.5959	.52255	3.6339	.46422	3.6571	.61036	1.981	
ISS2	3.6829	.57939	3.8021	.56587	3.8500	.63002	3.8500	.63002	4.292*	3 > 1
ISS3	3.0645	.69672	3.0388	.63883	2.9934	052144	3.0671	.68231	.941	
ISS4	3.0813	.73656	3.2313	.68558	3.2569	.68556	3.3524	.74351	3.478*	4 > 1
IEFLS	3.7807	.55753	3.7039	.55544	3.7824	.49912	3.8301	.64433	1.981	
GENE	3.1452	.57160	3.0739	.54859	3.0426	.50366	3.0236	.56741	1.535	

Note: 1 = 4 years below; 2 = 4-6 years; 3 = 7-9 years; 4 = 10 years above
* < 0.05; **0.01; ***0.000

Table 5. Means, standard deviations, *F*-radio, *the post hoc* comparison for the frequency of traveling to foreign countries

	none		1-3 times		4-6 times		7 times above			*Post hoc*
Scale	*M*	*SD*	*M*	*SD*	*M*	*SD*	*M*	*SD*	*F*	test
ISS	3.2652	.37420	3.4300	.40010	3.6516	.268909	3.3109	.57305	11.341***	1, 2 > 0
ISS1	3.5852	.51275	3.7725	.51307	3.8571	.37767	3.8000	.87178	7.607***	1 > 0
ISS2	3.8010	.55096	4.0045	.56271	4.0429	.45862	3.6286	.74322	6.346***	1 > 0
ISS3	2.9994	.59068	3.1303	.66393	3.6667	.47140	3.3333	.74536	7.584***	1, 2 > 0, 2 > 1
ISS4	3.2214	.69160	3.3665	.73117	3.8036	.65176	3.000	.90139	5.026**	2 > 0
IEFLS	3.7379	.53584	3.8607	.59174	4.1636	.57840	3.7333	.23094	3.752*	
GENE	3.0668	.53040	2.9805	.53040	3.2143	.69044	3.1714	.57071	1.536	

Note: 0 = none; 1 = 1-3 times; 2 = 4-6 times; 3 = 7 times above; * < 0.05; **0.01; ***0.000.

Table 6. Means, standard deviations, and *F*-radio for both gender

	Men		Women		
Scale (Variables)	*M*	*SD*	*M*	*SD*	*F*
ISS	3.2525	.40182	3.3203	.36161	3.252**
ISS1	3.5753	.54225	3.6444	.49392	2.802*
ISS2	3.7396	.58984	3.9037	.51215	17.791***
ISS3	3.0751	.65333	2.9770	.55270	9.648**
ISS4	3.2081	.77649	3.2748	.62324	10.401
IEFLS	3.6607	.58405	3.8398	.49621	8.506***
GENE	3.1157	.57451	3.0090	.48850	15.908**

Note: * < 0.05; **0.01, ***0.000

Table 5 reveals the result of comparing the mean score of each scale across students' frequency of traveling to foreign countries. The result found that, except GENE, each scale mean was increased for subjects who had traveled to other countries, from no experiences to 4-6 times. An ANOVA result also found that only the scale means for the GENE on the frequency of intercultural traveling experiences did not differ from one another, but there was a significant main effect ($p < 0.05$) on other scale scores, including (1) the overall ISS, F (3, 1156) = 11.341; (2) ISS1, F (3, 1176) = 7.607; (3) ISS2, F (3, 1175) = 6.346; (4) ISS3, F (3, 1178) = 7.584; (5) ISS4, F (3, 1181) = 5.026; and (6) IEFLS, F (3, 924) = 3.752 (see Table 4). The *post hoc* comparison showed that significant difference was found between students who had no experiences traveling to foreign countries and those who had traveled abroad 1-3 times in the overall ISS (MD none-1-3 times = -0.16912), ISS1 (MD none-1-3 times = -0.19392), ISS2 (MD none-1-3 times = -0.18456), and ISS3 (MD none-1-3 times = -0.16519). The findings suggest that those students who have more intercultural traveling experiences have a higher level of overall intercultural sensitivity and EFL interests. Particularly, they have a higher positive level of engagement, enjoyment, and confidence in interacting with foreign language speakers, as well as respect for cultural differences, than students who have had no traveling experiences. Students with or without prior intercultural experiences showed no significant difference in their degree of ethnocentrism.

Table 6 presents the result of t-test between genders, finding that, except the ISS3 and GENE, the mean scores of women in all scales (including four ISS subscales) were higher than men (see Table 6). The result of t test found that, except the ISS4 (t = -2.884, p < 0.05), significant differences existed between women and men on all scales, including the overall ISS (t = -3.022, p < 0.05), ISS1 (t = -2.291, p < 0.05), ISS2 (t = -5.111, p < 0.000), ISS3 (t = 2.792, p < 0.01), IEFLS (t = -5.049, p < 0.000), and GENE (t = 3.454, p < 0.01). The findings indicate that female students have more positive tendency of intercultural sensitivity and higher degrees of interaction engagement, respect for cultural differences, and EFL interests than male students, but the men have more confidence in intercultural interaction and a higher degree of ethnocentrism than women. Both genders showed no significant differences of interaction enjoyment when interacting with FL speakers.

Research Question 3: Which variables (students' demographic characteristics, FL interests, and ethnocentrism) are variable predictors significantly affecting the positive or negative level of intercultural sensitivity?

Multiple regression analysis was used to investigate which variable would more strongly predict the development of the overall ISS and its four subscales. Students' demographic characteristics (e.g., gender, duration of learning English, frequency of traveling to other countries), EFL interests, and ethnocentrism were computed as predictor variables and the ISS and its four subcomponents were calculated as variable criteria. The results of the regression analysis for the overall ISS are shown in Table 7. According to Cohen (1988), R < 0.10 is labeled as having a negligible effect, R < 0.30 as a "small" effect, R > 0.30 as "medium," R > 0.50 as "large," and R > 0.70 as "very large." The result showed the effect size is large for the overall ISS (R = 0.558). It also revealed statistically significant F (5, 864) = 78.036, p < .000 accounted for 31.1% of the variance. As predicted by the B and t values, the frequency of traveling to FL countries and IEFL were significant positive predictors, while ethnocentrism and the length of time spent learning English were negative predictors of the overall ISS. IEFLS was the strongest predictor (see Table 7). The results predict that students with lower ethnocentrism, more positive EFL interests, and less years of learning English are likely to have higher degrees of general intercultural sensitivity. The more frequently students travel to FL countries, the higher intercultural sensitivity they develop. Students' EFL interests were the most powerful factors contributing intercultural sensitivity development.

To determine the predictable variables contributing to each ISS subcomponent, multiple regression analysis was conducted to separately compute the influence of each of the four dependent variables (see Table 8). The results show that the effect size is large for the ISS1 (R = 0.629), medium for ISS 2 and ISS3 (R = 0.449, 0.429, respectively), and small for ISS4 (R = 0.263; see Table 9). All four dependent variables (DV) also showed statistically significant results: $F(5, 873) = 114.579$, $p < .000$ accounted for 39.6% of the variance in ISS1; $F(5, 875) = 44.298$, $p < .000$ accounted for 20.2% of the variance in respect for ISS2; $F(5, 874) = 39.359$, $p < .000$ accounted for 18.4% of the variance in ISS3; and $F(5, 877) = 13.071$, $p < .000$ accounted for 6.9% of the variance in ISS4. EFL interest was the strongest and most significant positive predicator in any of the four dimensions of ISS. On the other hand, ethnocentrism is identified as a significant negative predictor of ISS2 and ISS4, but as a significant positive predictor of ISS1 and ISS3. This predicts that students who have less ethnocentrism are more likely to engage with and show respect to FL speakers, but students who have higher ethnocentrism are more likely to feel confident in and enjoy intercultural interaction.

Furthermore, demographic variables were identified as a significant predictor of at least one dimension of intercultural sensitivity: Gender served as a significant negative predictor in ISS3, where ISS1, ISS2 and ISS4 showed no significant prediction of differences. Findings suggest that males are less willing to engage and feel confidence in intercultural interaction than females. Frequency of traveling to FL countries was a significant positive predictor in ISS3 and ISS4, which predict that the more frequently students travel to FL countries, the more confidence and enjoyment they develop.

Table 7. The result of regression analysis for the overall ISS

Predictors (independent variables)	B	SE	Beta	*t*	*P*-value
(constant)	2.028	.109		18.605	.000
1. Gender	-.025	.023	-.033	-1.100	.271
2. Length of time learning English	-.028	.014	-.060	-2.038	.042*
3. Frequency of traveling to FL countries	.071	.023	.089	3.120	.002**
7. IEFLS	.379	.020	.540	18.758	.000***
8. GENE	-.040	.020	-.057	-1.982	.048*
$R = 0.558$, $R^2 = 0.311$					

Note. $F(5, 864) = 78.036$***, $p < 0.000$; * < 0.05; **0.01; ***0.001

Table 8. The result of multiple regression analyses for four ISS subcomponents

Factor	Predictor variables	B	SEB	Beta	*t*	*P*-value
Factor 1: Interaction Engagement $R = 0.629$, $R^2 = 0.96$, $F(5,873) = 114.579$***	(constant)	1.216	.137		8.904	.000
	Gender	-.011	.029	-.011	-.388	.698
	Years of learning English	-.034	.017	-.054	-1.949	.052
	Frequency of traveling to FL countries	.055	.028	.052	1.959	.050
	IEFLS	.567	.025	.602	22.457	.000***
	GENE	.103	.025	.109	4.097	.000***
Factor 2: Respect for Cultural Differences $R = 0.449$, $R^2 = 0.202$, $F(5, 875) = 44.298$***	(constant)	3.085	.162		19.075	.000
	Gender	.019	.034	.017	.545	.586
	Years of learning English	-.031	.021	-.048	-1.514	.130
	Frequency of traveling to FL countries	.028	.033	.025	.825	.409
	IEFLS	.384	.030	.394	12.803	.000***
	GENE	-.209	.030	-.216	-7.061	.000***
Factor 3: Interaction confidence $R = 0.429$, $R^2 = 0.184$, $F(5, 874) = 39.359$***	(constant)	.995	.186		5.356	.000
	Gender	-.130	.039	-.107	-3.314	.001**
	Years of learning English	-.001	.024	-.001	-.024	.981
	Frequency of traveling to FL countries	.135	.039	.109	3.497	.000***
	IEFLS	.382	.034	.346	11.090	.000***
	GENE	.204	.034	.184	5.966	.000***
Factor 4: Interaction Enjoyment $R = 0.263$, $R^2 = 0.069$, $F(7, 868) = 13.071$***	(constant)	3.484	.231		15.052	.000
	Gender	-.071	.049	-.050	-1.445	.149
	Years of learning English	-.057	.030	-.066	-1.940	.053
	Frequency of traveling to FL countries	.127	.048	.088	2.662	.008**
	IEFLS	.178	.043	.138	4.154	.000***
	GENE	-.256	.043	-.198	-5.999	.000***

Note: * < 0.05; **0.01; ***0.001.

Discussion and Conclusion

This study explores the close relationships between each dimension of intercultural sensitivity (including four ISS components), EFL interests, and ethnocentrism. First, the results found that certain demographic variables—such as frequency of traveling to FL countries, length of time spent learning English, and gender—corresponded to significant differences in the overall ISS and its four ISS subcomponents. A comparison of the *p* value for the frequency of traveling to FL countries found significant differences in all scales (including four subscales). The results confirmed that those who have more intercultural experiences are more likely to develop intercultural sensitivity (including its four subcompoents) than those who have with little or no experience. A comparison of the *p* value also found significant difference in the overall ISS, ISS2, and ISS4. The results suggested that those who spend long durations of time learning English are more likely to develop intercultural sensitivity and more willing to interact with intercultural speakers. Students who spend more than 7 to 10 years learning English have significantly higher levels of respect for cultural differences and interaction engagement than those who learn English in less than 4 years. A comparison of the *t* value for gender also found significant differences in the overall ISS, ISS1, ISS2, and ISS3. The results demonstrate that female students are more likely to have intercultural sensitivity, and they have more confidence and are more willing to engage in intercultural contact than males. Female students' levels of respect for cultural difference are significantly higher than males.

The results of regression analysis found that two demographic variables, the frequency of traveling to FL countries and gender, served as significant predictors in overall intercultural sensitivity development. The category of traveling to FL countries emerged as a positively significant predictor in the overall ISS, ISS3, and ISS4. The category of gender emerged as a significant predictor in the overall ISS and ISS3. These results are similar to findings by Anderson (2006), Kim (2006), Kim and Goldstrein (2005), Kitasantas (2004), and Kitsantas and Meyres (2002), who found that intercultural experiences and gender differences directly influence certain degrees of intercultural sensitivity.

Second, demographic variables found significant differences in EFL interests and ethnocentrism. The comparison of *t* and *p* values found that three categories (academic majors, gender, and the frequency of traveling to other countries) showed significant difference. A conclusion can be drawn that those who have Business or Humanities majors and more traveling experiences have higher levels of EFL interests but lower ethnocentric attitudes than those who have Engineering majors and those without any intercultural traveling experiences. Female students have a higher level of EFL interest and less ethnocentrism than males. The results confirmed that the level of FL or EFL interests and attitudes are likely to be different according to individual variables, such as gender and age (e.g., Gardner, 1985), and intercultural experiences (e,g., Kim and Goldstein, 2005). Similarly, the degree of ethnocentrism differs according to individuals' characteristics, such as ethnicity and national status (e.g., Neupiep, Chaudoir and Mccroskey, 2001) and intercultural experiences (e.g., Anderson et al., 2006).

Regression analysis found that EFL interests are interrelated factors contributing the development of the overall ISS. IEFLS serves as a positive and significant predictor in each of its subcomponents. The results confirmed that the desire to affiliate with people who use another language and interest in FL are important precursors of the willingness to communicate in another language (Gardner, 1985; MacIntyre, 1998).

On the other hand, the result of regression analyses revealed that ethnocentrism negatively affected the ISS2 and ISS4. The result suggested that ethnocentric attitude had a direct influence on students' intercultural sensitivity development. Those who have a lower degree of ethnocentrism are more likely to accept cultural differences and enjoy interaction and communication. As Meuliep and Croskey (1997) have demonstrated, ethnocentrism influences social interaction. All intercultural exchange creates a lesser degree of ethnocentrism. Guan (1995) labels this type of interaction as "self-centered dialogue," where interactants use their own cultural standards to evaluate and communicate with others. High levels of ethnocentrism can result in misperceptions of people from different cultures and misinterpretation of their behavior (Meuliep and Croskey, 1997, p. 389).

The most interesting finding was that ethnocentrism was the significant and positive predictor in ISS 1 and ISS3. This demonstrated that those who have a higher degree of ethnocentrism are still more likely to have confidence and interest in interacting with intercultural speakers. MacIntye (1998) explains that communicative competence and communicative experiences, along with the interlocutor's patterns of personality variables, help determine L2 self-confidence, which is primarily defined by judgments of proficiency and feelings of apprehension. This interpretation can be used to imply that those students who have a higher degree of ethnocentrism might have higher perceived communication competence and a lower degree of anxiety, which leads them to have more confidence in communicating with FL speakers. Their high degree of ethnocentric attitudes likely makes them feel confident enough to answer and have the desire to speak, but their own evaluation and standards to judge others might prevent their intercultural understanding.

The study aimed to gather a better description of Taiwanese college students' intercultural sensitivities relative to their EFL interests and ethnocentrism. This study served as a starting point for conducting future studies to determine whether students' intercultural sensitivity may vary across different cultural, ethic, and national backgrounds.

REFERENCES

Ajzen, I. and Fishbein, M. (1980). *Understanding Attitudes and Predicting Social Behavior.* Englewood Cliffs, NJ: Prentice-Hall.

Anderson, P. H., Lawton, L., Rexeisen, R. J. and Hubbard, A. C. (2006). Short-term study abroad and intercultural sensitivity: A pilot study: *International Journal of Intercultural Relations, 30*, 467-469.

Baker, S. C. and MacIntyre, P. D. (2000). The role of gender and immersion communication and second language orientations. *Language Learning, 50*, 311-341.

Bateman, B. E. (2002). Promoting openness toward cultural learning: ethnocentric interviews for students of Spanish. *Modern Language Journal, 86*(3), 318-331.

Bateman, B. E. (2004). Achieving affective and behavioral outcomes in cultural learning: The case for ethnographic interviews. *Foreign Language Annals, 37*(2), 240-253.

Bennett, M. J. (1984). *Towards ethnocentrism: A development model of intercultural sensitivity*. Unpublished Paper presented at the Annual Conference of the Council on Intercultural Exchange. Minneapolis, MN.

Bennett, J. M. (1993). Toward ethniorelativism: A development model of intercultural sensitivity. In R. M. Paige (Eds.), *Education for the Intercultural Experiences* (2nd ed.) (pp. 21-71). Yarmouth, ME: Intercultural Press.

Bennett, J. M., Bennett, M. J. and Allen, W. (2003). Developing intercultural competence in the language classroom. In D. L. Lange and R. M. Paige (Eds.), *Culture as the Core: Perspectives on Culture in Second Langue Learning* (pp. 237-269). Greenwich, CN: Information Age Publishing, Inc.

Bhawuk, D. P. S. and Brislin, R. (1992). The measurement of intercultural sensitivity using the concepts of individualism and collectivism. *International Journal of Intercultural Relations, 16*(4), 413-436.

Chement, R. and Kruidenir, B. (1985). Aptitude, attitude, and motivation in second language proficiency: A test of Clement's model. *Journal of Language and Social Psychology, 4*. 21-37.

Chen, G. M. and Starosta, W. J. (1996). Intercultural communication competence: A synthesis. In B. Burleson (Eds.), *Communication Yearbook 19* (pp. 353-383). Thousand Oaks, CA: Sage.

Chen, G. M. and Starosta, W. J. (1997). A review of the concept of intercultural sensitivity. *Human Communication, 1*, 1-16.

Chen, G. M. and Starosta, W. J. (2000). The development and validation of the international communication sensitivity scale. *Human Communication, 3*, 1-15.

Chen, L. (2000). Perceptions of intercultural interaction and communication satisfaction: A study on initial counters. *Communication Reports, 15*(2), 133-147.

Council of Europe (1997). *The Sociocultural and Intercultural Dimensions of Language Learning and Teaching*. Stasbourg: Council of Europe.

Council of Europe (2001). *Common European Framework of Reference for Langue Learning, Teaching, Assessment.* Cambridge: Cambridge University Press.

Engle, L. and Engle, J. (2004). Assessing language acquisition and intercultural sensitivity development in relation to study abroad program design. *Frontiers: The Interdisciplinary Journal of Study Abroad, 5,* 219-36.

Fritz, W., Mollenberg, A. and Chen, G. M. (2002). Measuring intercultural sensitivity in different cultural context. *Intercultural Communication Studies, 11*, 165-176.

Gardner, R. C. (1985). *Social Psychology and Second Language Learning: The Role* of *Attitudes and Motivation.* London: Arnold.

Gardner, R. C. and MacIntyre, P. D. (1993). On the measurement of affective variables in second language learning. *Language Learning, 43*, 157- 194.

Gardner, R. C., Smythe, P. C. and Clement, R. (1974). *Attitudes and Motivation Test Battery* (rev. ed.). London, Ontario: University of Western Ontario.

Gardner, R. C., Masoret, A. M, Tennant, J. and Mihic, L. (2004). Integrative motivation: Changes during a year-long intermediate-level language. *Language Learning, 54*(1), 1-34.

Guan, S. J. (1995). *Intercultural Communication*. Beijing: Peking University Press.

Gudykunst, W. B. and Kim, Y. Y. (1997). *Communication with Strangers: Approach to Intercultural Communication*. New York: McGraw-Hill.

Kim, R. I. and Goldstein, S. B. (2005). Intercultural attitudes predict favorable study abroad expectations of American college students. *Journal of Studies in International Education, 9,* 265–278.

Kitsantas, A. (2004). Studying abroad: The role of college students' goals on the development of cross-cultural skills and global understanding. *College Student Journal*, 38(3), 441–452.

Kitsantas, A., and Meyers, J. (2001). Studying abroad: Does it enhance college student cross-cultural awareness? ERIC Document Reproduction Service No. ED 456 648.

Kramsch, C. (1993). *Context and culture in language teaching*. Oxford: Oxford University.

Levine, R. A., Campbell, D. T. (1972). *Ethnocentrism: Theories of Conflicts, Ethnic Attitudes, and Groups Behavior*. New York: John Wiley and Sons.

Lukens, J. (1978). Ethnocentric speech: Its nature and implications. *Ethnic Groups, 2*, 35-53.

MacIntyre, P. D. (1994). Variables underlying willingness to communicate: A causal analysis. *Communication Research Reports, 11*, 135–142.

MacIntyre, P. D. (1998). Conceptualizing willingness to communicate in a L2. *The Modern Language Journal, 82*, 545-562.

MacIntyre, P. D. and Charos, C. (1996). Personality, attitudes, and affect as predictors of second language communication. *Journal of Language and Social Psychology, 15*, 3-26.

Meyer, M. (1991). Development transcultural competence: Case studies of advanced foreign language learners. In D. Buttjes and M. Byrams (Eds.), *Mediating Language Culture* (pp. 136-158). Clevedon: Multilingual Matters.

Neuliep, J. R. (2002). Assessing the reliability and validity of the generalized ethnocentrism scale. *Journal of Intercultural Communication Research, 31*, 201-215.

Neuliep, J. W., Chaudoir, M. and McCroskey, J. C. (2001). A cross-cultural comparison of ethnocentrism among Japanese and United States college students. *Communication Research Report, 18*, 137-147.

Neuliep, J. W. and Croskey, J. C. (1997). The development of a U. S. and generalized ethnocentrism scale. *Communication Research Report, 14*, 385-398.

Nunnally, J.C. (1978). *Psychometric Theory*. New York: McGraw-Hill.

O'Dowd, R. (2003). Understanding the "other side": Intercultural Learning in Spanish-English email exchange. *Language Learning and Technology, 7*, 118-144.

Oxford, R. and Burry-Stock, J. (1995). Assessing the use of language learning strategies worldwide with ESL/EFL version of the strategy inventory for language learning SILL. *System, 23*, 1-23.

Paige, R. M., Jacobs-Cassuto, M. and Yershova, Y. (2003). Assessing intercultural sensitivity: An empirical analysis of the Hammer and Bennett intercultural development inventory. *International Journal of Intercultural Relations, 27*(4), 467–486.

Pederson, P. J. (2009). Teaching towards an ethnorelative worldview through psychology study abroad. *Intercultural Education, 20* (S1-2), S73-87.

Robinson-Stuart, G. and Nocon, H. (1996). Second cultural acquisition: Ethnography in the foreign language classroom. *Modern Language Journal, 80*(4), 431-449.

Sercu, L. (2002). Autonomous learning and the acquisition of intercultural communicative competence: Some implications for course development. Language, Culture and Curriculum, 15(1), 61-74.

Sercu, L. (2006). The foreign language and intercultural competence teacher: The acquisition of a new professional identity. *Intercultural Education, 17*(1), 55-72.

In: Stereotypes and Stereotyping
Editor: Claude Fields
ISBN: 978-1-63484-510-6

Chapter 6

YOUNG, BLACK, AND ENDANGERED: EXAMINING THE DEATHS OF TRAYVON MARTIN, MICHAEL BROWN, AND TAMIR RICE THROUGH A PSYCHOLOGICAL LENS

***Sarah E. Gaither*[1] *and Kristin N. Dukes*[2]**
[1] Psychology Department; Center for the Study of Race, Politics, and Culture, University of Chicago, IL, US
[2] Psychology Department, Simmons College, Boston, MA, US

ABSTRACT

The deaths of unarmed racial minorities across the United States have garnered widespread attention and speculation, yet the discussions surrounding why these events keep occurring remain limited. In this chapter, we apply a psychological lens to three notable cases. The shooting deaths of Trayvon Martin, Michael Brown, and Tamir Rice sparked a national debate surrounding race relations and racially biased shootings of unarmed minorities. Using psychological theory and findings, we identify and analyze factors that may have contributed to these deaths. Specifically we consider the roles that physical appearance and shooter bias may have played in all three cases. We also examine the biased media depictions that negatively portrayed Martin and Brown and influenced reactions to their deaths. Taken together, we contend that this evidence provides a probable narrative for the decisions to shoot Martin, Brown, and Rice while also starting a crucial discussion surrounding racial stereotyping, biased media representations, Stand Your Ground statutes, and needed police training paradigms. We conclude with recommendations for reform in each of these domains as a way to mitigate both future wrongful shootings and to reduce the overall bias experienced by racial minorities.

INTRODUCTION

On February 26, 2012 in Sanford, FL, Trayvon Martin, an unarmed 17-year old black male, was killed by a single gunshot to the chest by George Zimmerman, a neighborhood watch captain. Zimmerman was taken into custody, questioned, and released. Six weeks later, only after Martin's death attracted national media attention and the Sanford Police Department experienced substantial external pressure, George Zimmerman was charged with murder. He was ultimately acquitted of this charge (Alvarez and Buckley, 2013).

About two years later, on August 9, 2014 in Ferguson, Missouri, Michael Brown, Jr., an unarmed 18-year-old black male, was shot at least six times, including twice in the head by police officer Darren Wilson (Yan, 2014). Nearly a week later, the Ferguson, Missouri Police Department finally held a press conference to release the name of the officer involved in Michael Brown's death, but instead focused primarily on how Brown may have instigated the encounter rather than the racial nature surrounding this incident (Killoran, 2014; Taintor, 2014).

Then only a few months after Michael Brown's death,, on November 22, 2014 in Cleveland, Ohio, 12-year-old Tamir Rice, was fatally shot by Timothy Loehman, a Cleveland Police Officer, while Rice walked around a city park with a pellet gun. Loehman and another police officer Frank Garmback, responded to a 9-1-1 call that a black male was pointing a gun a people in the park. Video of the incident revealed that Loehman shot Rice without a verbal warning, less than two seconds after arriving on scene, despite the fact that the 9-1-1 caller had remarked that Rice was "probably a juvenile" and that the gun was most likely fake (Fieldstadt, 2015; LA Times, 2014). The city of Cleveland denied any wrongdoing regarding Tamir Rice's death and determined that Rice's death was caused by him failing to "exercise due care" (Fieldstadt, 2015).

With tragic events like the deaths of Trayvon Martin, Michael Brown, and Tamir Rice, people often seek reasons for why the violence has occurred. In the wake of Martin's death, a great deal of commentary focused on Martin's attire (i.e., a hoodie) the night of his death. Following Brown's death, many individuals focused on Brown's physical appearance relating him to a "giant" as an explanation for Officer Wilson's use of force. Similarly, law enforcement officials have cited Rice's size as a rationale for an "objectively reasonable" action to shoot. Protests emerged in response to all three shootings. Demonstrators held banners stating "I am Trayvon Martin," "Hands up, Don't Shoot," "Fake Gun, Real Target," and "Black Lives Matter" as a way of publicly acknowledging the questionable deaths of too many young black men. While some have recognized the potential role of race in these shootings, many have chosen to instead blame the victim rather than focusing on the psychological factors and biases that endanger so many young, black individuals across the United States.

Using a psychological lens, this chapter examines the deaths of Martin, Brown, and Rice by highlighting three factors surrounding their deaths: physical appearance, shooter bias, and biased media representations. We begin by summarizing research regarding how appearance is used when forming impressions of others (e.g., Fiske and Neuberg 1990; Maddox and Dukes, 2008) such as the racialization of certain types of attire including hoodies (Dukes, 2014). Next, we link these findings with research examining the shooter bias which is defined as the increased tendency to shoot unarmed black or minority suspects compared to white individuals (e.g., Correll, Park, Judd, and Wittenbrink, 2002; Mekawi and Bresin, 2015). We contend that these phenomena combined increase the likelihood of individuals choosing to shoot unarmed young black men. Lastly, we examine biased media portrayals of these incidences and black men more generally, to create a probable narrative for both the violent reaction toward Trayvon Martin, Michael Brown, and Tamir Rice and the rationalization of their shootings. We conclude by beginning the discussion for needed interventions to help reduce these occurrences.

"This Guy Looks Like He's up to No Good": How Physical Appearance Contributed to the Shootings of Trayvon Martin and Michael Brown

Social psychological research has shown that we rely on salient cues including physical appearance when forming impressions. In fact, race is one of the most salient characteristics people perceive (e.g., Freeman, Pauker, Apfelbaum, and Ambady, 2010; Ito and Urland, 2003; Montepare and Opeyo, 2002). Just seeing a black face can instantly activate stereotypes and racial biases without a perceiver's conscious awareness (e.g., Devine, 1989; Eberhardt, Goff, Purdie and Davies, 2004; Greenwald and Banaji, 1995). Accordingly, when encountering a young black male, we may automatically attend to specific physical features indicative of his racial category membership (e.g., dark-brown skin tone), categorize him as black, and subsequently activate stereotypes of blacks that become readily available to influence our subsequent impressions and behaviors (Bodenhausen and Macrae, 1998; Brewer, 1988; Fiske and Neuberg, 1990, Maddox and Dukes, 2008a). Furthermore we also rely on behavioral and situational cues to complete our impressions (Ableson, 1981; Ambady and Rosenthal, 1992; Duncan, 1976; Read, 1987), such as attending to a young black man walking in a "white" neighborhood.

As such, black men in the United States are commonly viewed as criminal, aggressive, and dangerous (Dukes and Overstreet, 2011; Maddox and Gray, 2002; Niemann, Jennings, Rozelle, Baxter, and Sullivan, 1994). Once Travyon Martin was categorized as a young black male by George Zimmerman, a slew of negative associations such as these were likely activated in Zimmerman's mind. Relatedly, research on racial phenotypicality bias (see Maddox, 2004), has determined that not all black Americans are perceived equally. Rather, individuals with more Afrocentric features (dark brown skin, broader nose, and fuller lips) are stereotyped to a greater degree (e.g., Blair Judd, Sadler and Jenkins, 2002; Maddox and Gray, 2002) and facilitate more automatic negative evaluations (Livingston and Brewer, 2002) than their low Afrocentric counterparts, causing even lighter skinned racial minorities to be remembered as darker than they actually are. Consequently, Martin's relatively dark brown skin, broader nose, and fuller lips left him susceptible to even greater stereotyping with deadly consequences.

Additionally, Martin's infamous hoodie potentially exacerbated Zimmerman's stereotypical perception of him. Like physical markers of race, attire can have a profound impact on the impressions we form. For example, while examining the role of attire in racial categorization one investigation found that racially ambiguous men wearing low-status, janitor attire were categorized as black, but when wearing high-status, business attire those same men were categorized as white (Freeman et al., 2011). Another study also examined the role of attire and racial stereotyping. In this study, participants were told that people can make accurate character judgments of others when only given minimal amounts of information about the person such as a simple photograph. Participants were then presented with photographs of men wearing "hip-hop" casual attire (e.g., oversized sports jerseys, gold chain necklaces) and professional attire (e.g., business suite with a tie) and asked to evaluate whether a number of traits and activities stereotypically associated with African American men applied to these men. Results revealed that black men dressed in hip-hop attire were stereotyped to a greater degree compared to their professionally dressed counterparts (Dukes and Maddox, 2008, see Figure 1). Further support for the racialization of attire, namely hoodies, can be found in research conducted even prior to Martin's death. In both a 2008 study conducted prior to Trayvon Martin's death and a 2013 study conducted after Trayvon Martin's death, when asked to list stereotypes associated with several racial and ethnic groups, participants listed hoodies for black men alongside traits like aggressive, lazy, criminal, and dangerous. Even more compelling, hoodies were associated exclusively with black men (Dukes, 2014). Therefore, this tendency to stereotype black men on the basis of their attire indicates that certain types of clothing may predict more biased perceptions of blacks.

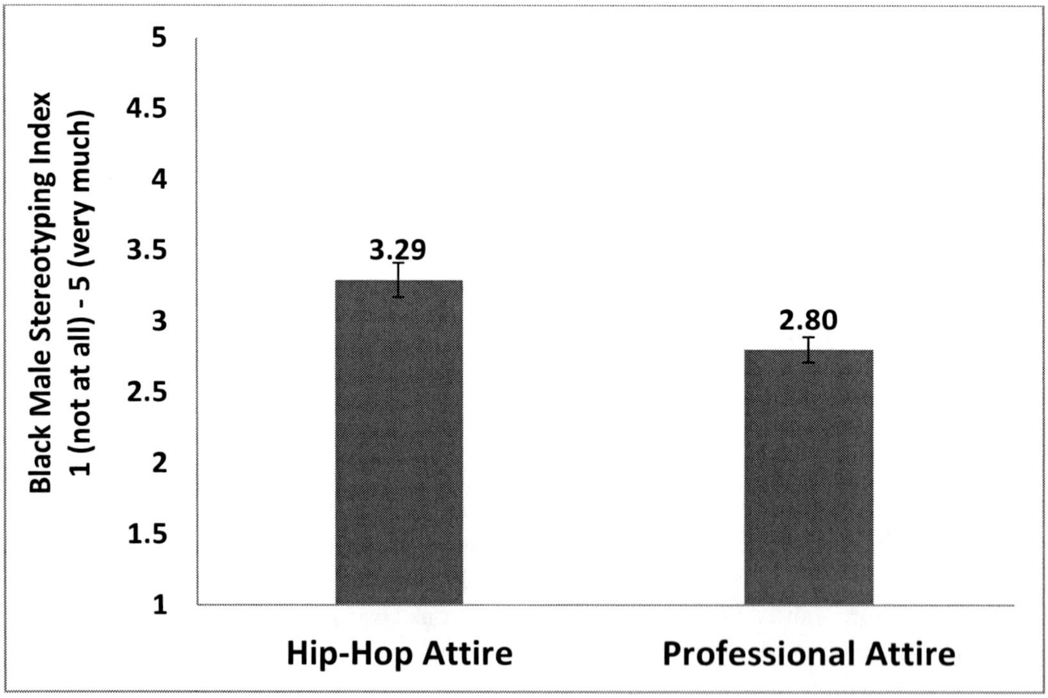

Figure 1. Participants stereotyped black men significantly more when wearing hip-hop attire than when wearing professional attire ($t(19) = 4.50$, $p < .001$, Cohen's $d = 1.53$).

According to the 9-1-1 transcript from Zimmerman's call that night, Zimmerman tells the dispatcher that Martin "looks like he's up to no good…or he's on drugs…" Zimmerman responded to the dispatcher's questions about Martin's appearance stating, "He looks black…[he is wearing] a dark hoodie." Thus, in light of this research underscoring the importance of appearance in impression formation, it is likely that Zimmerman unambiguously identified Martin as black due to his Afrocentric features and his attire creating a probable narrative for Zimmerman's mindset on the night of Martin's death.

A similar narrative can be developed when reflecting on Officer Wilson's reaction to Michael Brown. At 6'4," 292 lbs., Brown was a large man. On the day of his encounter with Officer Wilson, Brown was wearing an oversized white T-shirt, baggy khaki shorts, sneakers, and a baseball cap—a far cry from the professional attire research has shown to mitigate racial stereotyping of black men. His size, attire, race, and more specifically, his degree of Afrocentricity, were salient features contributing to Wilson's impression of him.

Likewise, Tamir Rice's race and perceived age are noteworthy physical features also likely contributing to Officer Loehman's reactions to him. Prior to arriving at the scene, the officers were given a physical description of Tamir Rice as a black male; however the 9-1-1 caller's repeated comment that Rice was probably a juvenile was not conveyed to responding officers. Police union representatives for Loehman stated that he believed that Rice was at least 20-years-old during the altercation. His perception of Rice as an adult is confirmed by police radio transcripts from the day of the shooting. Loehman's partner radioed in "shots fired, male down, um, black male, maybe 20…black hand gun (Izadi and Holley, 2014)." Other law enforcement agents interviewed about Rice's death also stated they believed he was much older than 12 (Mack and Koenrner, 2015).

There is a clear discrepancy between Rice's actual age, a 12-year-old boy, and his perceived age—an adult male in his early twenties. In fact, this tendency to perceive young black boys as older has been documented empirically. Black boys are perceived as less innocent or childlike (e.g., in need of protection or care) than non-black children. This differential emerges at the young age of 10 and continues across childhood such that the perceived innocence of black children aged 10-13 is equivalent to that of non-black children aged 14-17, and the perceived innocence of black children aged 14-17 is equivalent to that of non-black adults aged 18-21. Simply put, black children are often wrongly viewed as adults and this effect carries over into the criminal justice domain. For example, in a study where participants were presented with photographs of black, white, and Latino boys aged 10-17 who had purportedly committed crimes, participants overestimated the ages of black boys by an average of 4.5 years. Black boys were also rated as more culpable of the crime. This pattern was even more pronounced for felony crimes compared to misdemeanors. Moreover, this research also documents that perceived age predicts the use of force by police officers, stressing the role social perceptions and categorizations can play for black boys in particular (Goff, Jackson, Di Leone, Culotta, and DiTomasso, 2014).

Taken together, psychological research regarding one's physical appearance and impression formation suggests that Trayvon Martin, Michael Brown, and Tamir Rice were all potentially perceived as: physically intimidating, threatening, and aggressive black men deserving of lethal force, even if those stereotyped associations were unconscious. Unfortunately, this same implicit or unconscious prejudice also manifests itself through shooter bias which ultimately predicted these victims' fates.

"HE'S GOT SOMETHING IN HIS HANDS": SHOOTER BIAS AND UNARMED BLACK MEN

Shooter bias is defined as people being more likely to shoot unarmed black or racial minority suspects relative to unarmed white suspects (e.g., Correll et al., 2002). Several other cases beyond Martin, Brown, and Rice involving the shooting deaths of unarmed black men have garnered national attention in recent years. Some high-profile occurrences include the 1999 shooting death of Amadou Diallo, an unarmed immigrant from Guinea shot 19 times by four New York City police officers, and more recently, the 2013 shooting death of Jonathan Ferrell, an unarmed 24 year-old former Florida A&M University student and football player who was shot 10 times by a Charlotte-Mecklenburg, NC police officer. This tendency to shoot unarmed black men has also been documented empirically. Researchers argue that encountering a black man in an ambiguously dangerous situation automatically activates stereotypes of criminality associated with black men leading to the snap judgment to shoot (Markman, 2012). For example, in laboratory settings, participants playing a video game simulation where they decide to shoot or not shoot armed and unarmed individuals, participants were *more* likely to shoot unarmed black men and *less* likely to shoot armed white men (e.g., Correll et al., 2002). Furthermore, other research has shown that shooter bias is increased by exposure to stereotypes of blacks as criminal just prior to completing a shoot/don't shoot simulation, reinforcing the influence of stereotype activation in this process (Correll, Park, Judd and Wittenbrink, 2007). On the night Martin was shot, Zimmerman alerted the 9-1-1 dispatcher that Martin had "something in his hands," and consistent with research on the shooter bias phenomenon, Zimmerman most likely assumed that Martin was carrying a weapon when in fact we now know he was carrying a bag of Skittles.

Moreover, in line with work we summarized earlier in this chapter, shooter bias is also influenced by racial phenotypicality and attire. Recent studies show that individuals are more likely to shoot unarmed high Afrocentric black men in comparison to low Afrocentric black men (Kahn and Davies, 2011) and similarly, participants are more likely to shoot unarmed black men in casual attire than in professional attire (Kahn and Davies, 2007).

Because of this known association, racial minorities are often aware of how police officers and others perceive them. Although there is still debate surrounding the exact details of Brown's death, some bystanders reported that Brown had his hands up in the air during his encounter with Officer Wilson likely because Brown was aware of how commonly negative stereotypes link weapons and violence to black individuals. Within the black community it is known that having one's hands visible and in the air when a police officer is present is one approach toward mitigating shooter bias through attempting to purposefully disprove weapon stereotypes.

Alternatively, Tamir Rice wasn't afforded the opportunity to raise his hands during his encounter with law enforcement. Officer Loehman made a split-second, perhaps automatic, decision to shoot, without fully assessing the situation. There were mixed reports from Officers Loehman and Garmback regarding whether they asked Rice to show his hands and where Rice had his toy gun, but what is known, is that a 12-year-old boy with a pellet gun was shot instantly upon the officer's arrival (Shaffer, 2014). Surveillance footage of the encounter appears to contradict all of the officers' versions of the events leading up to Rice's death. Though there is no audio to this footage to confirm or deny the officers' claims that they asked Rice to show his hands, it is clear that Rice did not reach for anything in his waistband and that Loehman fired his weapon within two seconds of exiting his vehicle and was only 10 feet away from Tamir Rice (Izadi and Holley, 2014).

In sum, all three of these deadly encounters demonstrate how common shooter bias is in society and underscores the important role that stereotyping plays in the lives of young black men in particular. It is clear that these learned stereotypes predict people's behavior and actions toward blacks and other minorities in this society, stressing the need for researchers and policy makers to focus on creating changes and interventions that can help reduce bias and wrongful shootings. One avenue through which many stereotypes are learned and supported is the media. Therefore, changing media portrayals surrounding shootings such as these may be one step toward intervention. In other words, if we can at least provide equal positive and negative evidence, perhaps we can reduce some of the racial bias that exists in the U.S. resulting in a lower number of wrongful shootings.

"Dope-Smoking Gangsta Wannabe," "No Gentle Giant," and "Menacing": Characterizing Martin, Brown, and Rice Through Media Coverage

Past research highlights that blacks are more likely to be portrayed as criminals than victims, are pictured being physically restrained more often by law officials, and are displayed in the media more frequently for violent crimes in particular (e.g., Chiricos and Eschholz, 2002; Entman, 1992; Entman and Rojecki, 2000; Fishman, 1998). In the weeks following Zimmerman's arrest, images of Martin as a "gangsta" began to surface, seemingly legitimizing the conclusions Zimmerman drew about Martin and rationalizing Zimmerman's behavior. A Facebook account with photographs of a young black male shirtless and in baggy pants was falsely attributed to Martin (Collette, 2013; see Figure 2). Photographs of hip-hop artist The Game even circulated as the real Trayvon Martin (Emery, 2013). During the trial, Zimmerman's defense released photographs of Martin wearing a gold grill on his teeth and flipping off the camera. The defense also concentrated on text messages sent by Martin in the weeks prior to his death. These messages were full of misspellings and slang and focused on Marin's marijuana use and his suspension from school (Caputo, 2013), which are directly associated with commonly held black stereotypes including being uneducated and drug abusers (Dukes, 2014; Dukes and Overstreet, 2011). And following the verdict, National Rifle Association board member Ted Nugent characterized Martin as a "dope smoking, racist gangsta wannabe" and stated that Zimmerman did what anyone would have done in that situation (Alman, 2013).

Similarly, after his death, Michael Brown was characterized in a stereotypical manner in the media. In a press conference to address Michael Brown's shooting and to release the name of his shooter, the Ferguson police department chose to share footage of Brown purportedly robbing a convenient store prior to his death—facts that had nothing to do with Brown's shooting at all since that information was not known by the police officer who shot Brown (Killoran, 2014). In response to media leaked details of Officer Wilson's grand jury testimony and Brown's autopsy, social commentary shifted to characterizations of Brown as a "gentle giant," a nickname reportedly used by his family members. Like with Trayvon Martin, photographs of Michael Brown flipping off the camera surfaced and emphasized his past marijuana use, suggested by the presence of THC in his blood at the time of his death. During a segment on the HBO show Real Time with Bill Maher, Maher echoed this sentiment, stating that Michael Brown "wasn't a gentle giant. He was committing a robbery and he pushed that guy. He was acting like a thug, not a gentle giant" (Savali, 2014).

Figure 2. Widely circulated meme decrying bias in media coverage of the Trayvon Martin case, although ironically, the photograph on the right is not actually Trayvon Martin.

These rationalizations of Martin's and Brown's deaths demonstrate a sort of victim blaming consistent with previous research examining race and characterizations of victims. To our knowledge, no research has examined victim blaming responses in homicide cases; however, investigators have explored parallel questions of how victim race and respectability (e.g., sexual and social reputation) impact attributions of responsibility in acquaintance rape scenarios. For instance, one study found that black victims characterized as low in respectability were perceived as more responsible for their rapes than similarly characterized White victims (Dupuis and Clay, 2013). When applied to stereotypical media portrayals of Martin and Brown, these findings suggests that they continue to be blamed for their own deaths because they were widely characterized as lacking respectability.

Although Rice was not portrayed as stereotypically as Martin and Brown, the media still chose to also blame Rice for his own death. For example, some media outlets continuously stated that Rice should not have taken the orange colored tip off of his pellet gun since that is what marks a gun from being a real gun compared to a toy gun. They argue that is was this act that killed Rice—not the actual gun that shot him. Or, for example, covered by other media outlets, Cleveland Police Patrolman's Association President Steve Loomis was quoted saying, "He's menacing. He's 5-feet-7, 191 pounds. He wasn't that little kid you're seeing in pictures. He's a 12-year-old in an adult body" (Schutlz, 2015), highlighting the type of language that colors minority victims.

Yet, painting these victims with broad stereotypical strokes is regrettably all too predictable. Social psychological research has a revealed tendency for people to seek dispositional explanations over situational ones, especially when circumstances surrounding an incident are ambiguous (Jones and Harris, 1967; Duncan 1976). As details surrounding Martin's death were unveiled, very few of these details were actual fact; the only verified fact being Zimmerman shooting Martin. Similarly, conflicting accounts of Brown and Officer Wilson's altercation have surfaced - some eyewitnesses stating that Brown was attempting to surrender and Wilson stating that Brown "punched and scratched him repeatedly" (Schmidt, Apuzzo and Bosman, 2014). Again, the only verified fact is that an unarmed Michael Brown was shot to death by Officer Wilson. And as stated earlier, there is still ambiguity surrounding what officers Loehman and Garmback did or did not do when they approached Tamir Rice and why the 9-1-1 call about Rice was not relayed in full detail. However, perceptions of Martin, Brown, and Rice's behaviors as aggressive and threatening remain subjective. Research has demonstrated a lower threshold for labeling an ambiguous behavior as criminal and aggressive when someone is black (Correll et al., 2002; Duncan, 1976; Eberhardt et al., 2004). Consequently, individuals rationalizing Zimmerman's or Wilson's or Loehman's actions looked to these young black males' disposition for answers, causing many to focus on the ways in which they all fit the stereotypical black male mold.

"Black Lives Matter": Policy Implications and Needed Interventions

When tragedies like the deaths of Trayvon Martin, Michael Brown, and Tamir Rice occur, we search feverously for explanations and justifications for actions. Social commentary has focused on issues like controversial Stand Your Ground statutes and racial profiling. The research reviewed throughout this chapter suggests that the controversy surrounding Martin, Brown, and Rice's deaths is about more than standing one's ground and racism. It is an example highlighting how easily racial stereotypes can be applied while also depicting a pathway for tragic consequences such as the shooter bias phenomenon that has claimed the lives of others in similar contexts. Recognizing the role of such processes is an essential first step; however, action through application of existing research as well as continuing investigations in these areas is necessary in protecting the lives of raial and ethnic minority youth. Below we provide recommendations in four relevant areas: 1) media representations; 2) Stand Your Ground statues; 3) shooter-bias training; and 4) body-worn camera technology for law enforcement.

Combating Biased Media Representations

As mentioned earlier in this chapter, previous research has established clear biases concerning media representations of racial and ethnic minorities (e.g., Chiricos and Eschholz, 2002; Entman, 1992; Entman and Rojecki, 2000; Fishman, 1998) and the negative consequences of exposure to stereotypical depictions, such as an increase in shooter-bias (Correll et al., 2007). Perceptions of Martin, Brown, and Rice just prior to their deaths during their interactions with Zimmerman, Wilson, and Loehman respectively, were likely guided by such depictions. Furthermore, stereotypical representations and misguided portrayals of the incidences themselves in the media since their deaths have likely impacted the chances for justice. To decrease the likelihood of violence against unarmed minorities, significant changes must occur in media portrayals of racial and ethnic minorities going forward. This means encouraging media outlets to promote realistic and unbiased renderings of racial and ethnic minorities and holding other agencies accountable for the types of information they release to the media. For example, in the case of Michael Brown, this might mean holding the Ferguson Police Department accountable for the selective release of information about the case and inaction in preventing leaks of sensitive grand jury testimony. Among critics of those actions, the Department of Justice stated that the Ferguson Police Department's selective release of information such as the convenience store footage of Brown were "irresponsible and highly troubling" and called it "an inappropriate effort to influence public opinion about the case" (Pearce, 2014). This type of condemnation from officials and the general public is necessary for persuading media outlets to be more responsible and unbiased in their reporting and overall depictions of racial and ethnic minorities.

Equity in Stand Your Ground Statue Use

Future research should also investigate the circumstances under which people use lethal force as self-defense as well as the use of Stand Your Ground statues. Florida's Stand Your Ground law and similar self-defense statues give a person the right to use deadly force against a presumed attacker if the person has reasonable fear of the attacker (Wallace, 2008). Currently, 24 states have self-defense laws similar to Florida's Stand Your Ground law, and in these states, racial bias is prolific in the use of such laws. For instance, 78% of cases with black or Hispanic victims were seen as justified compared to 56% of cases with white victims. Overwhelmingly, cases with white perpetrators killing black victims were 354% more likely to be ruled justified relative to cases with white perpetrators killing white victims (Leber and Flatow, 2014).

While there is some data illustrating racial bias in the use of Stand Your Ground as a defense, researchers have not examined when people choose to use lethal force in self-defense or why racial bias occurs in the justification of lethal force empirically. Understanding the factors that contribute to people's decisions to use lethal force as self-defense as well as when and why judges and juries feel this force is justified is essential to combating racial bias in this domain and ensuring justice for victims. Policy makers should also carefully examine parameters around which an individual can stand their ground to ensure that clear instigators of altercations are held responsible for their behavior.

Shooter-Bias Training

To date research has merely focused on establishing when shooter bias occurs (i.e., more often toward black men). Although a few studies have attempted to change shooter bias outcomes using simple training paradigms, these types of interventions have yet to be extended to longitudinal formats or to actual real-world settings. Many laboratory investigations of shooter bias have relied on a shoot/don't shoot task, in which participants are instructed to shoot targets with weapons and not to shoot targets without weapons using a video game simulation (e.g., Correll et al., 2002, 2007; Correll, Park, Judd, Wittenbrink, Sadler and Keesee, 2007; Correll, Urland and Ito, 2006; Sim, Correll and Sadler, 2013). This work found that novice undergraduate students exhibited a greater degree of shooter bias in comparison to undergraduate student participants that received multiple sessions of training, showing some promising results of shooter bias training paradigms (Correll et al., 2007; Kahn and Davies, 2011; Sim et al., 2013). Other work involving actual police officers also shows that initially police officers were more likely to shoot unarmed black compared with unarmed white suspects, but that after extensive training with the task, that racial bias was eliminated (Plant and Peruche, 2005).

Therefore, this work suggests that targeted exposure to and training with shoot/don't shoot simulations can decrease shooter bias to a degree but it is clear that additional research is essential in pinpointing what specific types of training may actually reduce shooter bias for both the general population and police officers across the country. Moreover once these interventions and paradigms are more established, those interventions should become a mandatory part of training procedures for all police officers. If something as simple as a video game training paradigm can even marginally reduce shooter bias effects, it suggests that the answer to reducing shooter bias outcomes may not be as complex as originally thought.

Oversight through Body-Worn Camera Technology

Another promising intervention to combat shooter bias and excessive force by law enforcement in general, is the inclusion of cameras on uniforms or body-worn camera technology. Recent pilot programs requiring police officers to wear video cameras as a part of their uniform have shown significant decreases in use of force and positive reactions from the public. For instance, beginning February 2012, in one of the few empirical studies to date, the Rialto California Police Department randomly assigned half of their uniformed officers to wear small cameras that they are expected to activate anytime they leave a their patrols cars to interact with the public. Within the first year of the program, both the use of force decreased by nearly 60% and civilian complaints also decreased by 88% (Stross, 2013). An executive summary of research supported by the Department of Justice also recognizes the potential benefits of body-worn camera technology, noting that cameras could serve as a valuable source of feedback for training and performance evaluation (White, 2014).

To date, only five empirical studies have been conducted on the effectives of body-worn camera technology, but it is obvious that continued research in this area is essential in addition to figuring out additional ways to fundraise for this technology to be available for all police units across the country. This technology could also help to change media portrayals as well of both victims and police officers alike. Although this chapter has focused on the wrongful deaths of black males, these cameras can also protect police officers by accurately documenting their interactions. Therefore, these cameras can help right wrongful behavior that occur no matter which side in an incident may be at fault. By using these videos the media could actually change the story regarding racially charged incidences in particular.

Conclusion

In sum, we have highlighted various psychological factors that likely contributed to the deaths of Trayvon Martin, Michael Brown, and Tamir Rice, and shaped posthumous perceptions of these victims. Importantly, we have also pinpointed four main changes that can begin to positively affect the fates for future young, black men and other racial and ethnic minorities across the country: 1) altering media representations to aid in initiating changes in stereotype associations; 2) reanalyzing the use of policies such as Standing Your Ground to ensure it fairness to minorities; 3) expanding research on training programs to decrease shooter bias tendencies both longitudinally and to more police stations across the country; and 4) changing the norm for police officers wearing cameras while enforcing the law. Some of these changes are easier to initiate than others, but each of them can positively affect the treatment of young, black men to aid them in their hopefully transition them from being endangered to freely living. We cannot ask people to change their appearance, but we can at least try to get people to change their perceptions of outgroup members, or at a minimum, figure out methods to help change the context that endangers so many minority youth. It shouldn't be fact that the fate of racial minorities rests in the hands of others—their future should lie in their own hands. Instead, research needs to begin to pave a new pathway toward life for this population, so there will not be any more Trayvon Martins, Michael Browns, and Tamir Rices.

Author Note

This work was supported by a Ford Dissertation Fellowship and a Provost's Postdoctoral Scholarship from the University of Chicago awarded to Sarah Gaither. We would like to thank Judah Axe, Daren Graves, Saher Selod, and Sam Sommers for reading earlier versions of this chapter.

References

Alman, A. (2013, July 15). Ted Nugent calls Trayvon Martin 'dope smoking, racist gangsta wannabe.' *The Huffington Post.* Retrieved from http://www.huffingtonpost.com/2013/07/15/ted-nugent-trayvon-martin_n_ 3599437.html.

Alvarez, L. and Buckley, C. (2013, July 13). Zimmerman is acquitted in Trayvon Martin killing. *The New York Times.* Retrieved from http://www.nytimes.com/2013/07/14/us/george-zimmerman-verdict- trayvon-martin.html?pagewanted=all.

Ambady, N. and Rosenthal, R. (1992). Thin slices of expressive behavior as predictors of interpersonal consequences: A meta-analysis. *Psychological Bulletin, 111,* 256-274.

Blair, I. V., Judd, C.M., Sadler, M.S. and Jenkins, C. (2002). The role of Afrocentric features in person perception: Judging by features and categories. *Journal of Personality and Social Psychology, 83,* 5-25.

Bodenhausen, G. V. and Macrae, C. N. (1998). Stereotype activation and inhibition. In J. R.Wyer (Ed.), *Advances in social cognition* (Vol. 11, pp. 1– 52). Mahwah, NJ: Erlbaum.

Brewer, M. B. (1988). A dual process model of impression formation. In T. K. Srull and R. S. Wyer (Eds.), *Advances in social cognition* (Vol. 1, pp. 1– 36). Hillsdale, NJ: Erlbaum.

Chiricos, T. and Eschholz, S. (2002). The racial typification of crime and the criminal typification of race: The social construction of social threat by local TV news. *Journal of Research in Crime and Delinquency, 39,* 400-420.

Collette, C. (2013, March 28). "Fake" Trayvon Martin picture circulate on the web; image actually shows different person. Retrieved from http://http://www.wtsp.com/news/article/247194/19/Fake-Trayvon-Martin-picture-circulates-on-the-web-image-actually-shows-a-different-person.

Correll, J., Park, B., Judd, C. M. and Wittenbrink, B. (2002). The police officer's dilemma: Using ethnicity to disambiguate potentially threatening individuals. *Journal of Personality and Social Psychology, 83,* 1314-1329.

Correll, J., Park, B., Judd, C. M. and Wittenbrink, B. (2007). The influence of stereotypes on decisions to shoot. *European Journal of Social Psychology, 37,* 1102-1117.

Correll, J., Park, B., Judd, C. M. and Wittenbrink, B., Sadler, M. S. and Keesee, T. (2007). Across the thin blue line: Police officers and racial biases in the decision to shoot. *Journal of Personality and Social Psychology, 92,* 1006-1023.

Correll, J., Urland, G. and Ito, T. (2006). Event-related potentials and the decision to shoot: The role of threat perception and cognitive control. *Journal of Experimental Social Psychology, 42,* 120-128.

Devine, P.G. (1989). Stereotypes and prejudice: Their automatic and controlled components. *Journal of Personality and Social Psychology, 56,* 5-18.

Dukes, K.N. (2014). "Baggy pants, bling, durag, and a hoodie": Racialization of attire in stereotypes of black men. Poster presented at 15th Annual Meeting of the Society for Personality and Social Psychology, Austin, TX.

Dukes, K. N. and Maddox, K. B. (2008). Peripheral category cues and the moderation of Afrocentric Bias. Talk given at the 9th Annual Meeting of the Society for Personality and Social Psychology, Albuquerque, NM.

Dukes, K.N. and Overstreet, N. (2011). Black women = invisible women? Elucidating stereotypes and subtypes of black women. Poster presented at the 12th Annual Meeting of the Society for Personality and Social Psychology, San Antonio, TX.

Duncan, B. L. (1976). Differential social perception and attribution of intergroup violence. Testing the lower limits of stereotyping of blacks. *Journal of Personality and Social Psychology, 34,* 590-598.

Dupuis, E. C. and Clay, J. A. (2013). The role of race and respectability in attributions of responsibility for acquaintance rape. *Violence and Victims, 28(6)*, 1085-1095.

Eberhardt, J.L., Goff, P.A., Purdie, V.J. and Davies, P.G. (2004). Seeing black: Race, crime, and visual processing. *Journal of Personality and Social Psychology, 87,* 876-893.

Emery, D. (2013, July 4). This is not a picture of Trayvon Martin. Retrieved from http://urbanlegends.about.com/b/2013/07/04/this-is-not-a-picture-of-trayvon-martin.htm.

Entman, R. (1992). Blacks in the news: Television, modern racism and cultural change. *Journalism Quarterly, 69,* 341-361.

Entman, R.M. and Rojecki, A. (2000). *The black image in the white mind: Media and race in America.* Chicago: University of Chicago Press.

Fieldstadt, E. (2015, Feb 28). Fatal shooting of Cleveland boy Tamir Rice was caused by his own actions: City. *NBC News.* http://www.nbcnews.com/news/nbcblk/fatal-shooting-cleveland-boy-tamir-rice-was-caused-his-own-n314861.

Fishman, L.T. (1998). "The black bogeyman and white self-righteousness." pp. 109-25 In C.R. Maan and M.S. Zatz (Eds), *Images of color, images of crime: Readings.* (pp. 109-125). Los Angeles: Roxbury.

Fiske, S. T. and Neuberg, S. L. (1990). A continuum of impression formation, from category-based to individuation processes: Influences of information and motivation on attention and interpretation. *Advances in Experimental Social Psychology, 23,* 1-74.

Freeman, J.B., Pauker, K., Apfelbaum, E.P. and Ambady, N. (2010). Continuous dynamics in the real-time perception of race. Journal of Experimental Social Psychology, 46, 179-185.

Freeman, J.B., Penner, A. M., Saperstein, A., Scheutz, M. and Ambady, N. (2011). Looking the part: social status cues shape race perception. *PloS one,6(9),* e25107.

Greenwald, A.G. and Banaji, M.R. (1995). Implicit social cognition: Attitudes, self-esteem, and stereotypes. *Psychological Review, 102,* 4-27.

Ito, T.A. and Urland, G.R. (2003). Race and gender on the brain: Electrocortical measures of attention to the race and gender of multiply categorizable individuals. *Journal of Personality and Social Psychology, 85,* 616-626.

Izadi, E. and Holley, P. (2104, November 26). Video shows Cleveland officer shooting 12-year-old Tamir Rice within seconds. *Washington Post.* https://www.washingtonpost.com/news/post-nation/wp/2014/11/26/officials-release-video-names-in-fatal-police-shooting-of-12-year-old-cleveland-boy/.

Jones, E. E. and Harris, V. A. (1967). The attribution of attitudes. *Journal of Experimental Social Psychology, 3,* 1–24.

Kahn, K. and Davies, P. (2011). Differentially dangerous? Phenotypic racial stereotyping increases implicit bias among ingroup and outgroup members. *Group Processes and Intergroup Relations, 14,* 569-580.

Kahn, K. and Davies, P. (2007). Suits versus sweats: The influence of clothing type on decisions to shoot. Poster presented at the 8th Annual Meeting of the Society for Personality and Social Psychology, Memphis, TN.

Killoran, E. (2014, August 15). Ferguson police chief botches press conference to ID Mike Brown shooting officer. *International Business Times.* Retrieved from http://www.ibtimes.com/ferguson-police-chief-botches-press-conference-id-mike-brown-shooting-officer-1659786.

LA Times Staff (2014, November 26). Hear the 911 call about Tamir Rice: Gun is 'probably fake,' caller says. *Los Angeles Times.* Retrieved from http://www.latimes.com/nation/nationnow/la-na-nn-tamir-rice-911-call-20141126-htmlstory.html.

Leber, R. and Flatow. N. (2014, February 24). 5 disturbing fact about the state of Stand Your Ground on the second anniversary of Trayvon's death. *Think Progress.* Retrieved from http://thinkprogress.org/justice/2014/02/26/3332391/trayvon-martin-years/.

Mack, D. and Koerner, C. (2015, June 13). Cleveland officers thought Tamir Rice looked older than 12, report finds. *BuzzFeed News.* Retrieved from http://www.buzzfeed.com/davidmack/cleveland-sheriff-report-tamir-rice-death#.smJ81qD7W.

Maddox, K.B. (2004). Perspectives on racial phenotypicality bias. *Personality and Social Psychology Review, 8,* 383-401.

Maddox, K B. and Dukes, K. N. (2008). Social categorization and beyond. In N. Ambady and J. Skowronski (Eds.), *First impressions.* New York: Guilford Publications, Inc.

Maddox, K.B. and Gray, S. (2002). Cognitive representations of African Americans: Re-exploring the role of skin tone. *Personality and Social Psychological Bulletin, 28,* 250-259.

Markman, A. (2012, October 12). Shooter bias and stereotypes. *Psychology Today.* Retrieved from http://www.psychologytoday.com/blog/ulterior-motives/201210/shooter-bias-and-stereotypes.

Mekawi, Y. and Bresin, K. (2015). Is the evidence from racial bias shooting task studies a smoking gun? Results From a Meta-Analysis. *Journal of Experimental Social Psychology*, *61*, 120-130.

Montepare, J. M. and Opeyo, A. (2002). The relative salience of physiognomic cues in differentiating faces: A methodological tool. *Journal of Nonverbal Behavior, 26,* 43-59.

Niemann, Y. F., Jennings, L., Rozelle, R. M., Baxter, J. and Sullivan, E. (1994). Use of free responses and cluster analysis to determine stereotypes of eight groups. *Personality and Social Psychology Bulletin, 20,* 379-390.

Pearce, M. (2014, October 22). Justice department condemns Ferguson leak as effort to sway opinion. *Los Angeles Times.* Retrieved from http://www.latimes.com/nation/la-na-ferguson-leaks-20141022-story.html #page=1.

Plant, E. A. and Peruche, B. M. (2005). The consequences of race for police officers' responses to criminal suspects. *Psychological Science*, *16*(3), 180-183.

Read, S. J. (1987). Constructing causal scenarios: A knowledge structure approach to causal reasoning. *Journal of Personality and Social Psychology, 52,* 288–302.

Savali, K. W. (2014, October 25). Bill Maher: Michael Brown 'wasn't a gentle giant…he was acting like a thug. *News One.* Retrieved from http://newsone.com/3065680/bill-maher-michael-brown-wasnt-a-gentle-giant-he-was-acting-like-a-thug-video/.

Schmidt, M. S., Apuzzo, M. and Bosman, J. (2014, October 17). Police officer in Ferguson is said to recount a struggle. *New York Times.* Retrieved from http://www.nytimes.com. /2014/10/18/us/ferguson-case-officer-is-said-to-cite-struggle.html?_r=2.

Schultz, C. (2015, February 23). A city of two tales. *POLITICO Magazine.* Retrieved from http://www.politico.com/magazine/story/2015/02/tamir-rice-cleveland-police-115401_full.html?print#.VjdupX6rTIU.

Shaffer, C. (2014, November 23). Cleveland police officer shoots 12-year-old boy carrying BB gun. *Northeast Ohio Media Group.* Retrieved from http://www.cleveland.com/ metro/index.ssf/2014/11/cleveland_police_officer_shoot_6.html.

Sim, J. J., Correll, J. and Sadler, M. S. (2014). Understanding police and expert performance: When training attenuates (vs. exacerbates) stereotypic bias in the decision to shoot. *Personality and Social Psychology Bulletin, 39,* 291-304.

Stross, R. (2013, April 6). Wearing a badge, and a video camera. *The New York Times.* Retrieved from http://www.nytimes.com/2013/04/07/business/wearable-video-cameras-for-police-officers.html?_r=2&.

Taintor, D. (2014, August 16). How Ferguson police made the situation worse. *MSNBC.* Retrieved from http://www.msnbc.com/msnbc/ferguson-police-department-made-situation-worse.

Yan, H. (2014, October 22). Autopsy show Michael Brown was shot in the hand at close range. *CNN.* Retrieved from http://www.cnn.com/2014/10/22/justice/ferguson-michael-brown- autopsy/index.html.

Wallace, P. (2008). Stand your ground: Measure reasonable fear. *The Forensic Examiner, 17,* 74-77.

White, M. D. (2014). Police officer body-worn cameras: Assessing the evidence. Washington, DC: Office of Community Oriented Policing Services.

In: Stereotypes and Stereotyping
Editor: Claude Fields ISBN: 978-1-63484-510-6

Chapter 7

EVALUATING STEREOTYPES IN COUNTER-STEREOTYPIC OCCUPATIONS

***Fiona MacDougall*[1] *and Robert Nash*[2]**
[1]University of Aberdeen, Aberdeen, Scotland
[2]Bond Business school, Bond University, Gold Coast, Queensland, Australia

ABSTRACT

The contemporary workplace no longer exhibits rigid gender based stereotypes, rather it is, in theory at least, an area of equal opportunity for all. However, both anecdotal and empirical evidence suggests that individuals working in counter-stereotypic occupations (i.e., a female mechanic) still receive negative evaluations and are subject to discrimination. This study aimed to determine whether the negative evaluations these individuals receive map onto Fiske, Cuddy and Glick's (2006) universal warm-cold dimension of social perception. With the use of a Single Category Implicit Association Test (SC-IAT) stereotypicality was examined in relation to perceptions of warmth and coldness. The results revealed that individuals in counter-stereotypic occupations were perceived as cold. The theoretical and practical implications of implicitly associating coldness with counter-stereotypicality are discussed.

INTRODUCTION

Gender equality is an issue which has been rigorously fought for over centuries with the goal that individuals should no longer face discrimination simply due to their sex. The workplace is an area in which gender discrimination has been particularly rife, leading to the implementation of various pieces of legislation (e.g., UK Sex Discrimination Act, 1975; Equality Act 2010) with the aim of making the workplace an environment with equal opportunity for all. On the surface at least, men and women no longer dominate particular professions, overshadowing the opposite sex is behaviour the modern workplace tries extremely hard to avoid. Women are now routinely making a living through driving lorries, flying planes and working on building sites, with it being just as common to find males teaching, styling hair or providing childcare – this would have been almost unheard of not all that long ago.

Schuman, Steeh, Bobo and Krysan (1997) discovered through public opinion polls that the movement towards equal opportunity and the legislation put in place to prevent discrimination is almost universally accepted and supported. Unfortunately despite the legislation and workplace initiatives there is evidence to suggest that gender discrimination is still commonly found in the workplace today. Sheridan (2002) reported that whilst it appears that women are readily progressing into what was previously considered male dominant territory within the workplace - in particular higher-ranked positions within companies such as supervisory or management positions - the reality is that the majority of these roles are still in fact carried out by males. Women in the workplace are still exposed to a tougher time than males; progression within occupational fields is still mainly carried out by males with females being less frequently promoted. Woman also regularly receive a lower salary than their male counterparts, even when there is no difference between their occupational roles. Higher levels of stress and absenteeism are also found in women when compared to males (Lyness and Heilman, 2006). Interestingly Cuddy, Fiske and Glick (2004) found that female job applicants who were also mothers were subjected to higher levels of discrimination than females who do not have children, whereas they found no difference in employment possibilities for males whether they were fathers or not. This is an unfair prejudice in which women face discrimination simply for having a family whereas males are not subjected to this scrutiny (Cuddy et al. 2004). It is unclear why males do not face this discrimination but it is something which could be significantly hindering female progression within the workplace.

Discrimination in the workplace is not an issue which solely affects females; males are just as likely to experience discrimination although it is less commonly reported. Nursing has generally always been considered a female profession with females making up most of the nursing population. Lupton (2000) found that male nurses are subjected to continuous ridicule and abuse due to their occupation, constantly fearing being seen as less masculine. It is possible that there are so few males in nursing, and that it has not experienced the rises in gender equality that other industries have experienced due to the poor circumstances male nurses are frequently subjected to - possibly because the expectation that nurses are female is so strongly developed and therefore exceptionally hard to overcome (Macwilliams, Schmidt and Bleich, 2013). What this points to, however, is a situation in which, despite social and legislative changes, people performing non- traditional occupation roles (e.g., male nurse or female lorry driver) continue to face disadvantage. By drawing from theory and research in the domain of social cognition, the current thesis will attempt to provide some insight into why this might be the case.

Perceiving Others

Person perception is simply the process which comes into play when we are interacting with others in our environment, allowing us to understand and relate to them and leading to the formation of impressions. That is, the way in which we perceive others has a direct effect on how we interact and behave towards them. In this way, person perception is seen as an essential part of everyday life as interaction with others plays a large part in most aspects of day to day tasks, from getting on with colleagues to meeting new friends or catching up with old ones. The development of Bartlett's (1932) idea of schematic thinking in the person perception process has lead to what is now the generally accepted assumption - that it is in fact an individuals' schematic preconceptions which are the driving force in both their evaluations of and reactions towards others (e.g., Allport, 1954).

Macrae, Bodenhausen, Schloerscheidt and Milne (1999) emphasised the need for categorical thinking in person perception in order to deal with the cognitive demands of daily life. People only have a limited information-processing capacity and with the world being made up of complex and continuously changing stimuli it is no real surprise that 'short-cuts' are employed to reduce the cognitive load that the person perception process requires. To simplify and speed up person perception individuals rely heavily on the use of categorical thinking (Brewer, 1988), whereby others are perceived according to their social group (e.g., male or female). The process of categorization within person perception gives rise to the evaluation and formation of an impression of an individual, which in turn can often lead to stereotype-based judgements (Fiske and Neuberg, 1990). For instance, categorizing someone according to their sex may result in expectations about that person conforming to socially defined stereotypes. Whilst categorical thinking is an effective shortcut used commonly in person perception it is in fact a complicated process especially when there are many cognitive demands occurring at once. To this end, Macrae and Bodenhausen (2000) proposed three separate stages of categorical thinking which take place in person perception: category activation, category application and category inhibition.

Category activation - Allport (1954) initially claimed that category activation is unconditionally automatic, that it happens spontaneously and unconsciously every time we meet or think of someone. Once a category has been activated the stereotypical associations related to the category can lead to assimilation effects (Fiske, 1989). There are two proposed benefits to this assimilation process. First, quite simply assimilation makes the person perception process quick and easy, it allows for information to be streamlined and relies on preformed mental models so that individuals can quickly form impressions and successfully interact with others, whilst requiring minimal conscious effort on their part. Second, it is proposed that the assimilation process actually leads to the emphasis of counter-stereotypical information, highlighting the unexpected information so that it is effectively encoded in a way that individuals successfully remember the fact that that a particular individual does not conform to stereotypical expectations (e.g., Srull and Wyer, 1989).

It is highly probable that stereotype activation is due to an individual's inability to think in depth and accurately about others at a particular moment, whether it be due to a high cognitive load, time constraints or simply laziness (Fiske, Lin and Neuberg, 1999). Dijksterhuis, Spears and Lepinasse (2000) found that categorical assimilation only happens when participants are under a high cognitive load; conditions in which participants are solely focusing on target stimuli in the absence of distracters stereotypical expectations are not met. This challenges Allport's (1954) initial claim of unconditional automaticity in that context and state in which individuals interact with another person will affect whether or not a stereotype is activated (Wegner and Bargh, 1998). Nonetheless, once category activation has taken place, the application of this stereotypical information is then made possible.

Category application – It is essential to note that category activation and application are two distinct processes - even if a particular stereotype has been activated it does not necessarily mean that it will be applied. Depending on whether the information is perceived as consistent or inconsistent with stereotypical beliefs has an effect on the processing of target information, and how it may be applied. Objective judgements are based on evidence and facts, thinking critically and making decisions based on what is previously known and it has been found that objective judgements lead to assimilation with stereotypical expectancies. On the other hand, subjective judgements which are derived from emotions and personal preconceived beliefs tend to lead to contrasting ideas from what would stereotypically be expected (Kobrynowicz and Biernat, 1997). Schubert and Hafner (2003) agreed with the previously discussed findings that objective priming does result in a particular stereotype being activated through a process of assimilation; they also found that when participants were required to compare a primed social stereotype to themselves the assimilation process was stopped and resulted in contrasting behaviour. The act of having to relate yourself to the categorical thinking process was enough to eliminate stereotypical application towards others. Thus, it can clearly be seen that the way in which a stereotype is activated has large knock on effects on how the stereotype itself is later applied in the categorization process. This evidence all shows that even when stereotypical thinking may have already been activated the outcome of this categorical thinking will differ across situations. Stereotypical judgements may not necessarily be applied if they do not fit with the context in which an individual comes across the target in question.

Category inhibition – With discriminatory behaviour readily being viewed with distaste within society - not to mention the potential legal repercussions of such actions - it is no wonder that individuals try their best to inhibit stereotypical behaviour. Whatever an individual's reasons for inhibiting stereotypical behaviour whether it be due to fear of legal repercussions (Fiske, Bersoff, Borgida and Deaux, 1991), or simply because the idea of stereotypical behaviour distresses them as it disagrees with their own personal standards (Devine, Monteith, Zuwerink and Elliot, 1991), it can be seen throughout the literature as a prominent theme within categorising and stereotyping, with inhibition all too often failing to succeed. To be able to inhibit stereotypical thinking and behaviour, the perceiver first needs to be aware that the stereotypical representation has already been triggered. Wegner and Erber (1992) proposed the possibility that a conscious effort to inhibit a stereotype may in fact cause hyperaccessibility, making it more prominent in the mind than it previously would have been if inhibition had been avoided. The rebound effect caused by consciously inhibiting stereotypical behaviour can quite often be stronger than the initial categorisation effect would have been on its own, leading to more severe adverse effects (e.g., Macrae, Bodenhausen, Milne and Jetten, 1994a; Wyer, Sherman and Stroessner, 1998). Attempting to behave in line with societal expectations may actually be strengthening the effect of stereotypical behaviour. This could possibly be the reason why gender discrimination is still so prominent in the workplace. People know what is socially and legally expected of them and it is very easy to say what they are supposed to feel towards male nurses and female mechanics, but the research clearly shows that gender discrimination is still a regular occurrence. In attempting to inhibit discrimination individuals are actually heightening their stereotypical responses towards people in incongruent occupations. Therefore behaving in line with social expectations could, in fact, be leading to a greater level of discrimination in the workplace.

Sex-Role Stereotyping

As previously discussed gender discrimination in the workplace remains an issue and it is now of great interest as to why this behaviour is still happening. Flannigan, Miles, Quadflieg and Macrae (in press) were interested as to why people in counter-stereotypical occupations still face such high levels of discrimination despite all the legislation in place to prevent it. Flannigan et al. (in press) proposed that discrimination is still a prominent issue in the workplace because an implicit negativity is being associated with others when they don't perform the traditional roles expected of them (i.e., expectancy disconfirmation). They were interested to find out if there was an implicit, automatic association between positive and negative evaluations and stereotypical and counter- stereotypical targets. To investigate this they initially used an Implicit Association Test (IAT, Greenwald, McGhee and Schwartz, 1998) which measures the differential association between two target concepts with an attribute, making it possible to determine whether or not there was an association between a comparative dimension (positive or negative) and occupational stereotypicality. Results from the IAT confirmed that there was a relationship between positivity and negativity and stereotypicality. However the form of the IAT they employed is unable to provide information as to the direction of the association (e.g., an association between positivity and stereotypicality or negativity and counter- stereotypicality).

To further elucidate this issue, Flannigan et al. (in press) followed up this experiment with the use of the Single-Category Implicit Association Test (SC-IAT, Karpinski and Steinman, 2006). This is a modified version of the IAT which is able to measure the strength of the evaluative associations with a single attitude object (i.e., positivity or negativity and its association with stereotypicality). The results from the SC- IAT showed that negative evaluations were significantly associated with counter- stereotypicality. Flannigan et al. (in press) successfully supported their predictions that counter-stereotypic targets would receive negative evaluations from individuals. In so doing they provided initial evidence that people's automatic implicit evaluations of those in counter-stereotypical occupational roles might lie at the heart of their poor treatment in the workplace.

Dimensions of Person Perception

It is easy to say that people are readily perceived either positively or negatively, but what exactly constitutes as a positive or negative evaluation? Fiske, Cuddy and Glick (2006) identified two universal dimensions which can be used across all conditions of social cognition; warmth and competence. When interacting with others it is essential to quickly confirm whether someone is a friend or foe, whether they would cause harm and if they have the capability to act on those intentions. Warmth is the first dimension which is determined when perceiving an individual, deciding whether an individual's intentions are for good or bad is clearly beneficial to survival. The warmth judgement that is made determines whether someone implements approach or avoidance strategies (Cacioppo, Gardner and Berntson 1997). Second, the competence dimension is assessed, once it has been decided if another's intentions are good or bad it is then logical to determine how capable an individual is of successfully carrying them out.

Warmth and competence have been found to remain consistent across cultures and times (Asch, 1946; Wojciszke, Bazinska and Jaworski, 1998) - in all areas of life these two dimensions play a key role in evaluations of others. Since these two dimensions are universally applicable it makes sense to solely use these dimensions which have proved to be highly valid predictors of an individual, both in terms of interpersonal and intergroup social cognition. Although the two dimensions are conceptually separate, when people are evaluated on an individual basis it is often the case that judgments of warmth and competence will show consistency. That is, when people are judged individually, evaluations of warmth and competence tend to correlate positively and people are seen as warm and competent or cold and incompetent, (Judd, James-Hawkins, Yzerbyt and Kashima, 2005). This changes however when you move towards the judgement of social groups and not just an individual, then regularly the two dimensions do not correlate with one another in the same way (Yzerbyt, Provost and Corneille, 2005). It is very common for a social group to be thought of as warm and incompetent or cold and competent. It is important that the two dimensions can be used for the evaluation of both individuals and social groups so that a level of consistency is obtained across all social cognition research. Willis and Todorov (2006) found through the study of facial stimuli perception that people are making these crucial judgments on warmth and competence of other individuals in a fraction of a second. It is a credit to the person perception process that people are generally successfully able to evaluate others in such a short period of time, these evaluations have a major effect on how individuals interact, respond and treat others and it emphasises how streamlined a process person perception really is.

The Current Research

In bringing all the previously discussed research together it is reasonable to question whether the negative evaluations individuals in counter-stereotypical occupations receive (Flannigan et al., in press) can be broken down into the dimensions of warmth and competence proposed by Fiske et al. (2006) (i.e., a negative evaluation could mean an individual was seen as cold and incompetent). The aim of this current study is to determine whether the negative evaluations received by individuals in counter-stereotypic roles map onto Fiske et al.'s (2006) primary warm-cold dimension. With the use of a SC-IAT it will be possible to determine if there is a difference in the evaluations of warmth-coldness towards stereotypical and counter-stereotypical professionals, it will also be able to inform of us the direction of any found relationship. The SC-IAT is the most appropriate measure for this experiment as it has already been proven to be robust and reliable under various experimental conditions, and it allows for stereotypes to be assessed in relation to a single attitude (i.e., warm or cold), the inclusion of an IAT is not necessary under these circumstances. It is expected that the evaluations targets receive based on the warm – cold dimension will be very similar to the results of positive and negative evaluations found by Flannigan et al. (in press) therefore, it is hypothesised that there will be an association between individuals in counter-stereotypical roles and 'coldness.'

METHOD

Participants and Design Twenty one undergraduate students (15 female; M age = 19.8 years, SD = 1.9 years) from the University of Aberdeen participated in the study in exchange for course credit. The study had a single factor (warm vs. cold) within-participant design and was reviewed and approved by the School of Psychology Ethics Committee of the University of Aberdeen. All participants gave informed consent before taking part.

Stimulus Materials and Procedure

Participants arrived at the laboratory individually where they were met by a female experimenter. Participants were first required to complete two basic sorting tasks of warm and cold words (appendix A), and of stereotypic and counter-stereotypic occupational pictures (appendix B). They were corrected if they wrongly categorized stimuli. These tasks were used to ensure participants were familiar with the meaning of the target words, and were able to correctly identify stereotypical and counter-stereotypical occupational roles. To assess participant's true evaluative reactions towards individuals working in stereotypic and counter-stereotypic occupations they were then required to complete a standard computer based Single Category Implicit Association Test (SC-IAT; Karpinski and Steinman, 2006). The participants completed four trials (i.e., two practice blocks and two critical blocks) for both the warm and cold condition, in which a single evaluative dimension (i.e., warm or cold) shared a response key with an occupational stimuli (i.e., stereotypic targets), while the other response key only corresponded to occupational stimuli (i.e., counter – stereotypic targets). The specific details for each block of trials are shown in Table 1. The order of the experimental blocks (i.e., warm or cold versions) was counter-balanced across participants.

Table 1. Set up of trials for all categories in the SC-IAT. *A)* Represents the warm word version when combined with congruent and incongruent targets and *B)* demonstrates the cold word version of the SC-IAT

1 A)				
Block	**Trials**	**Function**	**Left-Key Response (E)**	**Right-Key Response (I)**
1	15	Practice	Congruent Picture + Warm Word	Incongruent Picture
2	30	Test	Congruent Picture + Warm Word	Incongruent Picture
3	15	Practice	Congruent Picture	Incongruent Picture + Warm Word
4	30	Test	Congruent Picture	Incongruent Picture + Warm Word
1 B)				
Block	**Trials**	**Function**	**Left-Key Response (E)**	**Right-Key Response (I)**
1	15	Practice	Congruent Picture + Cold Word	Incongruent Picture
2	30	Test	Congruent Picture + Cold Word	Incongruent Picture
3	15	Practice	Congruent Picture	Incongruent Picture + Cold Word
4	30	Test	Congruent Picture	Incongruent Picture + Cold Word

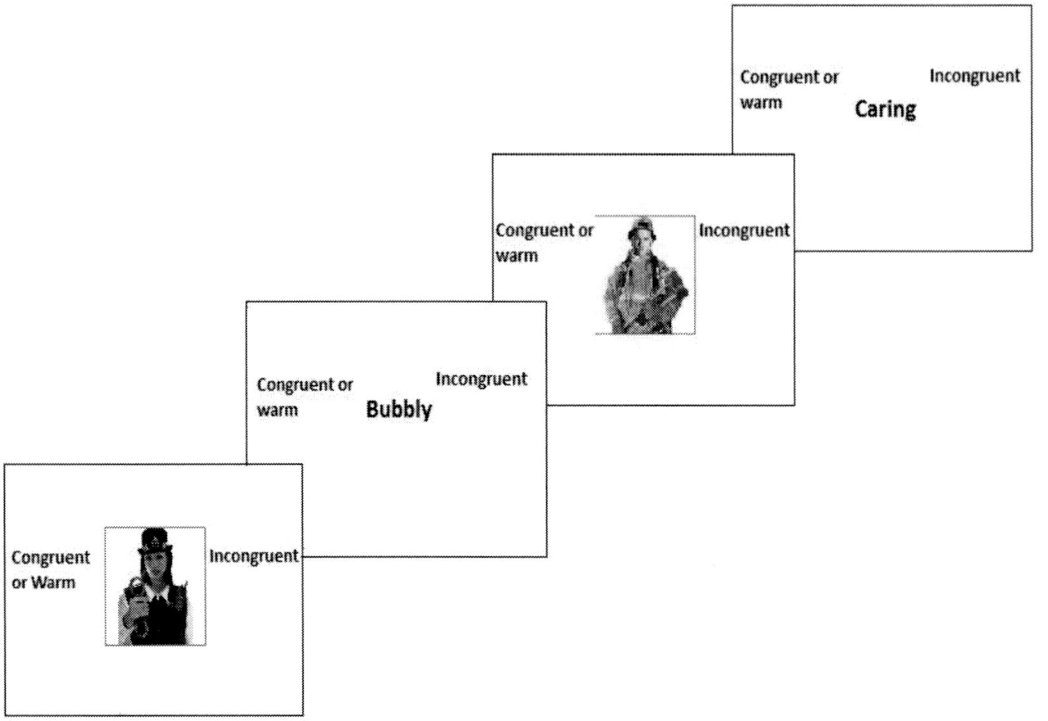

Figure 1. Example set-up of the warm trial condition from the SC-IAT showing an incongruent image followed by a warm word, a congruent image then another warm word, therefore the correct response pattern for this trial would be I, E, E and E.

Participants responded using the 'E' and 'I' keys on the keyboard to provide their response to the categorization between the target words and occupational sex-role images, category labels for both response keys were displayed on the screen to the left and right of the stimuli (see Figure 1). The target stimuli (both words and pictures) were always presented in the middle of the screen and were not removed until participants had made a response. If any errors were made the error trials were repeated again at the end of the block until the correct response was obtained for the trial in question. After all trials were completed participants were debriefed, and thanked for their assistance, and dismissed.

Data Analysis

By comparing response latencies between blocks which consisted of warm (or cold) words paired together with stereotypic targets and blocks in which they were paired with counter – stereotypic targets, it is possible to calculate a single – category implicit association score for each evaluative dimension (i.e., warm or cold) separately.

RESULTS

Data Cleaning and Reduction

Initially, practice trial blocks (i.e., 1 and 3) were removed and any trials in the remaining blocks (i.e., 2 and 4) with reaction times of less than 300ms or greater than 10000ms were excluded from analysis. Data were then reduced using the SC-IAT D-score algorithm proposed by Karpinski and Steinman (2006). Specifically, mean response times were computed for each of the two test blocks (i.e., blocks 2 and 4), along with pooled standard deviations for all the valid trials in these blocks. Next the mean difference between blocks 2 and 4 was calculated before being divided by the pooled standard deviation. For each participant this procedure was completed for both the warm and cold versions, the cold value was then subtracted from the warm value to reveal an overall SC- IAT value (i.e., D-score). D-Scores were coded such that positive scores showed an association between warmth and stereotypical occupations whilst negative scores indicated an association between cold and counter-stereotypicality.

SC-IAT Analysis

A paired samples t-test was used to compare SC-IAT D-scores between the warm and cold conditions. This revealed a significant effect, $t(20) = 3.99$, $p = .001$, whereby trials in the warm condition were accompanied by higher D-scores ($M = 0.11$, $SD = 0.36$) than trials in the cold condition ($M = -0.32$, $SD = 0.34$). This indicates that there was an association between the evaluative dimension (i.e., warmth or coldness) and target stereotypicality (see Figure 2). To further investigate this effect, follow-up single sample t- tests were used to compare D-scores from the warm and cold conditions (separately) with 0 (i.e., no association). It was found that there was no association between warmth and target stereotypicality, $t(20) = 1.33$, $p = .20$. However a significant association between coldness and stereotypicality was revealed, $t(20) = 4.29$, $p < .001$, whereby counter- stereotypical targets were seen to been associated with coldness.

DISCUSSION

Using a SC-IAT, the present study investigated whether the negative evaluations received by individuals in counter-stereotypic roles map onto Fiske et al.'s (2006) warm-cold dimension. The obtained results support the proposed hypothesis; individuals in counter-stereotypic roles were associated with coldness.

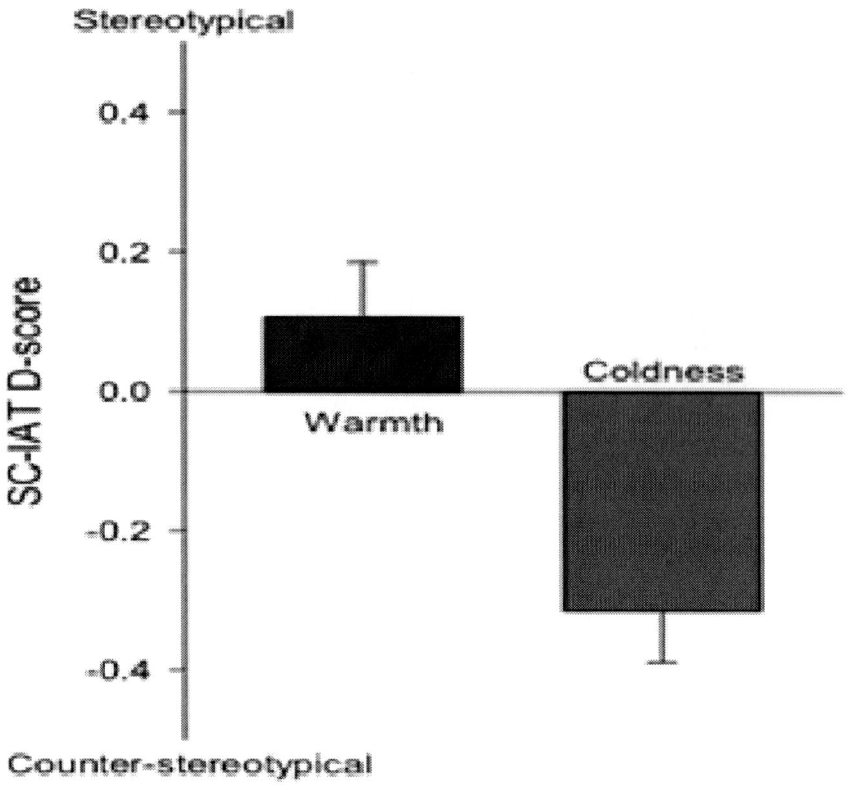

Figure 2. Graph revealing mean SC-IAT *D*-Scores showing the relationship between the evaluation dimensions (warm or cold words) with stereotypicality. Positive *D*-Scores (i.e., *D*-Score > 0) represent an association with stereotypical occupations whilst negative *D*- Scores (i.e., *D*-Score < 0) represent an association with counter-stereotypical occupations.

Results revealed that while counter-stereotypical targets were associated with cold evaluations, participants did not exhibit any significant response to congruent occupational images. Participants implicitly associated coldness with counter-stereotypical targets whilst there was no association found between the stereotypical targets and warmth. This is not an unexpected result, what we typically anticipate to be seen in our environment shouldn't evoke strong emotional responses. If something is presented to us which we would generally predict (i.e., stereotypical), it will not stand out enough to cause a shift in attentional resources. Various research using brain imagery techniques has successfully shown that there are differences in brain activity between exposure to congruent and incongruent stimuli. Horvitz (2000) presented findings showing different levels of recorded brain activity when participants experienced expected and unexpected stimuli across experimental trial blocks. The presentation of the unexpected stimuli (i.e., counter- stereotypical) resulted in increased dopamine levels in the striatum - the part of the basal ganglia system which reacts to environmental stimuli, and prepares for the initiation of behavioural responses. It was also found that the rate of dopaminergic neuronal firing in the midbrain also increased with the presentation of unexpected stimuli. Zink, Pagnoni,

Martin, Dhamala and Berns (2003) also found through the use of fMRI trials that there is a significant difference in the level of activity taking place in the nucleus accumbens when incongruent stimuli are presented to participants compared to when congruent stimuli are used. These studies all show that there is something biologically different occurring when individuals are exposed to congruent versus incongruent stimuli. The variation in the level of brain activity in response between congruent and incongruent stimuli shows that there is something fundamentally different about the processes taking place when we are exposed to unexpected information.

Mendes, Blascovich, Hunter, Lickel and Jost (2007) found that levels of uncertainty were increased in social interactions when individuals are exposed to unexpected circumstances. Mendes et al. (2007) found that when presented with stimuli which were typically unexpected participants experienced heightened cardiovascular responses, which is an indication of feeling threatened. All the previously discussed research is in support of the mismatch theory proposed by Johnston and Hawley (1994), the lack of response to congruent information is advantageous as to save limited cognitive resources, therefore, little time and energy is wasted on assessing something which was readily anticipated in the first place. This helps to streamline the perception of both people and their surroundings, making it as fast and efficient a process as possible.

The results of this study have successfully developed the findings of Flannigan et al. (in press) that people in counter-stereotypical occupations receive negative evaluations. Flannigan et al. (in press) found that individuals working in counter-stereotypic occupations are subject to negative evaluations, whilst those in stereotypical occupations were not subject to either a positive or negative evaluation. With the use of Fiske et al.'s (2006) universal dimensions of social cognition the negative evaluations found by Flannigan et al. (in press) were successfully broken down into more basic components.

The cold evaluations found in the present study exactly replicate the pattern of the negative associations, this supports the reliability of Flannigan et al.'s (in press) findings. The fact that the negative evaluations can successfully be broken down into the warm-cold element of Fiske et al.'s (2006) universal dimensions of social cognition is further support for the reliability of the two proposed dimensions - warmth and competence.

The obtained results were exactly as predicted, the reaction times of all responses which were used in the analysis were between 300ms and 10000ms. This supports the findings of Willis and Todorov's (2006) that these basic, fundamental yet crucial judgements of person perception are being made in extremely short time frames. This successfully shows that when under pressure or time constrains individuals can quickly evaluate others, labelling them as warm or cold without knowing anything about them and never having spoken to them. While it can clearly be seen that stereotypes can be activated within a fraction of a second, it does not necessarily mean that the application will follow.

A key issue which should be taken into account when considering this study is determining whether it falls into the category of activation or application (Macrae and Bodenhausen, 2000). There is no argument about the activation of stereotypical thinking; the results clearly show that categorical thinking has been activated. The ambiguity arises however when considering the level of application of these stereotypes which may be occurring. It could be argued that participants have to be applying the stereotype in question to have achieved the found results. On the other hand it could be argued that the SC-IAT is only capable of detecting activation and not application. As previously discussed, the activation of a stereotype does not mean it has to be applied. Participants may not have proceeded to carry out discriminatory behaviour towards target stimuli in counter-stereotypical occupations if they had been given the opportunity. Further research is needed to determine the level of application carried out after the activation of these negative and cold evaluations. While this may initially appear to be a relatively simple task it would require individuals to openly exhibit any type of discriminatory behaviour that they may feel towards incongruent targets. As people will go to great lengths to inhibit this type of behaviour being seen, such as partaking in deceptive behaviour and disguising their true opinions (Schuman et al., 1997; Fiske et al., 1991; Devine et al., 1991), actually obtaining true and reliable results would be extremely difficult. For these reasons it is sensible to assume that this study falls more heavily onto the side of category activation. While it may have some implications towards the category application side of the argument the ambiguity and uncertainty means any conclusions made on stereotype application based on these results would be extremely questionable, and therefore the reliability of such findings would be strongly up for debate.

Despite the mounting evidence showing the activation of negative evaluations in response to incongruent stimuli, not everyone in counter-stereotypical occupations are victims of discriminatory behaviour. Macrae and Bodenhausen (2000) proposed two processes which could be responsible for inhibiting stereotype application - inconsistency resolution and individuation.

Inconsistency Resolution

This is the process of realising and remembering that a particular individual does not conform to an anticipated stereotype, and therefore treating them in accordance with this stored information.

Individuation

Whilst someone may belong to a social group, individuation is the process of storing memories about somebody based on their personal identity and not group norms which they may be subject to.

These two processes come into play once categorical thinking has already been activated, leading to the successful inhibition of any discriminatory actions being carried out based on any stereotypical beliefs an individual may possess.

This study is robust and there are very few alterations which could be made to improve the quality of the method or results obtained. However, it could be further improved with a few additions or alterations, which in turn would produce both more developed and new findings to aid to the progression of the current research within this current field.

Firstly it would be of great interest to evaluate the responses towards male and female targets separately. There is a lot of evidence to suggest that reactions towards males and females in counter-stereotypical roles are not evenly balanced between the sexes, with males typically fairing worse than females. Eagly, Wood and Diekman (2000) presented findings revealing that men experience a tougher time in breaking free of the workplace discrimination in which they face. The stereotypes of occupations which are traditionally considered to be male professions are more conservative with very strict boundaries, leaving little room for diversity, also discovering that they are highly resistant to change. Traditionally female occupational stereotypes are considered to be more flexible and easily adaptable to changing circumstances. Wilbourn and Kee (2010) found that children struggle to think out of the confinements of preformed gender boundaries. Children were required to generate sentences based on forename-occupational stimulus pairings (e.g., Henry – Nurse, Kathy – Ballet dancer). Results revealed that children had the most difficulty when it came to generating sentences in response to male and counter- stereotypical occupations (e.g., Mark – Secretary). Flannigan et al. (in press) did in fact examine the difference between evaluations that the male and female targets received in their study. It was found that counter-stereotypical targets received negative evaluations, with this effect being most pronounced for males. With all the previous evidence showing that males are subject to stronger levels of discrimination it is no surprise that Flannigan et al. (in press) found that the negative evaluations were strongest for incongruent male targets. Taking the previous findings into consideration it would be reasonable to hypothesize that if we were to examine the warm-cold evaluations in relation to the gender of the targets, it would be found that males in counter-stereotypic occupations receive significantly colder evaluations than females.

It would also be of interest to include the second dimension of social cognition proposed by Fiske et al. (2006) – competence. Participants would be required to follow the exact same procedure as used with the warm-cold version of the SC-IAT; the only difference would be that the target words used would relate to either competence or incompetence. As the negative evaluation found by Flannigan et al. (in press) successfully broke down into the warm-cold dimension it is reasonable to predict that the competent- incompetent dimension will be just as successful. Therefore it could be predicted that individuals in counter-stereotypical occupations would also be seen as incompetent, an effect that would probably be most pronounced for males.

Following the success of the 2012 London Olympics, with team GB taking home 65 medal - 29 of which were gold – it is no real surprise that the sporting profession has quickly been but into the spotlight and is now under close scrutiny. Professional sports men and women are now common household names. Unfortunately the workplace for athletes is still an area wrought with discrimination. Female athletes receive less chances for participation than their male counterparts, receive reduced wages and women's teams are gifted with lesser funding and sponsorships (women's sports foundation). Unfortunately this discrimination towards athletes has a knock on effect towards participation levels, from basic and compulsory physical education classes in school right through to a professional level. Morrison and Nash (2012) looked at the participation levels in secondary school and examined the social and psychological factors affecting it.

They found that girls exhibited a greater 'need to belong' which was affecting participation rates. Girls are most likely to follow the norm of their class or particular group of friends to avoid discrimination even if it goes against their true feelings. Therefore, individuals are failing to participate in class, even when the activity in question is something which they enjoy, in doing so they are attempting to avoid scrutiny from their friends and classmates. These findings support the work of Cockburn and Clarke (2002) who found that girls who participate regularly fear being seen as 'socially inferior' in comparison to those who are more feminine and do not participate in PE and sport. With gender differences arising from such a young age it is no real surprise that female athletes are subject to a tougher time than their male counterparts. It would be of great interest to determine whether female athletes are subject to the same cold evaluations which other incongruent professionals face. Especially considering how infrequently athletes interact with society on a daily basis. Participants may feel more uncertainty towards female athletes simply due to their novelty, with people encountering them less frequently than other more 'day to day' non- stereotypical professionals (e.g., female doctor). The publicity surrounding certain sporting events may also have a large impact on how athletes are viewed within society. If it is found that sporting professionals are also subject to these implicitly negative associations it may be possible to explain the major gender differences found in sport, both at an amateur and professional level.

Overall the negative evaluations found by Flannigan et al. (in press) can successfully be broken down into the first fundamental dimension of social cognition proposed by Fiske et al. (2006) – warmth. Being able to break down these negative and undesirable evaluations which arise in response to stereotype activation means we are one step closer to being able to understand the process of stereotyping and workplace discrimination. Hopefully once an understanding of this complicated process has eventually been achieved it will allow for, as much as is possible, the elimination of workplace discrimination. This will allow for a fair working environment for all with equal opportunity available to everyone, this has been desired for many years yet it still seems to be rather a long way off until the effect of discriminatory behaviour is fully abolished.

CONCLUSION

Overall the results of this study have shown that participants rate targets in counter-stereotypical occupations as cold. This proves that whilst individuals claim to be comfortable with a male nanny or a female mechanic, they are in fact implicitly associating coldness with these professionals who are working in typically non- stereotypical occupations. These findings could be key to explaining why gender based discrimination in the workplace is still such a prevalent issue in society today. Perceiving a counter-stereotypical target in a negative light is often a snap decision made on instinct, not conscious choice. As such, it is near impossible for discrimination to be controlled for through legislation, which can only attempt to hide the symptoms of these cold evaluations.

REFERENCES

Allport, G. W. (1954). *The nature of prejudice*. Reading, MA: Addison-Wesley. Asch, S.E. (1946). Forming impressions of personality. *Journal of Abnormal Psychology, 41*, 258-290.

Bartlett, F. C. (1932). *Remembering: A study in experimental and social psychology*. Cambridge: Cambridge University Press.

Brewer, M. B. (1988). A dual process model of impression formation. In R. S. Wyer, Jr. and T. K. Srull (Eds.), *A dual-process model of impression formation: Advances in social cognition*, (Vol. 1, pp. 1–36). Hillsdale, NJ: Erlbaum.

Cacioppo, J. T., Gardner, W. L. and Berntson, G. G. (1997). Beyond bipolar conceptualizations and measures: The case of attitudes and evaluativespace. *Personality and Social Psychology Review, 1*, 3-25.

Cockburn, C. and Clarke, G. (2002). "Everybody's looking at you!": Girls negotiating the 'femininity deficit' they face in physical education. *Women's Studies International, 26*(6), 651-665.

Cuddy, A. J. C., Fiske, S. T. and Glick, P. (2004). When professionals become mothers, warmth doesn't cut the ice. *Journal of Social Issues, 60*, 701-718. Devine, P.G., Monteith, M.J., Zuwerink, J.R. and Elliot, A.J. (1991). Prejudice with and without compunction. *Journal of Personality and Social Psychology, 60*, 817–30.

Dijksterhuis, A. J., Spears, R. and Lepinasse, V. (2000). Reflecting and deflecting stereotypes: Assimilations and contrast in impression formation and automatic Behaviour. *Journal of Experimental Social Psychology, 37*, 286-299. Eagly, A. H., Wood, W. and Diekman, A. B. (2000). Social role theory of gender differences and similarities: A current appraisal. In T. Eckes and H. M. Trautner (Eds.), *The developmental social psychology of gender*, (pp. 123-174). Mahwah: Lawrence Erlbaum.

Fiske, S. T. (1989). Examining the role of intent: Toward understanding its role in stereotyping and prejudice. In J. S. Uleman and J. A. Bargh (Eds.), *Unintended thought*, (pp. 253–283). New York: Guilford.

Fiske, S. T., Bersoff, D. N., Borgida, E. and Deaux, K. (1991). Social science on trial: use of sex stereotyping research in Price Waterhouse v. Hopkins. *American Psychologist, 46*, 1049–60.

Fiske, S. T., Cuddy, A. J. C. and Glick, P. (2006). Universal dimensions of social cognition: warmth and competence. *Trends in Cognitive Science, 11*(2), 77-83.

Fiske, S. T., Lin, M. H. and Neuberg, S. L. (1999). The Continuum Model: Ten years later. In S. Chaiken and Y. Trope (Eds.), *Dual process theories in social psychology*, (pp. 231-254). New York: Guilford.

Fiske, S. T. and Neuberg, S. L. (1990). A continuum model of impression formation from category-based to individuating processes: Influences of information and motivation on attention and interpretation. In M. P. Zanna (Ed.), *Advances in experimental social psychology*, (Vol. 23, pp. 1–74). San Diego, CA: Academic Press.

Flannigan, N., Miles, L. K., Quadflieg, S. and Macrae, C.N. (in press). Seeing the unexpected: Counter-stereotypes are implicitly bad. *Social Cognition.*

Greenwald, A. G., McGhee, D. E. and Schwarz, J. L. K. (1998). Measuring individual differences in implicit cognition: The Implicit Association Test. *Journal of Personality and Social Psychology, 74*, 1464-1480.

Horvitz, J. C. (2000). Mesolimbocortical and nigrostriatal dopamine responses to salient non-reward events. *Neuroscience 96*, 651– 656.

Johnston, W. A. and Hawley, K. J. (1994). Perceptual inhibition of expected inputs: The key that opens closed minds. *Psychonomic Bulletin and Review, 1*, 56-72.

Judd, C. M., James-Hawkins, L. J., Yzerbyt, V. and Kashima, Y. (2005). Fundamental dimensions of social judgment: Understanding the relations between judgments of competence and warmth. *Journal of Personality and Social Psychology, 89*, 899–913.

Karpinski, A. and Steinman, R. B. (2006). The single category implicit association test as a measure of implicit social cognition. *Journal of Personality and Social Psychology, 91*, 16-32.

Kobrynowicz, D. and Biernat, M. (1997). Decoding subjective evaluations: how stereotypes provide shifting standards. *Journal of Experimental Social Psychology, 33*, 579–601.

Lupton, B. (2000). Maintaining masculinity: Men who do „women's work". *British Journal of Management, 11*, S33-S48.

Lyness, K. S. and Heilman, M. E. (2006). When fit is fundamental: Performance evaluations and promotions of upper-level female and male managers. *Journal of Applied Psychology, 91*, 777-785.

Macrae, C. N. and Bodenhausen, G. V. (2000). Social cognition: Thinking categorically about others. *Annual Review of Psychology, 51*, 93–120.

Macrae, C. N., Bodenhausen, G. V., Milne, A. B. and Jetten, J. (1994a). Out of mind but back in sight: Stereotypes on the rebound. *Journal of Personality and Social Psychology, 67*, 808–817.

Macrae, C. N., Bodenhausen, G. V., Schloerscheidt, A. M. and Milne, A. B. (1999). Tales of the unexpected: Executive function and person perception. *Journal of Personality and Social Psychology, 76*, 200–13.

Macwilliams, B. R., Schmidt, B. and Bleich, M. R. (2013). Men in nursing. *American Journal ofNursing, 113*, 38-44.

Mendes, W. B., Blascovich, J., Hunter, S. B., Lickel, B. and Jost, J. T. (2007). Threatened by the unexpected: Physiological responses during social interactions with expectancy-violating partners. *Journal of Personality and Social Psychology, 92*, 698-716.

Morrison, S. and Nash, R. (2012). The psychosocial influences on participation rates within Secondary School physical education. *Journal of Physical Education and Sport, 12(2)*, 147-156.

Pay Inequality in Athletes (n.d.). In *Women's Sports Foundation.* Retrieved April 13, 2013, from http://www.womenssportsfoundation.org/home/research/articles-and-reports/equity-issues/pay-inequity.

Schubert, T. W. and Hafner, M. (2003). Contrast from social stereotypes in automatic behaviour. *Journal of Experimental Social Psychology, 39*, 577-584.

Schuman, H., Steeh, C., Bobo, L. and Krysan, M. (1997). *Racial attitudes in America: Trends and interpretations*. Rev. ed. Cambridge, MA: Harvard University Press.

Sheridan, A. (2002), "What you know and who you know: 'Successful' women's experiences of accessing board positions." *Career Development International*, *7*(4), 203-210.

Srull, T. K. and Wyer, R. S. (1989). Person memory and judgement. *Psychological Review, 96*, 58-83.

Wegner, D. M. and Bargh, J. A. (1998). Control and automaticity in social life. In D. T. Gilbert, S. T. Fiske and G. Lindzey (Eds.), *Handbook of social psychology* (4th ed., Vol. 1, pp. 446–496). Boston, MA: McGraw-Hill.

Wegner, D. M. and Erber, R. (1992). The hyperaccessibility of suppressed thoughts. *Journal of Personality and Social Psychology, 63*, 903-912.

Wilbourn, M. P. and Kee, D. W. (2010). Henry the nurse is a doctor too: Implicitly examining children's gender stereotypes for male and female occupational roles. *Sex Roles*, *62*, 670-683.

Willis, J. and Todorov, A. (2006). First impressions: Making up your mind after a 100-ms exposure to a face. *Psychological Science*, *17*, 592–598.

Wojciszke, B., Bazinska, R. and Jaworski, M. (1998). On the dominance of moral categories in impression formation. *Society for Personality and Social Psychology*, *67*, 1245-1257.

Wyer, N. A., Sherman, J. W. and Stroessner, S. J. (1998). The spontaneous suppression of racial stereotypes. *Social Cognition*, *16*, 340-352.

Yzerbyt, V. Y., Provost, V. and Corneille, O. (2005). Not competent but warm . . . Really? Compensatory stereotypes in the French-speaking world. *Group Processes and Intergroup Relations*, *8*, 291-308.

Zink, C. F., Pagnoni, G., Martin, M. E., Dhamala, M. and Berns, G. S. (2003). Human striatal response to salient nonrewarding stimuli. *The Journal of Neuroscience*, *23*(22), 8092-8097.

In: Stereotypes and Stereotyping
Editor: Claude Fields
ISBN: 978-1-63484-510-6

Chapter 8

AGREEMENT AND ACCURACY OF NATIONAL STEREOTYPES IN FIVE CENTRAL EUROPEAN COUNTRIES

Martina Hřebíčková and Sylvie Graf
Institute of Psychology, Academy of Sciences of the Czech Republic, Czech Republic

ABSTRACT

In the chapter, we provide an overview of the current research on the accuracy of national stereotypes and introduce results of a research project on national stereotypes in five Central European countries. National stereotypes were operationalized as personality traits of typical country representatives. In Austria, the Czech Republic, Germany, Poland, and Slovakia, we measured stereotypes from ingroup as well as outgroup perspectives. Each typical country representative was rated by people from the same country as well as from the other countries in the central European region. We examined the consistency of national ingroup- and outgroup stereotypes across Czech participants differing in age, education and gender. We determined whether national stereotypes in central Europe are stable in time and whether national stereotypes converge across all countries under study. The main goal of our research was to compare both ingroup- and outgroup stereotypes with personality traits of real people living in the given countries to estimate if national stereotypes are accurate. Our results showed an agreement between Czech university students and Czech adults with different education level in their perception of Czech national stereotype and national stereotypes of other four countries, indicating stability of national ingroup stereotypes in time. The comparison of national ingroup stereotypes from the five central European countries resulted in a significant agreement between Czechs and Poles, Austrians and Germans, Czechs and Austrians, as well as Austrians and Poles. We found a good agreement among raters from different countries in their view on typical representatives of other countries – meaning that national stereotypes of a certain country rated from an outgroup perspective converge. National ingroup stereotype agreed with national outgroup stereotypes only in case of a typical German. The main finding of our research is that neither national ingroup stereotypes nor outgroup stereotypes correspond to personality traits of real people living in the given countries, indicating that national stereotypes are not accurate.

How to Examine Stereotype Accuracy?

Stereotypes can be defined as characteristics associated with certain social categories. Stereotypes are activated in the process of social categorization, during which people are assigned to – in the context meaningful – social categories. After inclusion into a certain social category, ascription of characteristics typical for the given category automatically ensues (Devine, 1989). Stereotypical characteristics may include typical *physical attributes* of members of a given category (e.g., Norwegians have blond hair), typical *reactions or behaviors* (e.g., Italians gesture exceedingly) or *personal characteristics* (e.g., Spaniards are lively) (Terracciano et al., 2005).

Research within personality psychology in general and studies presented in this chapter in particular conceive stereotypical characteristics as personality traits. Recently, the accuracy of stereotypes has been intensively investigated, especially of national stereotypes (Hřebíčková and Kouřilová, 2012, Hřebíčková and Graf, 2014; McCrae et al., 2007; Realo et al., 2009; Terracciano et al., 2005), regional stereotypes (Rogers and Wood, 2010) and gender stereotypes (Swim, 1994). Accuracy studies compare stereotypical characteristics to criteria representing reality (Funder, 1999). The research on stereotype accuracy typically examines to what extent stereotypical characteristics associated with certain social categories (i.e., personality traits typical of Czechs, an adult male) correspond to self- or observer-ratings of real people (i.e., personality traits of inhabitants of the Czech Republic, men aged from 21 to 59 years). In the past, it was difficult to find a frame of reference that would serve rating stereotypical characteristics and characteristics of real people within one study. Over the last 20 years, the Five-Factor Model based on lexical analysis of words used to describe personality became such a relational framework (Digman 1990; Goldberg, 1990). Research carried out in the framework of cross-cultural comparison and behavioral genetic studies provided evidence that the Five-Factor Model of personality contains versatile personality characteristics that can be measured reliably in different cultural contexts (McCrae, 2002, 2004; McCrae et al., 2000, 2005) and it can also be applied in the research on accuracy of stereotypes (Terracciano et al., 2005).

The chapter deals with national stereotypes of one's own and other countries in central Europe. We estimated accuracy of national stereotypes rated from ingroup and outgroup perspectives through comparison with ratings of real people living in the given countries. In our studies, we employed the Five-Factor Model of personality for both stereotypical and real people ratings.

Characteristics of the Five-Factor Model, NEO Inventory and National Character Survey

The Five-Factor Model (FFM) includes five general dimensions of personality commonly referred to as Neuroticism (*tense*, *restless*, *unstable* vs. *calm*, *relaxed*, *balanced*), Extraversion (*sociable*, *active*, *talkative* vs. *closed*, *taciturn*, *reclusive*), Openness to Experience (*innovative*, *inquisitive*, *with a rich imagination* vs. *conventional*, *realistic*, *insensitive*), Agreeableness (*good-natured*, *cooperative*, *trusting* vs. *bossy*, *aggressive*, *confrontational*) and Conscientiousness *(responsible*, *tidy*, *hardworking* vs. *aimless*, *sloppy*, *lacking perseverance*) (Digman 1990; Goldberg, 1990). Brief description of the Five-Factor Model dimensions is given in Table 1. We measured personality traits of real people with NEO Personality Inventory (NEO-PI-R; Costa and McCrae, 1992; Hřebíčková, 2004).[1]

Table 1. NEO Personality Inventory dimensions and facets (NEO-PI-R) and the National Character Survey scales (NCS)

Names of NEO-PI-R dimensions and facets and NCS scales	Brief characteristics of NEO-PI-R dimensions and facets	NCS scales
Neuroticism To what extent we are able to cope with mental stress		
N1: Anxiety	Anxiety of how everything turns out.	*relaxed* vs. *anxious*
N2: Angry, Hostility	Feeling of anger and bitterness.	*balanced* vs. *irascible*
N3: Depression	Experiencing grief and despair.	*happy* vs. *depressive*
N4: Self–Consciousness	Feeling of embarrassment, shame or discomfort.	*confident* vs. *self-conscious*
N5: Impulsiveness	Succumbing to temptation (food, alcohol, cigarettes, drugs, shopping).	*in control* vs. *impulsive*
N6: Vulnerability	Tendency to be absorbed by urgent events or stressful situations, tendency to act in panic.	*mentally balanced* vs. *vulnerable*
Extraversion To what extent are we social, active and energetic		
E1: Warmth	Friendliness, affection and fondness of others.	*cold* vs. *warm*
E2: Gregariousness	Sociability, search for social contacts.	*reclusive* vs. *sociable*
E3: Assertiveness	Dominance and vigorous self-assertion.	*conforming* vs. *assertive*
E4: Activity	Vigor, tendency to live life at a fast pace.	*slow* vs. *active*
E5: Excitement Seeking	Prioritization of exciting experiences and distinctive sensory stimuli.	*avoiding exciting experiences and stimuli* vs. *adventurous*
E6: Positive Emotions	Optimism and a sense of happiness.	*serious* vs. *hilarious*
Openness to experience To what extent are we open to new experience		
O1: Fantasy	Creating an interesting inner world, imagination and fantasy.	*practical* vs. *with rich fantasy*
O2: Aesthetics	Sense of art and beauty, sensitivity.	*not caring about art* vs. *sensitive to the perception of art and beauty*
O3: Feelings	Ability to evaluate and experience, alone and with others, a large number of positive and negative emotions.	*insensitive* vs. *sensitive*

[1] NEO Personality Inventory (NEO-PI-R, Costa, McCrae, 1992) was translated into more than 30 languages (McCrae, 2002) and was used in international projects Personality Profiles of Cultures (PPOC, McCrae et al., 2005a,b; Terracciano et al., 2005) and Adolescent Personality Profiles Across Cultures (APPAC, De Fruyt et al. 2009; Löckenhoff et al., 2009; McCrae et al., 2010). The Czech version of NEO-PI-R (Hřebíčková, 2004) was applied in the research of agreement between self-reports and observer ratings (McCrae et al., 2004a), age trends of the five dimensions of personality (McCrae et al., 2004b), relationship between personality and the subjective well-being (Hřebíčková, Blatný & Jelínek, 2010) or in cluster analysis to derive personality types (Hřebíčková & Urbánek, 2006).

Table 1. (Continued)

Names of NEO-PI-R dimensions and facets and NCS scales	Brief characteristics of NEO-PI-R dimensions and facets	NCS scales
O4: Actions	Prioritization of the new and diverse before the routine and familiar.	*favoring habit* vs. *favoring change*
O5: Ideas	Intellectual curiosity, openness to new and unconventional ideas.	*with limited interests* vs. *open to accept new ideas*
O6: Values	Willingness to verify social, political and religious values, non-dogmatic thinking.	*clings to tradition* vs. *tolerant and embracing new ideas*
Agreeableness	To what extent are we welcoming of other people	
A1: Trust	Tendency to trust others.	*suspicious* vs. *credulous*
A2: Straightforwardness	Honorable and direct behavior.	*wily* vs. *honest*
A3: Altruism	Generosity, thoughtfulness and desire to help others.	*selfish* vs. *generous*
A4: Compliance	Preference for cooperation instead of competitiveness.	*competitive* vs. *cooperating*
A5: Modesty	Humility in front of others.	*pretentious* vs. *modest*
A6: Tender–Mindedness	Caring, compassion and sympathy for others.	*unsympathetic* vs. *compassionate*
Conscientiousness	To what extent we fulfill our obligations	
C1: Competence	Readiness and ability to effectively address challenges.	*incompetent* vs. *competent*
C2: Order	Art of being able to organize everything properly, proceed in a methodical way.	*unsystematic* vs. *systematic*
C3: Dutifulness	Compliance, reliability	*unreliable* vs. *conscientious*
C4: Achievement Striving	Tendency to put up challenging task and fulfill them.	*without goals and ambitions* vs. *ambitious*
C5: Self–Discipline	Ability to motivate oneself to complete the task and resist interference.	*hesitant* vs. *persistent*
C6: Deliberation	Ability to think through things in advance.	*imprudent* vs. *prudent*

For rating of national stereotypes the National Character Survey (NCS; Terracciano et al., 2005) was created. The NCS contains 30 five-point bipolar scales defined by two to three adjectives, or short phrases on each pole. The 30 NCS scales correspond to the 30 facets of the NEO-PI-R. Overview of the NEO-PI-R and NCS facets or scales, their brief characterization and examples of adjectives from the NCS are presented in Table 1. Comparison of characteristics of real people and stereotypical characteristics using the same, universal personality traits answered the question about the extent to which stereotypes are accurate.

Methodological Aspects of Accuracy Research

We were not interested in correlations between the specific characteristics of the Five-Factor Model used for the rating of stereotypes and real people but rather in the *correlation between the full profiles* of stereotypical and real personality characteristics (i.e., profile correlation approach). When comparing profiles of characteristics, the magnitude of correlation can be distorted. Any two profiles can look similar not only because they contain an identical rate of given characteristics but also because they correspond to an average profile. Participants tend to respond in a certain way, for example they may assign a lower degree of Neuroticism and a higher degree of Extraversion, Openness to Experience, Agreeableness and Conscientiousness regardless of who is being judged. As a result of such response style, the profiles correlate with each other, a bias known as the "generalized other" (Cronbach, 1955). In our research, we removed the bias by means of standardization – transformation of raw scores to T-scores ($M = 50$, $s = 10$) using mean and standard deviations from an international data set for NCS and American normative data for NEO-PI-R (for more details on the transformation of data into T-scores, see Hřebíčková and Graf, 2014).

To determine the correspondence between profiles, we calculated the intra-class correlation (ICC) across 30 NCS scales, and/or NEO-PI-R facets using the "double-entry" method (Griffin and Gonzales, 1995)[2]. McCrae (2008) believes that intraclass correlations are more appropriate for the comparison of profiles than Pearson correlation due to their sensitivity to differences in the shapes of profiles.

Accuracy of National Stereotypes in International Projects

The main outcome of the PPOC project led by Robert McCrae was a paper published in Science (Terracciano et al., 2005). In 49 countries (cultures), data were obtained from self-reports and observer-ratings using NEO-PI-R. The second group of respondents (university students) rated a typical representative of their country using NCS. The aim of the study was to determine whether self-reports and observer ratings on the traits from the Five-Factor model corresponds to ratings of national stereotypes on the same personality traits. The accuracy of national stereotypes in 49 countries was estimated using intraclass correlations between profiles of national stereotypes and profiles of self-reports and observer-ratings of real people. Profiles of national stereotypes significantly correlated with profiles based on self-reports of real people only in two out of the 49 countries (Japan and Poland). When comparing profiles of national stereotypes with observer-ratings of real people, convergence was found only in respondents from Australia, Lebanon and Poland. Therefore, the study concluded that national stereotypes do not correspond to personality traits of people living in a given country (Terracciano et al., 2005).

[2] For example, if we wish to compare the profile of the characteristics of the ingroup stereotype of a typical Czech (profile A) with the outgroup stereotype of a typical Czech according to Slovak respondents (profile B), we arrange the variables into two columns. In the first column, we place T-scores of 30 characteristics of A profile and beneath them T-scores of 30 characteristics of B profile. In the second column we organize the variables the other way round (T-scores of 30 B profile characteristics and then T-scores of 30 A-profile characteristics). "Double entry" intraclass correlation is the Pearson correlation between the two columns of variables.

Research on national stereotypes within the PPOC project has been criticized for the fact that respondents were solely college students (McGrath and Goldberg, 2006). Moreover, in some countries, the sample was relatively small (e.g., in the Czech Republic, N = 71). In addition, critics predicted that outgroup stereotypes (ratings of a typical member of a particular country by people from other countries) may correspond with ratings of real people better than national ingroup stereotypes (McGrath and Goldberg, 2006).

Another objection to the PPOC project pointed out different methods used for self-reports and observer-ratings (NEO-PI-R) and ratings of national stereotypes (NCS). The shortcoming was addressed by Realo et al. (2009) who examined the accuracy of national stereotypes in six countries in the Baltic Sea region (Finland, Estonia, Latvia, Lithuania, Poland and Belarus) and Russia. The authors employed NCS for both stereotypical characteristics and characteristics of real people in those countries. The results did not provide unequivocal support for previous findings of the PPOC project. In all countries, national ingroup stereotypes (ratings of own nation) correlated positively with ratings of real people from the given countries. In half of the countries, Estonia, Finland, Poland, and Russia, the correlation was a statistically significant. Using the same method (NCS) for ratings of real people and stereotypical characteristics helped avoiding bias in the magnitude of correlation between profiles derived from two different methods. However, due to the fact that the same group of respondents rated real people and national stereotypes, their findings might suffer from other biases. When assessing own personality or groups to which respondents belong (the ingroup) the ratings may suffer from a tendency to present own personality or ingroup in a better light (self-enhancement bias; Kwan et al., 2008; ingroup favoritism; Hewstone, Rubin, Willis, 2002).

Accuracy of National Stereotypes in Five Central European Countries

In our research project, we addressed all above outlined points criticizing previous studies on accuracy of national stereotypes. We focused on stereotypes of typical country representatives in central Europe, (Austria, the Czech Republic, Germany, Poland and Slovakia). National stereotypes in all countries were measured from ingroup as well as outgroup perspectives. Participants rated typical representatives of the five central European countries on the NCS

Profiles of traits of real people (rated on NEO-PI-R) living in the given countries represented a criterion for accuracy of national stereotypes. The profiles of traits of real people were adopted from normative data published in NEO-PI-R manuals in the respective countries, or from published data[3]. NEO-PI-R differs from NCS in wording of items as well as in the number of items. In order to eliminate the effect of methods on the convergence between national stereotypes and real people personality traits, we compared the stereotypical profiles from the NCS with profiles of real people derived both from the NEO-PI-R and from

[3] We employed profiles of real people rated on NEO-PI-R from manuals containing Czech, Polish and German normative data (Hřebíčková, 2004; Ostendorf, Angleitner, 2004; Siuta, 2007). Self-reports of Austrians on NEO-PI-R were taken from McCrae (2002, pp. 120-125), observer ratings by Slovak respondents were obtained within the PPOC. For more information about participants see Hřebíčková and Graf (2014).

the NCS. This means that we used NCS (in the Czech Republic) for both stereotype ratings and self-reports of real people. To eliminate the self-enhancement bias, self-reports and ratings of national stereotypes were provided by different respondents. We will first introduce results on the convergence between ratings of national stereotypes by different groups of respondents and in time. Second, we will examine the correspondence between national ingroup and outgroup stereotypes in central Europe. Lastly, we will focus on the accuracy of national stereotypes.

Do Czech Respondents Agree in Ratings of National Stereotypes?

A large set of respondents from the Czech Republic allowed us to examine the consistency of ratings of national stereotypes in different groups. We investigated whether people coming from different parts of the Czech Republic, people completing the questionnaire in paper or electronic form, men and women, adults and college students differed in rating of a typical representative of their own nation and neighboring nations. The results showed that men and women did not differ in rating the personality traits of typical representatives of the five central European countries. The method of administration (pencil and paper for adults and online data collection in case of university students) also did not lead to differences in ratings of national stereotypes. When comparing similarities between the ingroup and outgroup-stereotypes rated by different age groups and people from different parts of the Czech Republic, most respondents agreed when rating stereotypes of typical Germans. College students from different parts of the Czech Republic and adults perceived them virtually identically. High correlation was also recorded among college students from different parts of the Czech Republic when rating a typical Czech. However, college students agreed less with adults in ratings of a typical Czech. Generally, in ingroup stereotype ratings (i.e., ratings of a typical Czech) and ratings of four outgroup stereotypes (i.e., typical representatives of neighboring nations) students from different parts of the Czech Republic agreed more than student versus adult participants. Thus, the level of agreement in ratings of national stereotypes is influenced rather by participants' age than their place of residence. More information about consistency of national stereotypes in the Czech sample can be found in the study by Hřebíčková and Kouřilová (2012).

Are Ratings of National Stereotypes Stable in Time?

Previous studies within the Five-Factor Model showed that major socio-political events do not have a significant impact on rating of national stereotypes. A typical American was rated almost identically by respondents in various countries including Lebanon before and after the US invasion to Iraq (Terracciano and McCrae, 2007). Realo et al. (2009) observed stability of national ingroup stereotypes in respondents from Estonia and Poland. In our research, we were able to confirm the stability over time of four national ingroup stereotypes after five years because all the countries in our research (excluding Austria) participated in the PPOC project in 2003. The intraclass correlation between the profiles of national ingroup stereotypes after five years was .87 in Poland, .82 in the Czech Republic, .81 in Germany and .78 in Slovakia (all correlations $p <. 001$). The relatively high correlations indicate that perception of national ingroup stereotypes in four Central European countries remains stable and fundamentally unchanged over the period of five years. Other studies, however, suggest that stereotypes change after a prolonged period of time (Ferjenčík, 2006; Madon et al., 2001). It is therefore possible that the period of five years used in our research and research by Realo et al. (2009) is not long enough for a shift in the perception of national stereotypes to occur. Another possible explanation for the stability found in our study is the fact that we included only personality characteristics that can be more stable over time than other characteristics (e.g., behavioral). Future research should compare ratings of stereotypes over longer time periods to disentangle the contradictory findings.

Do National Ingroup Stereotypes in Central Europe Converge?

In our research, we compared the profiles of ingroup stereotypes in five central European countries to determine the extent to which the convergence depends on the affiliation to two different language groups (Slavic vs. Germanic). Figures 1 and 2 show the profiles of national ingroup stereotypes separately for countries speaking Slavic (1) and Germanic languages (2). The horizontal axis shows the five dimensions of the Five-Factor Model and 30 NCS facets. The vertical axis shows the values of T-scores that can be interpreted as follows: T-scores below 44 indicate a low level on a given dimension (N, E, O, A, C) or facet (N1 - S6); T-scores in the range 45 to 55 are interpreted as ambivalence, and T-scores greater than 55 represent a high degree of those characteristics. The curves represent the course of stereotypical profiles. 10 intraclass correlations ranged from -.03 to .62; *Mdn* = .13. Statistically significant agreement was observed between Czech and Polish ingroup stereotypes (ICC = .62; $p < .001$), German and Austrian ingroup stereotypes (ICC = .55; $p < .01$), Austrian and Czech ingroup stereotypes (ICC = .50; $p < .01$), and Polish and Austrian ingroup stereotypes (ICC = .45; $p < .05$). German participants converged in their ratings of their typical country representative with Austrian participants rating their country representative, and Polish participants with Czech participants; corroborating the hypothesis about stronger agreement within language and cultural groups. However, the Austrian ingroup stereotype also corresponded to Czech and Polish ingroup stereotypes indicating that the agreement does not depend exclusively on the same cultural and language background. The Slovak ingroup stereotype did not converge with either of the other four ingroup stereotypes (correlations close to zero, *Mdn* = .04), meaning that Slovak participants rated characteristics of their typical country representative in contrast to how participants from the other four countries rated their typical representatives.

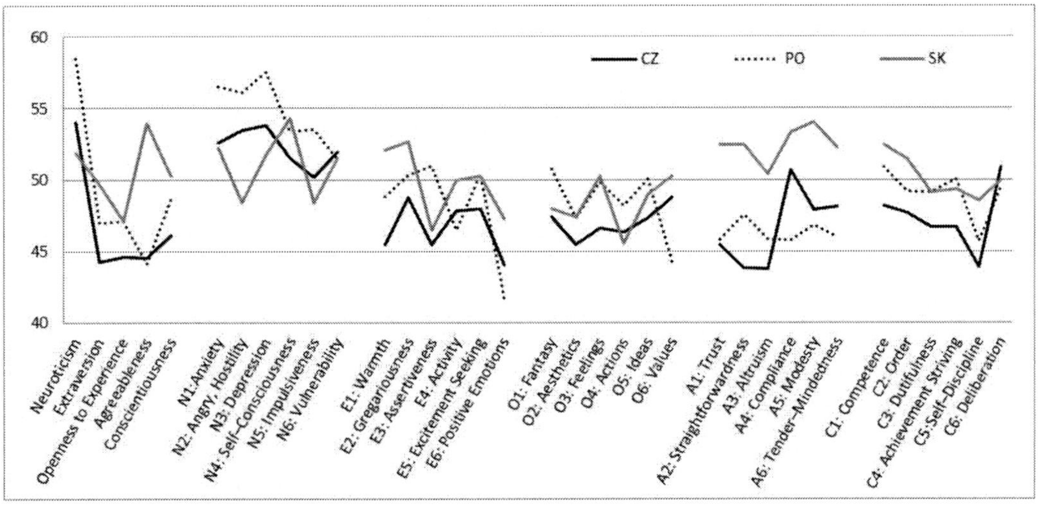

Figure 1. Profiles of ingroup stereotypes in three Slavic countries.

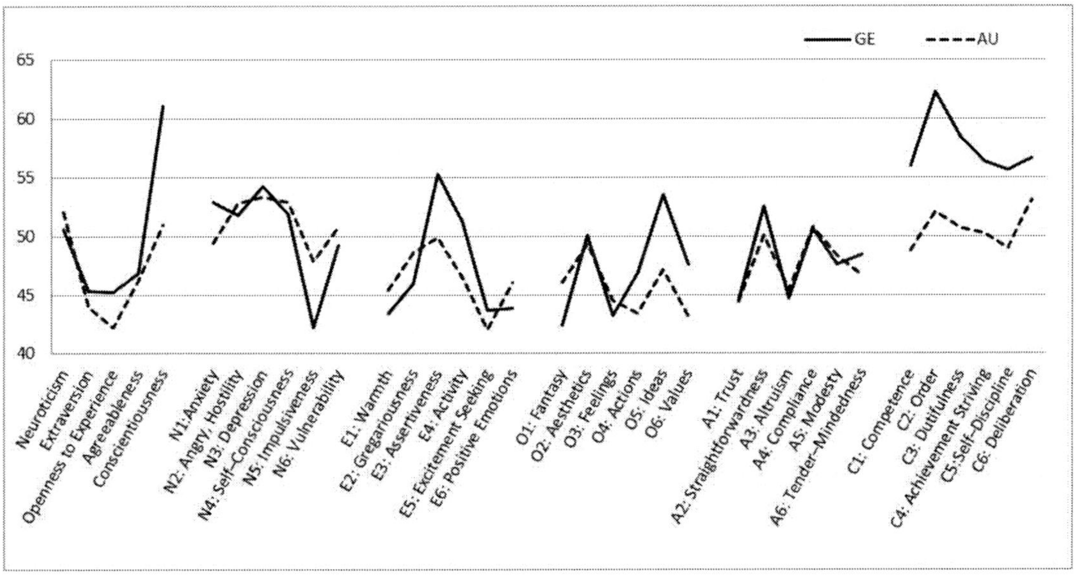

Figure 2. Profiles of ingroup stereotypes of the typical Austrian and German.

Do National Outgroup Stereotypes in Central Europe Converge?

Our research design where participants from all countries rated stereotypes of all included countries allowed to estimate the degree of agreement in national stereotypes rated from outgroup perspective. The level of agreement between outgroup stereotypes can help us revealing mechanisms that influence sharing of national stereotypes. From a total of 46 intraclass correlations, 39 were statistically significant, showing good agreement between different profiles of national outgroup stereotypes. The highest level of agreement was found in ratings of a typical German (*Mdn* ICC = .93), whereas lower level of agreement was found in outgroup stereotypes of the other four countries (*Mdn* ICC = .77 for a typical Austrian, *Mdn* ICC = .52 for a typical Czech; *Mdn* ICC = .65 for a typical Pole, *Mdn* ICC = .57 for a typical Slovak). Like Czech respondents from different parts of the Czech Republic, participants from the four neighboring countries also perceived a typical German in a similar way. We found a high agreement in ratings of Austrian outgroup stereotypes. Respondents from the three Slavic countries (the Czech Republic, Poland and Slovakia) agreed in their ratings of a typical Austrian, while German participants rated a typical Austrian in a different way. In outgroup stereotypes of the three Slavic countries, the highest agreement was found in ratings of a typical Pole. Austrian and German participants saw Poles similarly, while participants from the other two Slavic countries agreed less in the perception of a typical Pole. In Slovak outgroup stereotypes, only four out of 10 intraclass correlations were statistically significant. When rating a typical Slovak, Austrian and German participants again agreed. Similar pattern of results occurred in Czech outgroup stereotypes. The highest agreement was found between Austrian and German participants. On the other hand, Slovak participants disagreed with Austrian and German participants in their perception of a typical Czech especially in characteristics corresponding to dominance when they rated Czechs as assertive, energetic, ambitious and rebellious. The past coexistence in a common state where Slovaks perceived Czechs as the dominant older brother (Kosatík, 2010) is thus reflected also in ratings by Slovak university students despite the fact that they have spent more than half of their life in the independent Slovakia.

People belonging to the same language group agreed in their ratings of national outgroup stereotypes more than people from different language groups. Austrian and German participants agreed in their perception of their Slavic neighbors more than members of the three Slavic countries. Likewise, when rating a typical Austrian, respondents from Slavic countries agreed more with each other as compared to German respondents. Sharing of outgroup stereotypes is therefore influenced by linguistic and cultural proximity of people providing their ratings.

Do National Ingroup and Outgroup Stereotypes in Central Europe Converge?

In their research on perception of a typical American in 49 countries, Terracciano and McCrae (2007) demonstrated a high level of agreement between American ingroup stereotype and outgroup stereotypes (ICC = .71). Similarly, Realo et al. (2009) found an agreement between ingroup- and outgroup stereotypes of a typical Russian (ICC = .40). In our research, the comparison of national ingroup- and outgroup stereotypes from central Europe showed that respondents agree only in their ratings of a typical German (*Mdn* ICC = .76). In none of the other countries the ratings of national stereotype of own nation agreed with corresponding ratings by participants from abroad.

Based on the past studies, we can assume that ingroup stereotypes and outgroup stereotypes correspond only in case of typical representatives of global powers with economic and political influence, such as the US, Germany and Russia. On the other hand, in case of smaller and less important countries, ingroup stereotypes tend to differ from outgroup stereotypes. People are able to learn more information about global superpowers and their inhabitants who play a significant role in history, politics and economy from the media and fiction than about smaller and less important countries. Stereotypes of typical representatives of global powers are thus shared across countries, yielding convergence between profiles of ingroup and outgroup stereotypes.

Research on convergence of national stereotypes can contribute to detection of mechanisms that are involved in stereotype formation. One possible mechanism is mirroring (Terracciano and McCrae, 2007; Realo et al., 2009). Mirroring describes a situation where respondents from one country rate their national ingroup stereotype in contrast to national stereotype of a neighboring country. Mirroring occurs when a typical representative of a neighboring country is attributed a high degree of a certain characteristic, a typical representatives of own country a low degree of the same characteristic and vice versa. For example, Canadians described themselves as friendly, but not sufficiently assertive, in contrast to how Americans perceive themselves and are perceived by others (unkind and assertive; Terracciano et al., 2005). Thus, Canadians define their ingroup stereotype in some characteristics against what they think about Americans. Realo et al. (2009) found mirroring in the Baltic Sea Region. The mirroring of regional stereotypes was observed in northern and southern Italy by McCrae et al. (2007). In our research, mirroring occurred in Slovak ingroup stereotype and German outgroup stereotype. Slovak participants rated their typical representative as warm, optimistic, with a rich imagination, open to experiencing emotions and friendly, which is in direct contrast to their ratings of a typical German who was perceived as assertive, with a low degree of warmth and agreeableness, but with a high degree of conscientiousness. To some extent, national stereotypes play a compensating function (Kervyn, Yzerbyt and Judd, 2010). When rating two social groups, people tend to perceive one of the groups as high and the other group as low on one dimension (e.g., warmth). Employing a compensatory mechanism, the first group is then viewed as low and the other group as high on the other dimension (i.e., competence). While dominant groups are perceived as high on competence/Conscientiouss but low on warmth/Agreeableness, subordinate groups are perceived as low on competence but high on warmth.

National ingroup stereotype of Slovaks (from one of the youngest and also the smallest European nations) in contrast to how Slovaks see typical German corresponds to the stereotype content model (SCM; Fiske, Cuddy, Glick, Xu, 2002). The SCM postulates that strong and dominant groups are attributed a high degree of competence, but a small degree of warmth, while subordinate social groups and their members are perceived as warm but incompetent.

Independent Slovakia was established in 1993 and the ongoing construction of national identity possibly highlights differences between own and foreign groups (Plichtová, Lášticová, Petrjanošová, 2009). Another reason for the attempts of Slovak participants to differentiate themselves from their neighbors may be the marginal position of Slovakia in central Europe. Slovakia is geographically located in its eastern part, and is the smallest of the countries surveyed. The same characteristics also apply to the position of Estonia in the Baltic Sea Region, where mirroring was found (Realo et al., 2009).

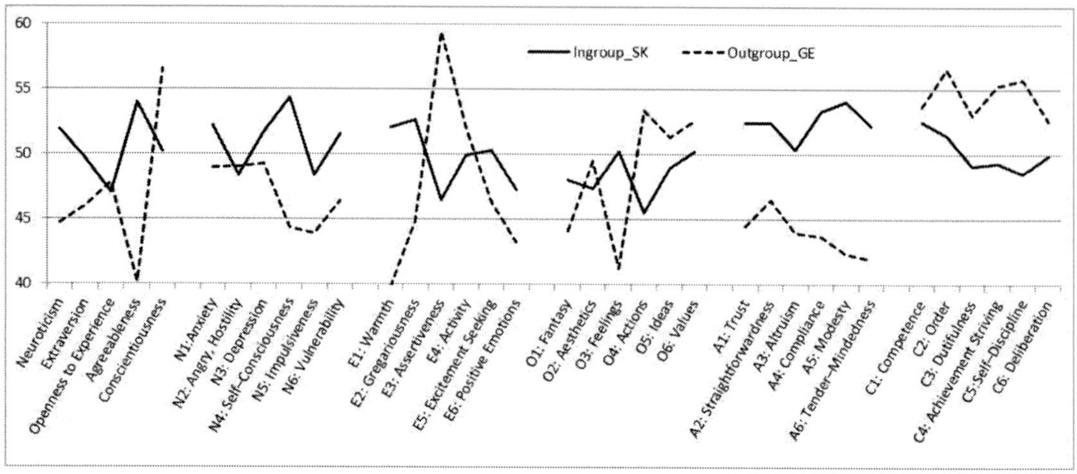

Figure 3. Profiles of ingroup stereotypes of a typical Slovak and outgroup stereotype of a typical German by Slovak participants.

We showed that mirroring, as compared to compensation, is a broader mechanism influencing the content of ingroup stereotypes on other than just two dimension of social perception. Our results confirmed that there are other dimensions on which participants systematically differentiate their ingroup from relevant outgroups. The perception of national stereotypes is typically influenced by economic prosperity. Stereotypes of wealthy countries and regions were perceived as disagreeable, cold, less sociable, pessimistic and not showing emotions, but at the same time as conscientious, assertive, active and rational. Participants from less affluent countries and regions then rated their ingroup stereotype as directly opposite on these relevant characteristics, manifesting itself in mirroring.

Do National Stereotypes Correspond to Ratings of Real People?

The main objective of our research project was to determine the accuracy of national stereotypes – whether the profiles of ingroup and outgroup stereotypes correspond with ratings of real people. We computed two kinds of agreement: ICCs between national ingroup stereotypes and ratings of real people represented by self-reports and observer ratings (when available) established *ingroup accuracy*. To determine the *outgroup accuracy*, we computed ICCs between ratings of real people and outgroup stereotypes from the respective countries. In Poland, Austria and Slovakia only one type of rating of real people was available – either self-reports or observer ratings. In Germany and the Czech Republic both types of ratings were available. The Czech sample comprised group of university students and adults who rated their own personality using NCS scales. Thus, in the Czech Republic, we obtained six intraclass correlations indicating the degree of agreement between Czech ingroup stereotype and the profiles of real people (self-reports and observer ratings on NEO-P-R and self-reports on NCS). The German sample yielded two correlations, and samples from other three countries one correlation, a total of 11 intraclass correlations that ranged from -.41 to .61, *Mdn* = .13.

We found a medium level of agreement between Polish ingroup stereotype and self-reports of Poles (ICC = .61, $p < .001$) and between ingroup stereotype from Czech adults and ratings of Czechs on NCS (ICC = .51, $p < .01$). The medium level of agreement between the ingroup stereotype of a typical Pole and self-reports of real Poles was also found in two previous studies (Realo et al., 2009; Terracciano et al., 2005). Poles, in contrast to other nations, are able to rate characteristics of their typical representative in accordance with how real Poles rate themselves – as neurotic, a little friendly and moderate in the remaining three characteristics of the Five-Factor Model. Intraclass correlations in the Czech sample ranged from .06 to .51 ($p < .01$), *Mdn* = .22. Czech stereotype rated by Czech adults corresponded to characteristics of real Czechs more than the Czech stereotype rated by college students. In Slovakia, Austria and Germany no agreement between ingroup stereotypes and characteristics of real people was found, all intraclass correlations were negative.

While ingroup stereotypes corresponded with characteristics of real people in Poland and the Czech Republic, outgroup stereotypes did not agree with ratings of real people in any of the five central European countries. 37 intraclass correlations expressing a degree of agreement between outgroup stereotypes and characteristics of real people ranged from -.48 to .25, *Mdn* = -.18. We found positive but statistically non-significant correlation only in Poland. With respect to the German-speaking countries, we found negative correlations between outgroup stereotypes and profiles of real people. In the Czech Republic and Slovakia the correlation was close to zero. Similar findings about medium degree of agreement between characteristics of real people with ingroup stereotypes and low or no agreement with outgroup stereotypes was reported by Realo et al. (2009). Although participants from six countries around the Baltic Sea agreed in their perception of a typical Russian, none of the outgroup stereotypes correlated with self-reports of real Russians.

CONCLUSION

The key findings of our research can be summarized as follows: 1) rating of national ingroup stereotypes has not significantly changed in five years, indicating that ingroup stereotypes are stable over time; 2) college students from different parts of the Czech Republic did not differ in their perception of a typical representative of their own nation and neighboring nations, meaning national stereotypes are consistent. 3) Outgroup stereotypes corresponded with each other, especially in case of a typical German. Respondents from four central European countries perceived a typical German almost identically. In the case of other countries, outgroup stereotypes correspond more if people who provided the ratings belonged to the same language group. 4) National outgroup stereotypes did not correspond with ingroup stereotypes with the exception of a typical German, who was perceived similarly by German participants and participants from other countries. 5) Ratings of real people from five countries corresponded with national ingroup stereotypes only in Poland and the Czech Republic; 6) outgroup stereotypes did not correspond with ratings of real people in any of the five countries. We can conclude that members of neighboring nations are unable to rate national stereotypes of their neighbors more accurately than people ratings characteristics of their own nation.

ACKNOWLEDGMENTS

This research was supported by a grant 13-25656S from the Czech Science Foundation and by RVO: 68081740 from the Institute of Psychology, Academy of Sciences of the Czech Republic.

REFERENCES

Costa, P. T. & McCrae, R. R. (1992). Revised NEO Personality Inventory (NEO-PI-R) and NEO Five-Factor Inventory (NEO-FFI) professional manual. *Odessa, FL: Psychological Assessment Resources*.

Cronbach, L. J. (1955). Process affecting scores on "understanding others" and "assumed similarity." *Psychological Bulletin*, *52*, 177-193.

Devine, P. G. (1989). Stereotypes and prejudice: Their automatic and controlled components. *Journal of Personality and Social Psychology*, *56*, 5-18.

Digman, J. M. (1990). Personality structure: Emergence of the five-factor model. *Annual Review of Psychology*, *41*, 417-440.

Ferjenčík, J. (2006). Sémantické obrazy seba a typických príslušníkov vybraných národov u slovenských vysokoškolákov: Porovnanie v odstupe desiatich rokov [Semantic pictures of self and typical members of selected nations in Slovak university students: Comparison after ten years]. *Československá psychologie*, *50*, 50-63.

Fiske, S. T., Cuddy, A. J. C., Glick, P. & Xu, J. (2002). A model of (often mixed) stereotype content: Competence and warmth respectively follow from perceived status and competition. *Journal of Personality and Social Psychology*, *82*, 878-902.

Funder, D. (1999). Personality judgment: A realistic approach to person perception. San Diego, CA: Academic Press.

Goldberg, L. R. (1990). An alternative "description of personality": The Big-Five factor structure. *Journal of Personality and Social Psychology*, *59*, 1216-1229.

Griffin, D. and Gonzales, R. (1995). Correlational analysis of dyad-level data in the exchangeable case. *Psychological Bulletin*, *118*, 430-439.

Hewstone, M., Rubin, M. and Willis, H. (2002). Intergroup bias. *Annual Review of Psychology*, *53*, 575-604.

Hřebíčková, M. (2004). NEO osobnostní inventář podle NEO-PI-R P.T. Costy a R.R. McCraee [NEO Personality Inventory according to P.T. Costa and R.R. McCrae]. Praha: Testcentrum.

Hřebíčková, M. and Urbánek, T. (2001). NEO pětifaktorový osobnostní inventář (podle NEO Five-Factor Inventory P.T. Costy a R.R. McCraee). Praha: Testcentrum.

Hřebíčková, M. and Urbánek, T. (2006). Typologie osob: Aplikace shlukové analýzy v NEO osobnostním inventáři [Typology of Persons: Application of cluster analysis in NEO Personality Inventory]. *Československá psychologie*, *50*, 5, 405-418.

Hřebíčková, M., Blatný, M. and Jelínek, M. (2010). Osobnost jako prediktor osobní pohody v dospělosti [Personality as a predictor of subjective well-being in adulthood]. *Československá psychologie*, *54*, 32-42.

Hřebíčková, M. and Kouřilová, S. (2012). Jak se vidíme, jak nás vidí a jací jsme: porovnání českého národního auto- a heterostereotypu s posuzováním reálných Čechů v kontextu pětifaktorového modelu osobnosti [How do we see ourselves, how are we seen and how we are: Comparison of Czech national auto- and heterostereotypes with ratings of real people in context of five-factor model of personality]. *Československá psychologie*, *56*, 1-18.

Kervyn, N., Yzerbyt V. and Judd, C. M. (2010). Compensation between warmth and competence: Antecedents and consequences of negative relation between the two fundamental dimensions of social perception. *European Review of Social Psychology*, *21*, 155–187.

Kosatík, P. (2010). České snění [Czech dreeming]. Praha: Torst.

Kwan, V. S. Y., John, O. P., Robins, R. W. and Kuang L. L. (2008). Conceptualizing and assessing self-enhacement bias: A componential approach. *Journal of Personality and Social Psychology*, *94*, 1062-1077.

Löckenhoff, C. E., De Fruyt, F., Terracciano, A., McCrae, R., De Bolle, M., Costa, P. T. and 43 Members of the Adolescent Personality Profiles of Cultures Project (2009). Perceptions of Aging across 26 Cultures and their culture-level correlates. *Psychology and Aging*, *24*, 941-954.

Madon, S., Guyll, M., Aboufadel, K., Montiel, E., Smith, A., Palumbo, P. and Jussim, L. (2001). Ethnic and national stereotypes: The Princeton trilogy revisited and revised. *Personality and Social Psychology Bulletin*, *27*, 996-1010.

McCrae, R. R. (2002). NEO-PI-R data from 36 cultures: Further intercultural comparisons. In: A. J. Marsella (Series Ed.) and R. R. McCrae and J. Allik (Eds.), The Five-Factor Model Across Cultures, New York: Kluwer Academic Publishers/Plenum,105-125.

McCrae, R. R. (2008). A note on some measures of profile agreement. *Journal of Personality Assessment*, *90*, 105-109.

McCrae, R. R., Costa, P. T., Ostendorf, F., Angleitner, A., Hřebíčková, M., Avia, M., Sanz, J., Sánchez-Bernardos, M., Kusdil, E., Woodfield, R., Saunders, P. and Smith, P. (2000). Nature over nurture: Temperament, personality, and lifespan development. *Journal of Personality and Social Psychology*, *78*, 173-186.

McCrae, R. R., Costa, P. T., Martin, T. A, Oryol, V. E., Rukavishnikov, A. A., Senin, I. G., Hřebíčková, M. and Urbánek, T. (2004a). Consensual validation of personality traits across cultures. *Journal of Research in Personality*, *38*, 179-201.

McCrae, R. R., Costa, P. T., Hřebíčková, M., Urbánek, T., Martin, T. A, Oryol, V. E., Rukavishnikov, A. A. and Senin, I. G. (2004b). Age differences in personality traits across cultures: Self-report and observer perspectives. *European Journal of Personality*, *18*, 2, 143-157.

McCrae, R. R., Terracciano, A. Khoury, B., Nansubuga, F., Kneževič, G., Djuric Jocic, D. and Camart, N. (2005a). Universal features of personality traits from the observer's perspective: Data from 50 cultures. *Journal of Personality and Social Psychology*, *88*, 547-561.

McCrae, R. R., Terracciano, A., Leibovich, N. B., Schmidt, V., Shakespeare-Finch, J., Neubauer, A. and Djuric Jocic, D. (2005b). Personality Profiles of Cultures: Aggregate Personality Traits. *Journal of Personality and Social Psychology*, *89*, 407–425.

McCrae, R. R., Terraciano, A., Realo, A. and Allik, J. (2007). Climatic warmth and national wealth: Some culture-level determinants of national character stereotypes. *European Journal of Personality*, *21*, 953-976.

McCrae, R. R., Terracciano, A., De Fruyt, F., De Bolle, M., Gelfand, M. J., Costa, P. T. and 42 Collaborators of the Adolescent Personality Profiles of Cultures Project (2010). The Validity and Structure of Culture-Level Personality Scores: Data from Ratings of Young Adolescents. *Journal of Personality*, *78*, 815-838.

Mcgrath, R. E. and Goldberg, L. R. (2006). How to measure national stereotypes? *Science*, *311*, 776-777.

Ostendorf, F. & Angleitner, A. (2004). NEO-Persönlichkeittsinventar nach Costa und McCrae. Revidierte Fassung [NEO Personality Inventory according to Costa and McCrae. Revised]. Göttingen, Germany: Hogrefe.

Plichtová, J., Lášticová, B. and Petrjanošová, M. (2009). Konštuovanie slovenskosti vo verejnom priestore. Bratislava: Kabinet výzkumu sociálnej a biologickéj komunikácie SAV.

Realo, A., Allik, J., Lonnqvist, J. E., Verkasalo, M., Kwiatkowska, A., Kööts, L. and Renge, V. (2009). Mechanisms of the national character stereotype: How people in six neighbouring countries of Russia describe themselves and the typical Russian. *European Journal of Personality*, *23*, 229-249.

Rogers, K. H. and Wood, D. (2010). Accuracy of United States regional personality stereotypes. *Journal of Research in Personality*, *44*, 704-713.

Siuta, J. (2007). Inwentarz osobowości NEO-PI-R Paula T. Costy i Roberta McCrae. Aplikacija polska. Podręcznik [NEO Personality Inventory NEO-PI-R of Paul Costa and Robert McCrae. Polish version. Questionnaire]. Warszawa: Pracownia Testów Psychologicznych.

Swim, J. K. (1994). Perceived versus meta-analytic effect sizes: An assessment of the accuracy of gender stereotypes. *Journal of Personality and Social Psychology*, *66*, 21-36.

Terracciano, A., Abdel-Khalek, A. M., Ádám, N., Adamovová, L., Ahn, C. k., Ahn, H. n. and McCrae, R. R. (2005). National character does not reflect mean personality trait levels in 49 cultures. *Science*, *310*, 96-100.

Terracciano, A. and McCrae, R. R. (2007). Perceptions of Americans and the Iraq invasion: Implications for understanding national character stereotypes. *Journal of Cross-Cultural Psychology*, *38*, 695-710.

In: Stereotypes and Stereotyping
Editor: Claude Fields
ISBN: 978-1-63484-510-6

Chapter 9

AGING AND AGEISM: THE ROLES OF IDENTITY PROCESSING STYLES AND SELF-CONSCIOUSNESS

Robert M. Kirk[1] and Yiwei Chen[2,*]
[1]Adams State University, Colorado, US
[2]Bowling Green State University, Ohio, US

ABSTRACT

In the new millennium, older adults face a number of challenges in attempting to stay connected to a changing world. Ageism was first described by Butler (1969) as age discrimination or "prejudice by one age group toward other age groups." Younger adults often see older adults as burdensome or as nonproductive members of society. Utilizing Whitbourne's (1987) identity process theory, the present study examined the roles of identity processing styles (i.e., assimilation, accommodation, and balance) and self-consciousness factors (i.e., insight, self-reflection, and public self-consciousness) on individuals' susceptibility to ageism.

Self-report data were collected in-person and online from 564 adults (69% female) between the ages of 18-89. Results showed full support for the identity process hypotheses such that identity assimilation increased with age, identity accommodation decreased with age, and identity balance was not related to age. In addition, full support was found for the ageism hypotheses: age and identity processing styles significantly predicted ageism. Age was negatively associated with ageism. Identity assimilation and identity accommodation were positively related to ageism, whereas identity balance was negatively associated with ageism. In addition, insight increased with age, self-reflection decreased with age, and public self-consciousness also decreased with age. More importantly, self-consciousness components moderated the relationship between age and identity accommodation. Specifically, self-reflection increased the likelihood of an accommodative style with increasing age. Findings are discussed with implications for successful aging.

Keywords: older adults, aging, ageism, identity processing styles, self-consciousness

---

* Correspondence to: Yiwei Chen, Ph.D. Professor of Psychology, Psychology Department, Bowling Green State University, Bowling Green, OH 43551, ywchen@bgsu.edu.

INTRODUCTION

There is an abundance of literature, predominantly within Western cultures, which indicates that older adults face a number of challenges in attempting to stay connected to a world that often sees them as burdensome or incapable of being productive members of society (Macnicol, 2006; Giles and Reid, 2005; Nelson, 2002, 2005). Ageism was first described by Butler (1969) as "prejudice by one age group toward other age groups" (p. 243), most notably when younger adults discriminate against older adults, especially in youth-oriented cultures. Ageism is a form of prejudice and discrimination that individuals are susceptible to as they progress through the life course. Thus, the primary purpose of the present study was to examine the relationship between age and ageism, and the roles of identity processing styles and self- consciousness in combating the negative effects of ageism.

Chen, Pethtel, and Ma (2010) suggested that stereotypes might guide our beliefs in the absence of other information and that these stereotypes were not always invalid or malicious. However, they pointed out that while these stereotypes could be useful timesavers, they may lead to negative consequences depending upon our stereotypic beliefs. This is a valid concern given that they found older adults to be more susceptible to age-stereotypic information. In accordance with cognitive aging theory, Chen and Blanchard-Fields (2000) emphasized that "stereotypic thoughts can result in inaccurate perceptions and judgments" (p. 703). This statement is evidenced at the societal level by Palmore (2001) who reported that nearly 80% of older Americans claim to have been the recipient of ageism, which demonstrates just how prevalent age discrimination really is for many older adults. This finding illustrates that there are many older Americans who feel the presence of ageism in their own culture, sometimes even from their own age group.

Although ageism is commonly experienced via extrinsic sources, its pervasive influences can and often do become internalized, much to the detriment of older adults. Levy's (1996) study on cognitive performance of older adults found that memory ability decreased when negative age primes were used whereas memory performance was enhanced when positive age primes were used. As is often the case with "-isms" (i.e., racism, classism, sexism, etc.), ageism not only affects one's thought processes, but also behaviors and the well-being of those who are targets of this form of prejudice and discrimination. This appears to be the case even for those who are not considered "typical" targets of ageism. Bargh, Chen, and Barrows (1996) found that the walking speed of college-aged adults actually decreased after being primed with negative age stereotypes. Consistent findings were found by Hausdorff, Levy, and Wei (1999), who reported that the walking speed of a sample of 47 community-dwelling older adults actually increased after being primed with positive age stereotypes.

While Nelson (2002) pointed out that research on ageism is "only about one-tenth of that devoted to racism" (Giles and Reid, 2005, p. 389), it is not hard to identify ageism in everyday life. Ageism is prevalent in youth-oriented cultures (Palmore, 2001) and often perceived as socially acceptable. Levy and Banaji (2004) elucidate that negative aging stereotypes can implicitly affect people's thoughts, feelings, and behaviors. They describe that ageism is not a hatred of sorts, but rather a widespread, institutionalized acceptance of negative beliefs about older adults. Although such negative stereotypes are often met with benevolent indifference or passive acceptance, they do possess the ability to make an individual highly self-conscious about one's own age and produce negative perceptions of the aging process.

To examine these implicit views within an educational setting, 82 students enrolled in an undergraduate-level adult development and aging class at a large Midwestern university took an Age Implicit Association Test (IAT). The results of this exercise (Kirk, 2013) showed that an overwhelming majority of students demonstrated a strong implicit preference for younger adults. Less than 5% of the students showed no preference for either age group while none of the college-aged students showed an implicit preference for older adults over younger adults. Although this was only a classroom exercise used purely for pedagogical reasons, it nevertheless lends support to Levy and Banaji's (2004) work which highlights a drastic imbalance in the implicit preferences that people exhibit toward younger adults. Macnicol (2006) said that our "everyday social judgments are frequently age-based, even if we consciously deny it" (p. 3). Drawing from Baltes' (1987) lifespan perspective on aging, Baltes, Lindenberger, and Staudinger (2006) posit that lifespan development occurs via dynamic interactions between growth, maintenance, and regulation of loss. They emphasize four critical factors in this process, one of which is the lack of cultural support structures or "old-age friendly" supporting systems. So the question must be asked, how does one age successfully in a youth-oriented culture such as the United States? Fortunately, despite ageism and a variety of challenges that older adults face today, most of them are able to remain resilient and maintain a positive sense of self (Cotter and Gonzalez, 2009). Whitbourne's (1987) identity process theory presents three identity processing styles (i.e., assimilation, accommodation, and balance) that individuals use to form perceptions of the aging self.

The Identity Processing Theory

The identity process theory (IPT) is a contemporary framework that emphasizes cognitive models of the aging self (Whitbourne, 1987; Whitbourne and Collins, 1998; Whitbourne, Sneed and Skultety, 2002). It has theoretical ties to both Jean Piaget and Erik Erikson. The IPT borrows terminology from Piaget's cognitive theory (1975/1977) in which the core tenets are identity assimilation, identity accommodation, and identity balance (i.e., equilibrium, in Piagetian terms). An important distinction must be made in the utilization of these terms. While Piaget coined them to reference cognitive/intellectual development within children and adolescents, Whitbourne adopted these terms to represent cognitive identity processes from an aging perspective. Sneed and Whitbourne (2003) explicate that identity assimilation refers to the maintenance of self-consistency where an individual strives to preserve self-defining schemas. Conversely, identity accommodation refers to making changes in one's own cognitive perceptions of self. Identity accommodation should not become so prominent with age, however, that one's sense of self is based predominantly on perceptions of others or experiencing the "ups and downs" of life. Rather, a person should be able to adjust these perceptions of self as needed while also maintaining a coherent and integrative sense of identity. That is, individuals maintain a balance between who they perceive themselves to be as unique individuals while making the necessary adjustments to accommodate for the life changes invariably associated with aging.

Whitbourne, Sneed, and Skultety (2002) made a parallel of assimilators, accommodators, and balanced individuals with the metaphorical roles of egoists, politicians, and scientists. Identity assimilators were perceived as "egoists" in the sense that they seek self-enhancement, even to the point of distorting self-information which reflects poorly on them in an apparent attempt to avoid negative affect. From a theoretical perspective, assimilators are reluctant to acknowledge changes associated with aging to the extent that these age-related changes are discrepant from a youthful identity the individual wishes to possess or retain (Whitbourne, 1996). There are both costs and benefits associated with being an assimilator. On one hand, assimilators tend to be optimistic, take pride in their accomplishments, and typically perceive themselves as healthy. On the other hand, overuse can lead to social isolation, exhaustion from defense against identity-discrepant information, and failure to engage in important age-related compensatory activities (Whitbourne et al., 2002). Assimilators may, for instance, disregard the inevitable and natural signs of physical aging and "cause themselves harm in attempting to engage in activities formerly within the range of competence" (p. 32).

Identity accommodators were likened to "politicians" who lack a core sense of identity and who are viewed more as products of public performance. Negative affect and anxiety occur when they fail to gain public approval or acceptance. Theoretically, identity accommodators overreact and overgeneralize the consequences associated with age-related changes in physical and cognitive ability. This could be especially dangerous within youth-oriented cultures where older persons are often perceived as feeble, incapable, or burdensome. Accommodators may embrace old age stereotypes all too readily at the expense of their own well-being. Although negative, these age stereotypes do provide a concrete set of external self-referents which may cause older adults to passively accept the notion of being "over the hill," thereby leading to a lack of engagement in preventative or compensatory activities which are beneficial to the aging process (Whitbourne et al., 2002).

Lastly, they made a parallel of identity-balanced individuals to "scientists" who use a flexible and pragmatic approach to make changes or adjustments in self-perceptions based on identity-salient discrepancies. These individuals are able to maintain a core understanding of who they are while also being able to make necessary changes in perceptions of self (i.e., accommodations based on age-relevant information). Individuals who utilize an identity-balanced approach to aging are the theoretical ideal. They are in the best position to age successfully, due to an adaptive, cognitively flexible identity style (Whitbourne et al., 2002).

Erikson's psychosocial theory of development is another foundation from which identity process theory draws. Erikson (1963) suggested that one of life's greatest psychosocial challenges is developing a secure sense of self or identity. Posing the question "Who am I?" is an acceptable and logical starting point to address this issue. But unfortunately, the theory provides little detail on how to measure such a construct objectively. Whitbourne et al. (2002) explicate that the next milestone in identity literature beyond Erikson was Marcia's (1966) work on operationalizing identity in terms of "identity statuses." But research and theory have struggled since then with respect to expanding on Marcia's basic concepts, particularly beyond adolescence and young adulthood. We suggest that maintaining a secure sense of identity is an integral psychosocial process across the adult lifespan, even into later years. Retirement, for example, is a major life event for most working adults, in which a number of anxiety-inducing changes may make older adults question or reevaluate their sense of identity. During these significant transitions, an identity "crisis" (in Eriksonian terms) may be brought to the forefront of our adult lives.

It is during such times that identity styles and adjustment capacities become critical to our sense of self and well-being. The extant literature on aging trajectories of Whitbourne's identity process theory has essentially been restricted to middle-aged and older adults. Drawing from a community-based sample of 173 participants between the ages of 42-85, Sneed and Whitbourne (2003) reported that identity assimilation increased with age, identity accommodation decreased with age, and identity balance was not found to be age-related. Previous work by Whitbourne and VanManen (1996) did examine identity statuses in a sample of young and middle-aged adults, but this work was rooted in the theoretical groundings of Marcia (1966). Therefore, the conceptualization of identity and the methodology used to measure it were considerably different than that of the IPT. There is an urgent need for a true lifespan developmental examination of identity processing styles across adulthood. The present study examined age differences in the identity processing styles with a sample of a wide age range. We hypothesized that (a) identity assimilation would increase with age, (b) identity accommodation would decrease with age, and (c) identity balance would not be related to age. It is also a goal of the present study to examine how the different identity processing styles influence ageism.

Ageism

With respect to ageism, a solidified and balanced sense of identity should act as a buffer to the deleterious effects of negative age stereotypes. Sneed and Whitbourne (2001) highlighted one model of particular interest to the identity process theory, Brandtstadter and Greve's (1994) model of successful aging. It contended that aging successfully partially results from the "accommodative shift" of assimilative coping strategies. According to this model, three interdependent processes serve to stabilize and protect older individuals from the psychological, biological, and social changes inherent to the aging process. These processes help to maintain a positive view of the self and personal development through: (1) instrumental and compensatory activities which aim to prevent and alleviate losses in domains relevant to self-esteem and identity (e.g., regular exercise, use of a hearing aid); (2) accommodative changes or readjustments to personal goals and aspirations which counteract negative self-evaluations (e.g., plant a garden instead of build a house); and (3) immunizing mechanisms which mitigate the impact of self-discrepant evidence (e.g., rationalize poor test performance, devalue/discredit negative feedback). In essence, successful aging involves combating both negative age-related changes, and external sources of negative age information through the self-selection of information and environments that help maintain a positive view of the aging self. It also involves the ability to disengage in blocked goals and activities in order to develop new goals or aspirations in accord with one's abilities. A clear association between this model and the identity process model can be made when comparing the fundamental components of these two theories. An important distinction, however, is that Whitbourne's identity model is centered on pre-existing self-schemata and how these self-concepts persist or change with age while Brandtstadter's successful aging model is primarily focused on goal-orientation and how goal adjustments are made with age.

In terms of defense mechanisms which may help ward off negative effects of ageism, a proposed identity assimilation effect (IAE) has been observed in a number of aging studies (Whitbourne and Collins, 1998; Sneed and Whitbourne, 2001; Whitbourne and Sneed, 2002).

The IAE was hypothesized to result from an individual's desire to maintain a positive perception of self in the face of increasingly threatening factors that depict aging as a negative state of existence (Whitbourne and Sneed, 2002). This phenomenon was first discovered by Whitbourne and Collins (1998) who found that assimilation was linked to increased levels of self-esteem in older adults. Although identity assimilation is predominantly viewed as a defensive cognitive strategy with potentially negative consequences, it would appear that maintaining a certain degree of consistency may prove useful in buffering against age-related decline, as it has been associated with heightened levels of self-worth (Whitbourne and Sneed, 2002). Specifically, denial may serve as a functional operating mechanism for the IAE. This contention is supported by other research which has shown that older adults possessed the highest denial scores of any age group across a sex- and age-stratified random sample from varying socioeconomic backgrounds (Diehl, Coyle and Labouvie-Vief, 1996).

Baltes and Baltes' (1990) lifespan developmental perspective may provide a theoretical framework to understand the identity assimilation effect through the selective optimization with compensation (SOC) model. Among the essential premises of this framework are two propositions stating that the balance between gains and losses becomes less positive with age and that the self, paradoxically, remains resilient with age. To combat inevitable cognitive, physical, and social restrictions to retain levels of subjective well-being, the SOC model contends that successful aging is, in part, the result of compensatory processes which operate via mechanisms intended to selectively optimize certain domains. Compensation promotes resiliency and helps offset losses through the selection and optimization of individual strengths, positive attributes, and optimal conditions. Given that a core tenet of identity assimilation is consistency, older adults may look to optimize their self-perceptions by selectively emphasizing qualities, information, and experiences which are consistent with a positive view of the aging self, thereby compensating for identity-discrepant information or negative perceptions of the aging self.

Consistent with the SOC model (Baltes and Baltes, 1990), other lifespan theorists have proposed that successful aging partially results from a shift in one's social and emotional motivations (Carstensen, 1992, 1995). The socioemotional selectivity theory (SST) contends that, as future time is perceived as limited, "older adults structure their social worlds to optimize emotionally meaningful, and therefore gratifying, experiences and to avoid potentially negative interactions" (Carstensen, Fung and Charles, 2003, p. 108). Among the imperative aspects of the SST is an age-related positivity effect wherein changes begin to emerge not only in social and environmental choices, but also in older adults' attention and memory (Mather and Carstensen, 2005; Kennedy, Mather and Carstensen, 2004), emotion regulation and coping strategies (Scheibe and Blanchard-Fields, 2009; Carstensen and Mikels, 2005), and cognitive processing of positive and negative information (Carstensen, Fung and Charles, 2003). These shifts may also help to explain a decrease in identity accommodation with age. The positivity effect, combined with the compensatory motives of the SOC model, may contribute to a decrease in accommodative styles as people get older with the intent of combating negative self information or age stereotypes from the outside world. Decreased accommodation promotes consistency in one's sense of identity and is found to be inversely related to self-esteem in older adults (Sneed and Whitbourne, 2001). Thus, it is hypothesized in the present study that (a) age would show a negative association to ageism given that individuals' perceptions of aging tend to change as they get older, (b) identity assimilation would positively predict ageism, (c) identity accommodation would also positively predict ageism, perhaps due to a lack of stability in self-defining schemata, and (d) identity balance would negatively predict one's susceptibility to ageism.

Self-Consciousness

The IPT model suggests that older adults place greater emphasis on internal or private forms of self-perception and less importance on external or public forms of self-awareness. It is at the intersection of these changing social, emotional, and cognitive domains that identity-defining schemata converge with self-consciousness factors. Self-consciousness is an ideology as old as philosophy itself and an area of interest for construct measurement within the field of psychology for the last several decades. There exists a substantial body of research pertaining to the notion of self-consciousness (Fenigstein, Scheier and Buss, 1975; Scheier and Carver, 1985; Piliavin and Charng, 1988; Creed and Funder, 1998; Rankin, Lane, Gibbons, and Gerrard, 2004). But what does it mean to be self-conscious? Over the last few decades, many researchers have studied this construct and associated it with numerous outcomes, often the presence of clinical conditions or various indicators of well-being. However, there has been much debate and discrepancy in the literature over what self-consciousness actually is and how it should be measured. Historically, the standard for measurement was set by Fenigstein, Scheier, and Buss (1975) when they developed the Self-Consciousness Scale. Through principal-components analysis using varimax rotation, 38 items explained 43% of the variance across three latent factors: public self-consciousness (i.e., a general awareness of the self as a social object that has an effect on others), private self-consciousness (i.e., attending to one's inner thoughts and feelings), and social anxiety (i.e., a discomfort in the presence of others). Public self-consciousness and social anxiety have traditionally been negatively-valenced constructs associated with such outcomes as eating disorders, generalized anxiety, depression, and lowered self-esteem (Sawaoka, Barnes, Blomquist, Masheb and Grilo, 2012; Nilly and Winquist, 2002; Heatherton and Polivy, 1991) while private self-consciousness has elicited mixed results across studies.

The overarching concept of self-consciousness is a subordinate category nested within the neuroticism trait encompassed by the "Big 5" or five-factor personality model by Costa and McCrae (1992). In the 1980s, Scheier and Carver (1985) created a revised version of the Self-Consciousness Scale, retaining the three latent factors (i.e., private self-consciousness, public self-consciousness, and social anxiety) while modifying the items used to explain them. Other researchers, such as Wicklund and Gollwitzer (1987), criticized the dichotomization of private and public self-consciousness claiming that a separation of the two is conceptually flawed. More criticism followed when discrepant findings indicated that private self-consciousness was not a unidimensional construct, but consisted of two distinct subcomponents: insight and self-reflection (Grant, Franklin and Langford, 2002). In this new 4-factor conceptualization of self-consciousness, findings for insight (a.k.a. internal state awareness) have generally been positive and consistent across studies (Creed and Funder, 1998; Harrington and Loffredo, 2011) while self-reflection has shown greater variance (Lyke, 2009; Harrington and Loffredo, 2011), but generally relates negatively to measures of well-being (Creed and Funder, 1998; Trapnell and Campbell, 1999; Grant, Franklin and Langford, 2002; Harrington and Loffredo, 2007). A potential explanation for the inconsistencies in self-reflection findings, according to Trapnell and Campbell (1999), is that some studies confound self-reflection and rumination. Rumination is a concept often found in clinical psychology; it refers to a psychologically maladaptive form of self-attention wherein individuals excessively dwell or ruminate on the past or negative aspects of the self. If self-reflection confounds with rumination, it makes intuitive sense that the overarching construct of self-consciousness is nested within the neuroticism trait under the five-factor model. Insight and self-reflection, then, appear to be theoretically distinct elements within the realm of private self-consciousness. Insight offers positive benefits for the individual whereas self-reflection is associated with negative outcomes.

A third and final approach to self-consciousness takes a cognitive-behavioral approach to the association between self-consciousness and social anxiety. With the obvious presumption that consciousness itself is a cognitive ability, the subsequent behavior is likely to be one of social anxiety if an individual is excessively self-conscious in public settings. This model is unique in the sense that it is not customary for researchers to eliminate social anxiety from the measurement model. Among others, Schlenker and Leary (1982) have argued that "the cognitive state of the individual mediates both affective arousal and behavior" and these cognitive states are "dispositional antecedents of social anxiety" (p. 641). The consideration of self-consciousness as a dispositional/cognitive antecedent to social anxiety is a critical distinction in the proposed model from the past models in the literature. This approach to self-consciousness assumes that people who are highly preoccupied with public opinion or have a greater need for public approval are more likely to be socially anxious. Hence, cognition precedes the psychophysiological manifestation of anxiety within this context, thereby justifying the theoretical argument that social anxiety need not be a measurement property assessed concurrently with public and private self-consciousness. Due to this inherent conceptual distinction, social anxiety was not measured as a cognitive state of self-consciousness in the present study.

Public self-consciousness has historically and still currently is measured as a unidimensional construct (Fenigstein, Scheier and Buss, 1975; Scheier and Carver, 1985; Davis, 1991; Evans, Baer and Segerstrom, 2009). According to Scheier and Carver (1981), public self-consciousness refers to a tendency to focus attention on the self as a social object (i.e., the self as seen by others). It has been consistently shown over time to predict a wide variety of negative outcomes, including depression (Saboonchi, Lundh and Ost, 1999), social anxiety (Mor and Winquist, 2002), and eating disorders (Striegel-Moore, Silberstein and Rodin, 1993). For all intents and purposes, public self-consciousness appears to be a negatively-valenced attribute in the realm of self-awareness processes. Private self-consciousness refers to a tendency to focus on more covert aspects of the self (i.e., thoughts, feelings/emotions, etc.) from a self-derived, introspective point of view (Agatstein and Buchanan, 1984). As previously stated, private self-consciousness was also once thought to be a unidimensional construct, but is now commonly viewed as consisting of two distinct subcomponents: insight (internal state awareness) and self-reflection (Brunkrant and Page, 1984; Piliavin and Charng, 1988; Creed and Funder, 1998; Grant, Franklin and Langford, 2002). In the present study, insight was conceptualized as a positively-valenced element while self-reflection was treated as a negative component within the realm of private self-consciousness.

An awareness of self, whether externally derived or internally generated, has an inherent theoretical tie to one's sense of identity. It is at the crossroads of self-awareness and one's sense of identity that self-consciousness factors and identity processing styles meet. If the core age-related social, emotional, and motivational shifts posited by the SST (Carstensen, 1992) and SOC model (Baltes and Baltes, 1990) are valid, these cognitive antecedents should combine with socioemotional motivations to elicit a compensatory identity assimilation effect in older adults. In other words, as people get older, they may be able to increase positive experiences and emotions by avoiding, discrediting, or devaluing negative self-information and negative age stereotypes from the outside world. By utilizing an assimilative processing style, they may seek to maintain a positive view of the aging self.

Similar to that of the IPT, the literature on self-consciousness is limited from an adult developmental perspective, particularly so for constructs which demonstrate measurement validity. A considerable amount of research in this area has focused on adolescence and young adulthood. Davis and Franzoi (1991) found relative stability in self-consciousness measures while Rankin, Lane, Gibbons, and Gerrard (2004) found that public self-consciousness decreased as private self-consciousness increased with age in two adolescent samples. It should be noted that both studies utilized an antiquated (i.e., unidimensional private self-consciousness) and questionable technique for assessing self-consciousness. Davis and Franzoi (1991) did not test measurement validity while Rankin et al. (2004) reported unacceptable fit indices for their confirmatory factor analysis, yet utilized their construct anyway. Sneed and Whitbourne (2003) studied IPT and self-consciousness in middle and later adulthood. Although their work did not find age to be a significant predictor for any of the three self-consciousness factors, these findings must be considered in light of the limitations of the study. First and foremost, construct validity is paramount in attempting to explain their non-significant findings. Consistent with a body of literature which supports the separation of private self-consciousness into two distinct subcomponents (Watson, Hickman, Morris, Stutz and Whiting, 1994; Watson, Morris, Ramsey, Hickman and Waddell, 1996; Grant, Franklin and Langford, 2002), Sneed and Whitbourne (2003) acknowledged this distinction in their work, but did not adjust for these theoretical and empirical discrepancies with a psychometrically sound measure. Rather, they merely divided the antiquated private self-consciousness scale (Fenigstein, Scheier and Buss, 1975) into two separate hypothetical dimensions and measured them accordingly. Additionally, the Cronbach alpha they reported for the internal state awareness (insight) subscale was $\alpha = .55$, lower than what is typically deemed an acceptable coefficient for internal consistency. Another limitation is that only middle-aged and older adults were represented in their work. The present study addressed this issue with a sample that is representative of the entire adult lifespan (i.e., included younger adults).

There is extant literature (Kirk and Chen, 2012; Rankin et al., 2004) suggesting age-related changes in self-consciousness. In contrast to work conducted by Sneed and Whitbourne (2003), Kirk and Chen (2012) found that insight demonstrated a significant positive association to age, as well as significant moderation effects on the relationship between intrinsic motivation and positive emotions. Furthermore, it was found that rumination was also associated with age, showing a significant decrease across the adult lifespan. Kirk and Chen's (2012) study did not, however, examine the association between age and public self-consciousness. Given age-related decreases in identity accommodation (Sneed and Whitbourne, 2001; 2003) and previous research showing a decrease in public self-consciousness among younger cohorts (Rankin et al., 2004), it was hypothesized that there would be a significant negative association between age and public self-consciousness across adulthood. Consistent with our previous work on private self-consciousness (Kirk and Chen,

2012), it was anticipated that insight would increase with age while self-reflection would decrease across the adult lifespan.

From an IPT standpoint, self-consciousness factors have had mixed associations to identity processing styles. Internal state awareness or insight was not significantly related to identity assimilation or accommodation in Sneed and Whitbourne's (2003) work, but was found to be positively associated with identity balance ($r = .35$, $p < .01$). Self-reflection was not significantly related to identity assimilation or balance, but had a positive association to identity accommodation ($r = .46$, $p < .01$). Similarly, public self-consciousness exhibited a non-significant association to identity assimilation and balance, but was found to have a significant positive relationship with identity accommodation ($r = .49$, $p < .01$). Based on the changing social, emotional, and motivational dynamics posited by the SST (Carstensen, 1992) and SOC model (Baltes and Baltes, 1990), it was expected that (a) insight would have a significant moderation effect on the association between age and identity balance, perhaps due to increased self-understanding and identity balance as people get older. In addition, it was expected that (b) self-reflection would significantly moderate the association between age and identity accommodation. Specifically, self-reflection was expected to interact with age to increase the utilization of an accommodative processing style (Whitbourne, Sneed and Skultety, 2002; Sneed and Whitbourne, 2003). With respect to public self-consciousness, the more credence one gives to outside sources of information, the more likely they may be to make adjustments based on that information, which could prove detrimental for older adults. If external sources of ageism are indeed a threat to older adults' sense of identity, then (c) negatively-valenced public self-consciousness would moderate the relationship between age and identity accommodation. Specifically, public self-consciousness would interact with age to increase the likelihood of an accommodative processing style across the adult lifespan.

The Present Study

To summarize, the primary goal of the present study was to better understand age-related changes in identity processes and self-consciousness as protectants against ageism. These associations have not been sufficiently addressed in the current literature from an adult developmental perspective. The present study anatomized these relations in order to better understand what cognitive, social, and developmental processes contribute to a secure sense of self throughout adulthood. Specifically, the present study (I) investigated age differences in identity processing styles within a sample that represents the entire adult lifespan, (II) examined the influence of identity processing styles and age on ageism, (III) assessed age-related changes in self-consciousness factors, and (IV) explored the potential moderating effects of self-consciousness factors on the associations between age and identity processing styles.

In accordance with the IPT's contention that self-consistency is a defensive aging mechanism with positive benefits for older adults (Sneed and Whitbourne, 2001), it was hypothesized that (I): (a) identity assimilation would increase with age, (b) identity accommodation would decrease with age, and (c) identity balance would not be related to age and remain stable across the adult lifespan. With respect to the association between identity processing styles, age, and susceptibility to ageism, it was hypothesized that (II): (a) age would show a negative association to ageism given that individuals' perceptions of aging tend to change as they get older, (b) identity assimilation would positively predict ageism scores based on the theoretical contention that it is a defensive coping strategy, (c) identity accommodation would also positively predict ageism scores due to a lack of stability in self-defining schemata, and (d) identity balance would negatively predict one's susceptibility to ageism on account of its consistent, yet adaptive nature.

With regard to self-consciousness factors, it was hypothesized that (III): (a) insight would increase with age, (b) self-reflection would decrease with age, and (c) public self-consciousness would also decrease with age. In terms of moderation effects, it was hypothesized that (IV): self-consciousness factors would moderate the associations between age and identity processing styles. Specifically, (a) insight would interact with age to increase identity balance, (b) self-reflection would interact with age to increase identity accommodation, and (c) public self-consciousness would interact with age to increase identity accommodation across adulthood.

METHOD

Participants

Five hundred and sixty-four adults (69% female) between the ages of 18-89 ($M = 41.7$, $SD = 19.3$) participated in the current work. Data were collected from undergraduate students at a large Midwestern university ($N = 244$), from community-dwelling residents in the Northwest Ohio region ($N = 196$), and online through the use of SurveyGizmo ($N = 124$). The sample was 84.6% Euro-American (white), with the largest percentage being married (44.1%), followed closely by single individuals (39.7%). Younger participants reported being physically healthier, which resulted in a significant negative association between age and self-reported physical health ($r = -.23$, $p < .01$). See Table 1 for descriptive statistics of demographic variables.

Measures

Demographics Questionnaire. Standard background and demographic information (i.e., race/ethnicity, self-reported health, education, annual income, sex/gender, etc.) were collected through an initial questionnaire before measures of identity processing styles, self-consciousness, and ageism were administered. These variables were used as controls and for descriptive purposes during analysis.

Identity and Experiences Scale — Assimilation, Accommodation and Balance. The Identity and Experiences Scale (IES), developed by Whitbourne, Sneed, and Skultety (2002), was a 33-item measure which assessed the extent to which an individual utilizes identity assimilation, identity accommodation, or identity balance to formulate self concepts.

Each subscale of the IES contains 11 items. The assimilation component of this scale was designed to assess the level of consistency in one's identity schema (e.g., generally try to avoid change in my life or how I see myself). Cronbach's alpha for this subscale was $\alpha = .81$. Items for the accommodation component were intended to measure the plasticity of one's identity and how willing an individual is to either question or modify his/her concept of self based on experiences and/or opposing information (e.g., have many doubts and questions about myself). Cronbach's alpha for the accommodation subscale was α = .91. The identity balance portion of the measure was developed to assess the extent to which an individual maintains a sense of self, but is also willing to make changes or adjustments when necessary (e.g., feel confident in "who" I am but am willing to learn more about myself). Cronbach's alpha for the balance subscale was α = .85. All items were assessed along a continuum, a 7-point scale where 1 = *not like me* and 7 = *completely like me*. It should be noted that all subscales were combined into a single 33-item scale in randomized order during the collection process. As suggested by Whitbourne, Sneed, and Skultety (2002), however, scoring was performed separately for all three subscales and there was no aggregate score for the full measure.

Table 1. Demographic Variables (N = 564)

Variable	Level	# of participants	% of participants
Education	No degree/diploma	16	2.8
	H. S. Diploma/GED	299	53.0
	Associate's Degree	71	12.6
	Bachelor's Degree	123	21.8
	Master's Degree	43	7.6
	Doctoral Degree	12	2.1
Annual Income	Less than 20,000	171	30.3
	20,000-39,000	64	11.3
	40,000-59,000	88	15.6
	60,000-79,000	82	14.5
	80,000-99,000	37	6.6
	100,000 or more	118	20.9
Self-Reported Health	Poor	9	1.6
	Fair	104	18.4
	Good	331	58.7
	Excellent	120	21.3
Marital Status	Single	224	39.7
	Married	249	44.1
	Divorced	43	7.6
	Widowed	26	4.6
	Cohabiting	22	3.9
Race/ Ethnicity	Euro-American (white)	477	84.6
	African-American (black)	66	11.7
	Asian	6	1.1
	Hispanic	13	2.3
	Native American	1	0.2
	Other	1	0.2

Private Self-Consciousness. In the current work, private self-consciousness was measured as two distinct subcomponents: insight and self-reflection. The Self-Reflection and Insight Scale (SRIS) was designed by Grant, Franklin, and Langford (2002) as an improvement on the private self-consciousness subscale of the Self-Consciousness Scale developed by Fenigstein, Scheier, and Buss (1975). The 8-item subscale for insight was used to assess what is often considered an "internal state awareness" to private self-consciousness (e.g., I usually have a very clear idea about why I've behaved a certain way). The coefficient alpha for internal consistency was $\alpha = .84$. The 12-item self-reflection subscale was used to assess the typically-negative dimension of private self-consciousness (e.g., I frequently take time to reflect on my thoughts). The coefficient alpha for internal consistency was $\alpha = .90$. The SRIS is a self-report measure that assessed these two constructs along a 7-point continuum where 1 = *strongly disagree* and 7 = *strongly agree*. The private self-consciousness subscales were scored separately to create two distinct composite scores, one for insight and one for self-reflection.

Public Self-Consciousness. The public aspect of self-consciousness was measured using the revised version of Scheier and Carver's (1985) Self-Consciousness Scale. The public subscale of this measure was a 7-item questionnaire which assessed the individual's tendency to focus on aspects of the self which are a matter of public display (e.g., I care a lot about how I present myself to others). Cronbach's alpha for internal consistency was $\alpha = .85$. All items were assessed along a continuum, a 4-point scale where 1 = *not at all like me* and 4 = *completely like me.*

Fraboni Scale of Ageism—Revised. Ageism was measured using the revised version of Fraboni, Saltstone, and Hughes' (1990) Fraboni Scale of Ageism (FSA), which was further assessed and validated by Rupp, Vodanovich, and Crede (2005). The FSA-R was a 23-item scale which assessed negative perceptions of older adults and aging (e.g., feeling depressed around old people is probably a common feeling). Cronbach's alpha for this scale was $\alpha = .87$. All responses were assessed along a continuum, a 7-point scale where 1 = *strongly disagree* and 7 = *strongly agree*, and all items were aggregated to form a single composite score.

Design and Procedure

All participants were asked to respond to a series of surveys measuring the variables of interest. Participants either had access to these surveys through a web link posted online via SurveyGizmo or by hard copy while data were collected in-person. Undergraduate and community samples who chose the electronic survey rather than a physical copy of the measures were directed to the appropriate web address where they were first presented with an informed consent page. They could either click "Next" to give consent or discontinue if they chose not to participate. For all who provided consent, they then began by answering a number of background/demographic questions.

Participants were then presented with the aforementioned measures in randomized order: IES (Assimilation, Accommodation, and Balance), SRIS (Self-Reflection and Insight), SCS-R (Public Self-Consciousness subscale), and the FSA-R (ageism scale). This process was identical for data collected in-person, except that participants signed a physical copy of the informed consent form and completed the measures by hand. Online respondents recruited through networking followed the same procedure outlined above for participants who chose to fill out the electronic survey via SurveyGizmo. The data collection process took approximately six months to complete. Students were compensated with course credit while community-dwelling residents and online respondents participated for free.

RESULTS

Hierarchical multiple regression was used to test all hypotheses for the current project. Main effects for Hypothesis I and III were tested by entering age as a continuous independent variable in separate linear models using components of identity processing styles (i.e., assimilation, accommodation and balance) and self-consciousness (i.e., insight, self-reflection, and public self-consciousness) as dependent variables. In the first step, all control variables (i.e., gender, education, annual income, and self-reported physical health) were entered into the model, followed in the second step by the predictor variable (age).

While some associations were significant between control variables and dependent measures within and across models tested, none changed the directionality or significance of the associations between the target independent and dependent variables.

Hypothesis II was tested using the same method described for Hypothesis I and III, but instead of outcome variables, the identity processing styles and age were used as predictors of aggregate ageism scores after first controlling for gender, education, annual income, and self-reported physical health. Interaction effects were tested according to Hypothesis IV by first performing a linear transformation on the independent and moderator variables. This was done by centering the variables at their mean to adjust for the shared variance between main effects and the interaction term (Cohen, Cohen, West and Aiken, 2003). In the first step, control variables were entered, followed in the second step by centered age and self-consciousness variables, followed in the third step by the interaction term itself. Three separate hierarchical models were run to test the potential moderating effects of insight, self-reflection, and public self-consciousness.

Hypothesis I

Table 2. Hierarchical Regression Analysis for Variables Predicting Identity Assimilation (N = 564)

	Model 1			Model 2		
Variable	*B*	*SE B*	*β*	*B*	*SE B*	*β*
Gender	-3.96	.97	-.17**	-4.03	.90	-.17**
Education	-1.16	.42	-.12**	-1.38	.39	-.15**
Annual Income	.81	.25	.14**	.07	.25	.01
Health (self-report)	-1.11	.67	-.07	.47	.64	.03
Age				.23	.02	.40**
R2	.06			.19		
F for change in R2	7.04**			91.32**		

Note. *$p < .05$; **$p < .01$.

In accordance with previous research, full support was found for the IPT hypotheses. It was found that (a) age predicted significant increases in identity assimilation (β = .40, $t(559) = 9.56, p < .01$) across the adult lifespan, lending support to Whitbourne's proposal of an identity assimilation effect with age. See Table 2.

Consistent with this finding, (b) age predicted significant decreases in identity accommodation (β = -.39, $t(559) = -9.24, p < .01$) throughout the adult lifespan. See Table 3. As expected, (c) identity balance was not related to age (β = .04, $t(559) = 0.91, p = .36$).

Table 3. Hierarchical Regression Analysis for Variables Predicting Identity Accommodation (N = 564)

	Model 1			Model 2		
Variable	*B*	*SE B*	*β*	*B*	*SE B*	*β*
Gender	3.11	1.21	.10*	3.20	1.13	.11**
Education	-.33	.52	-.03	-.06	.48	-.01
Annual Income	-1.28	.31	-.18**	-.38	.31	-.05
Health (self-report)	.65	.83	.03	-1.27	.80	-.06
Age				-.27	.03	-.39**
R2	.06			.13		
F for change in R2	6.56**			85.42**		

Note. *$p < .05$; **$p < .01$.

Hypothesis II

Table 4. Hierarchical Regression Analysis for Variables Predicting Ageism (N = 564)

	Model 1			Model 2		
Variable	*B*	*SE B*	*β*	*B*	*SE B*	*β*
Gender	-6.91	1.61	-.18**	-6.71	1.56	-.18**
Education	-.94	.69	-.06	-.12	.67	-.01
Annual Income	-.57	.42	-.06	-.05	.42	-.01
Health (self-report)	.10	1.10	.004	-.05	1.01	-.002
Age				-.09	.05	-.10*
Identity Assimilation				.27	.07	.16**
Identity Accommodation				.23	.06	.17**
Identity Balance				-.29	.08	-.16**
R2	.04			.13		
F for change in R2	4.66**			13.80**		

Note. *$p < .05$; **$p < .01$.

Full support was found for the ageism hypotheses. Results showed that (a) age itself negatively predicted ageism scores (β = -.10, $t(559) = -1.97, p < .05$). Conversely, (b) identity assimilation positively predicted ageism scores (β = .16, $t(559) = 3.62, p < .01$) throughout adulthood. Results demonstrated that (c) identity accommodation also positively predicted ageism scores (β = .17, $t(559) = 3.77, p < .01$). Finally, (d) identity balance was the only processing style to negatively predict ageism (β = -.16, $t(559) = -3.78, p < .01$). See Table 4.

Hypothesis III

Full support was found for the self-consciousness hypotheses. It was found that (a) age predicted significant increases in insight, the typically-positive subcomponent of private self-consciousness (β = .32, $t(559)$ = 7.42, p < .01). See Table 5. Results showed that (b) age significantly predicted decreases in self-reflection, the typically-negative subcomponent of private self-consciousness (β = -.27, $t(559)$ = -6.01, p < .01). See Table 6. Lastly, (c) age also significantly predicted decreases in public self-consciousness (β = -.24, $t(559)$ = -5.34, p < .01) across the adult lifespan. See Table 7.

Table 5. Hierarchical Regression Analysis for Variables Predicting Insight (N = 564)

	Model 1			Model 2		
Variable	*B*	*SE B*	β	*B*	*SE B*	β
Gender	-.93	.74	-.05	-.98	.71	-.05
Education	.81	.32	.11*	.67	.30	.09*
Annual Income	.91	.19	.21**	.46	.19	.10*
Health (self-report)	.40	.51	.03	1.37	.50	.11**
Age				.14	.02	.32**
R2	.08			.16		
F for change in R2	9.77**			55.10**		

Note. *p < .05; **p < .01.

Hypothesis IV

Partial support was found for the moderation hypotheses. Results demonstrated that (a) the interaction between age and insight was non-significant (β = -.09, $t(559)$ = -1.66, p = .09). However, (b) a significant interaction effect was found between age and self-reflection on identity accommodation (β = .08, $t(559)$ = 1.98, p < .05), decreasing the strength of the negative association between age and identity accommodation across the adult lifespan.

Table 6. Hierarchical Regression Analysis for Variables Predicting Self-Reflection (N = 564)

	Model 1			Model 2		
Variable	*B*	*SE B*	β	*B*	*SE B*	β
Gender	2.80	1.27	.09*	2.86	1.24	.09*
Education	2.48	.54	.20**	2.67	.53	.22**
Annual Income	-.86	.33	-.12**	-.22	.34	-.03
Health (self-report)	.81	.87	.04	-.56	.88	-.03
Age				.20	.03	-.27**
R2	.05			.11		
F for change in R2	5.86**			36.15**		

Note. *p < .05; **p < .01.

Table 7. Hierarchical Regression Analysis for Variables Predicting Public Self-Consciousness (N = 564)

	Model 1			Model 2		
Variable	*B*	*SE B*	*β*	*B*	*SE B*	*β*
Gender	1.64	.47	.15**	1.66	.46	.15**
Education	-.27	.20	-.06	-.20	.19	-.05
Annual Income	-.12	.12	-.04	.09	.13	.03
Health (self-report)	.65	.32	.09*	.20	.33	.03
Age				-.06	.01	-.24**
R2	.04			.08		
F for change in R2	4.17**			28.57**		

Note. *$p < .05$; **$p < .01$.

See Table 8. Finally, (c) the interaction term between age and public self-consciousness was also non-significant ($\beta = -.01$, $t(559) = -0.20$, $p = .84$).

Table 8. Hierarchical Regression Analysis showing Moderation Effects of Self-Reflection on the Association between Age and Identity Accommodation (N = 564)

	Model 1			Model 2			Model 3		
Variable	B	SE B	β	B	SE B	β	B	SE B	β
Gender	3.11	1.21	.11*	2.64.	1.11	09*	2.73	1.11	.09*
Education	-.33	.52	-.03	-.58	.48	-.05	-.72	.49	-.06
Annual Income	-1.28	.31	-.18**	-.33	.30	-.05	-.40	.30	-.06
Health (self-report)	.65	.83	.03	-1.16	.79	-.06	-1.16	.78	-.06
Age				-.24	.03	-.34**	-.23	.04	-.33**
Self-Reflection				.20.	.04	21**	.23	.04	.24**
Age x Self-Reflection							.004	.002	.08*
R2	.06			.22			.23		
F for change in R2	6.56**			58.02**			3.91*		

Note: Age and Self-Reflection were centered at their means.
*$p < .05$ **$p < .01$.

CONCLUSION

This work had four primary objectives: (I) test the associations between age and identity processing styles, (II) examine the associations that age and identity processing styles have to one's susceptibility to ageism, (III) examine the associations between self-consciousness and aging, and (IV) determine whether self-consciousness factors would moderate the relationships between age and identity processing styles.

Age Differences in Identity Processing Styles

The findings of Hypothesis I offer support for the aging trajectories of Whitbourne's identity process theory and are the first to do so using a large sample with a wide age range that encapsulates the entirety of adulthood. Results confirm an apparent identity assimilation effect whereby individuals use a more assimilative processing style as they get older. This indicates that the proposition of identity assimilation as a defensive coping strategy (Whitbourne and Collins, 1998; Sneed and Whitbourne, 2001; Whitbourne and Sneed, 2002) may hold true, particularly given the results of Hypothesis II which showed a positive linear relationship between identity assimilation and ageism. A de-emphasis on external sources of age-relevant information may assist individuals in maintaining a positive view of the aging self, especially if they hold ageist views themselves. This may prove particularly useful in youth-driven cultures where getting older is often perceived as a "bad thing" (Macnicol, 2006; Giles and Reid, 2005; Nelson, 2002; Nelson, 2005). Consistent with these findings is the negative association found between age and identity accommodation. If individuals are less likely to integrate others' negative views of aging into their own core sense of self, then they may be able to reduce the perception of aging as a negative experience and, in turn, increase overall health and well-being. These results further support the theoretical contentions of Carstensen's (1992; 1995; 2004) socioemotional selectivity theory and a proposed positivity effect wherein older adults show a preference for positive experiences, relationships, and information and take efforts to minimize negative information, emotions, and experiences. Consistent with the work of Whitbourne et al. (2002), identity balance was not found to be age-related in our sample.

Age, Identity Processes, and Susceptibility to Ageism

The results of Hypothesis II fully supported the expected associations between age, identity processing styles, and susceptibility to ageism. A significant negative association was found between age and aggregate ageism scores, suggesting that individuals tend to hold fewer negative perceptions of aging as they themselves get older. These findings certainly make intuitive sense. As previously stated, ageism is a form of "uncontrolled" prejudice and discrimination that we are all susceptible to as we get older. Unlike racism, sexism, classism, and other "isms," the very nature of aging causes a unique, unavoidable shift in our in-group/out-group status as we progress through the natural life course. By no means, however, does this imply that individuals have no control over the impact that ageism has on them. Herein lies support for the associations proposed between identity processing styles and one's susceptibility to ageism. The positive linear relationship between identity assimilation and aggregate ageism scores lends support to Whitbourne et al. (2002), who posited that the IAE is a defensive coping mechanism and that assimilators are resistant to age-relevant information which may cause discrepancies in self-perceptions of ability and competence. Identity accommodation also positively predicted ageism scores, suggesting that if an individual is more likely to internalize outside sources of negative age information, they are also more likely to subscribe to ageist attitudes and beliefs themselves. These results have obvious implications for overall well-being given the associations that previous research has demonstrated between age stereotypes and physical and cognitive performance (Levy, 1996; Hausdorff, Levy and Wei, 1999).

Finally, identity balance showed the strongest predictive ability on ageism, demonstrating a significant decrease in aggregate ageism scores across adulthood. These findings support Whitbourne et al.'s (2002) theoretical contention that balanced individuals are the "aging ideal" and are best-prepared to handle the inevitable ups and downs of life without significant impingement on one's sense of identity. To be able to maintain a positive and consistent view of the self throughout adulthood presents obvious benefits, but the current results further highlight the importance of being able to make age-related adjustments in order to avoid the pitfalls of ageism.

Age Differences in Self-Consciousness

The results of Hypothesis III fully supported the expected age-related changes in self-consciousness. These results were consistent with previous work (Kirk and Chen, 2012; Rankin et al., 2004) and contradicted other research (Davis and Franzoi, 1991). Insight, the theoretically and empirically positive subcomponent of private self-consciousness (Creed and Funder, 1998; Harrington and Loffredo, 2011; Kirk and Chen, 2012) was found to increase with age in the current sample. These findings suggest that as people get older, they tend to use a more beneficial, internally-oriented form of self-consciousness, one that results in positive self-understanding and change for the individual. A negative association was found between age and self-reflection. As opposed to insight, this subcomponent of private self-consciousness has been associated with negative outcomes and, in some research, likened to clinical rumination (Trapnell and Campbell, 1999). The current findings indicate that the division of private self-consciousness into two distinct components has merit, as self-reflection appears to decrease with age while insight appears to increase as people get older. The final proposition of Hypothesis III was supported by a negative linear association between age and public self-consciousness. These findings are consistent with an overall decrease in identity accommodation across adulthood. If individuals become less publicly self-conscious as they get older, it makes intuitive sense that they would also become less concerned about physical appearance and the opinions of others as it relates to their own sense of identity.

Moderation Effects of Self-Reflection on Age and Identity Accommodation

The expected moderation effects of Hypothesis IV were partially supported, such that self-reflection significantly moderated the association between age and identity accommodation. Previous research (Whitbourne et al., 2002; Sneed and Whitbourne, 2003) and the results of Hypothesis I have demonstrated a decrease in identity accommodation with age. This negative association was qualified by an interaction effect of self-reflection on the association between age and identity accommodation, demonstrating that people with higher levels of self-reflection were more likely to use an accommodative identity style than those who were low in self-reflection. Whitbourne and Sneed (2002) stated that identity accommodators are "compelled to seek information about themselves to assuage their feelings of self-doubt and low self-esteem" (p. 261). From a self-consciousness standpoint, given that self-reflection is perceived more as a form of internal self-doubt than insightful self-awareness, it is logical that higher levels of self-reflection would lead to an increase in an accommodative processing style. The interaction between age and insight on identity balance was non-significant in our sample. The anticipated interaction effect between age and public self-consciousness on identity accommodation was also non-significant. It is possible that there is a beneficial element to these so-called "negative" aspects of self-consciousness. Post hoc analyses revealed that public self-consciousness significantly moderated the association between age and identity balance ($\beta = .14$, $t(559) = 2.98$, $p < .01$). These results suggest that a certain degree of public self-consciousness may actually be beneficial for individuals in achieving a balanced sense of identity.

LIMITATIONS AND FUTURE DIRECTIONS

There were a number of limitations to the study. First, it utilized a cross-sectional design to determine age differences in identity processing styles and self-consciousness across the adult lifespan. While this method is telling of between-person differences over time, it does not provide insight into within-person differences and how they may change for the individual across adulthood. A longitudinal design is better suited in providing this information. A cross-sequential design may be better still in providing both between-group and within-group differences over time. Future work may want to consider collecting from different age groups at multiple points over an extended period. A cross-sequential design could illuminate any potential cohort differences that may exist between generations.

Another limitation was that we utilized survey methodology which consisted of only self-report data. Such data may be influenced by social desirability; particularly so for the ageism scale. Given that this measure explicitly assessed one's negative attitudes of older adults, it is possible that participants may have felt the desire to respond in a more favorable manor, one which does not reflect their true attitudes or beliefs. The self-report data for identity processes and self-consciousness may also include inaccurate self-perceptions. Future work may want to consider collecting other reports (i.e., from family or close friends) to compare responses.

The generalizability of results must also be considered. The majority of the sample identified as "white" (84.6%), and "female" (69%). While the sample was fairly representative of the region in which the majority of the data were collected (Northwest Ohio), future work may want to collect a more balanced gender sample which includes greater racial and ethnic diversity. Greater heterogeneity could lend further support to the generalizability of results.

A final recommendation for future research is to potentially examine how gender plays a role in identity processes, self-consciousness, and susceptibility to ageism. Our work found significant gender differences across several of the models tested. Of particular interest is the finding that gender had a stronger association to ageism than any of the identity processing styles. Further assessing these constructs with respect to the influence of gender may reveal additional insights from a developmental perspective.

Contributions and Implications

As previously stated, a principal contention of this work was that older adults can partially combat the negative effects associated with ageism through internal mechanisms which contribute to a secure sense of self or identity throughout adulthood.

Consistent with the identity process theory, results suggested that there are cognitive identity styles which show both positive and negative associations to one's susceptibility to ageism. This work lends support to previous research on identity processing styles (Whitbourne and Collins, 1998; Sneed and Whitbourne, 2001; Whitbourne and Sneed, 2002) and offers new understanding from an ageism paradigm. It seems clear that identity styles play an important role in one's susceptibility to ageist attitudes. Both identity assimilation and accommodation positively predicted ageism scores while identity balance negatively predicted ageism.

These findings lend support to Whitbourne's contention that identity-balanced individuals are the "aging ideal" (2002). Results also suggest that factors other than age may be responsible for the theoretical ideal of maintaining a balanced (i.e., consistent, yet adaptive) sense of identity. Future work may want to examine more stable constructs (temperament, intelligence, etc.) as predictors of the relative stability found for identity balance across the adult lifespan. In light of post hoc findings, it may also prove beneficial to further examine how self-consciousness relationships which were not hypothesized a priori in the current work (i.e., public self-consciousness) may interact with age to promote a balanced sense of identity throughout adulthood.

If identity balance is indeed the optimal identity style from an aging perspective, it is plausible that such results may extend further into the well-being literature.

Future studies should consider these constructs as they relate to measures of psychological or subjective well-being. It could prove worthwhile to test these associations in determining significant differences in emotional experience and overall life satisfaction from an adult developmental perspective; they may hold valuable information for successful aging.

References

Agatstein, F. and Buchanan, D. (1984). Public and private self-consciousness and the recall of self-relevant information. *Personality and Social Psychology Bulletin, 10,* 314-325.

Baltes, P. B. (1987). Theoretical propositions of life-span developmental psychology: On the dynamics between growth and decline. *Developmental Psychology, 23,* 611-626.

Baltes, P. B. and Baltes, M. M. (1990). Psychological perspectives on successful aging: The model of selective optimization with compensation. In P. B. Baltes and M. M. Baltes (Eds.), *Successful aging: Perspectives from the behavioral sciences* (pp. 1-34). New York, NY: Cambridge University Press.

Baltes, P. B., Lindenberger, U. and Staudinger, U. M. (2006). Life span theory in developmental psychology. In R. M. Lerner and W. Damon (Eds.), *Handbook of child psychology: Vol. 1, Theoretical models of human development* (6th ed., pp. 569-664). Hoboken, NJ: Wiley.

Bargh, J. A., Chen, M. and Burrows, L. (1996). Automaticity of social behavior: Direct effects of trait construct and stereotype activation on action. *Journal of Personality and Social Psychology, 71,* 230-244.

Burnkrant, R. E. and Page, T. J., Jr. (1984). A modification of the Fenigstein, Scheier, and Buss self-consciousness scales. *Journal of Personality Assessment, 48,* 629-637.

Butler, R. N. (1969). Age-ism: Another form of bigotry. *Gerontologist, 9,* 243-246.

Carstensen, L. L. (1992). Social and emotional patterns in adulthood: Support for socioemotional selectivity theory. *Psychology and Aging, 7,* 331-338.

Carstensen, L. L. (1995). Evidence for a life-span theory of socioemotional selectivity. *Current Directions in Psychological Science, 4,* 151-156.

Carstensen, L. L., Fung, H. H. and Charles, S. T. (2003). Socioemotional selectivity theory and the regulation of emotion in the second half of life. *Motivation and Emotion, 27,* 103-123.

Carstensen, L. L. and Mikels, J. A. (2005). At the intersection of emotion and cognition: Aging and the positivity effect. *Current Directions in Psychological Science, 14,* 117-121.

Cavanaugh, J. C. and Blanchard-Fields, F. (2011). *Adult development and aging* (6th ed.). Belmont, CA: Wadsworth.

Chen, Y. and Blanchard-Fields, F. (2000). Unwanted thought: Age differences in the correction of social judgments. *Psychology and Aging, 15,* 475-482.

Chen, Y., Pethtel, O. and Ma, X. (2010). Counteracting age stereotypes: A self-awareness manipulation. *Educational Gerontology, 36,* 702-717.

Cohen, J., Cohen, P., West. S. G. and Aiken, L. (2003). *Applied multiple regression/correlation analysis for the behavioral sciences.* (3rd ed.). New Jersey: Lawrence Erlbaum Associates.

Costa, P. T., Jr. and McCrae, R. R. (1992). *Revised NEO Personality Inventory (NEO PI-R) and NEO Five-Factor Inventory.* Odessa, FL: Psychological Assessment Resources.

Cotter, V. and Gonzalez, E. (2009). Self-concept in older adults: An integrative review of empirical literature. *Holistic Nursing Practices, 23,* 335-348.

Creed, A. T. and Funder, D. C. (1998). The two faces of private self-consciousness: Self-report, peer-report, and behavioral correlates. *European Journal of Personality, 12,* 411-431.

Davis, M. H. and Franzoi, S. L. (1991). Stability and change in adolescent self-consciousness and empathy. *Journal of Research in Personality, 25,* 70-87.

Diehl, M., Coyle, N. and Labouvie-Vief, G. (1996). Age and sex differences in strategies of coping and defense across the life span. *Psychology and Aging, 11,* 127-139.

Erikson, E. H. (1963). *Childhood and society* (2nd ed.). New York: Norton.

Evans, D. R., Baer, R. A. and Segerstrom, S. C. (2009). The effects of mindfulness and self-consciousness on persistence. *Personality and Individual Differences, 47,* 379-382.

Fenigstein, A., Scheier, M. F. and Buss, A. H. (1975). Public and private self-consciousness: Assessment and theory. *Journal of Consulting and Clinical Psychology, 4,* 522-527.

Fraboni, M., Saltstone, R. and Hughes, S. (1990). The Fraboni Scale of Ageism (FSA): An attempt at a more precise measure of ageism. *Canadian Journal on Aging, 9,* 56-66.

Giles, H. and Reid, S. A. (2005). Ageism across the lifespan: Towards a self-categorization model of ageing. *Journal of Social Issues, 61,* 389-404.

Goldberg, L. R. (1999). A broad-bandwidth, public-domain, personality inventory measuring the lower-level facets of several five-factor models. In I. Mervielde, I. J. Deary, F. De Fruyt, and F. Ostendorf (Eds.), *Personality psychology in Europe* (Vol. 7, pp. 7-28). Tilburg, The Netherlands: Tilburg University Press.

Grant, A. M., Franklin, J. and Langford, P. (2002). The Self-Reflection and Insight Scale: A new measure of private self-consciousness. *Social Behavior and Personality: An International Journal, 30,* 821-835.

Harrington, R. and Loffredo, D. A. (2007). Private self-consciousness factors and psychological well-being. *The Journal of Psychiatry, Psychology, and Mental Health.* Retrieved December, 29, 2011 from http://www.scientificjournals.org.

Harrington, R. and Loffredo, D. A. (2010). Insight, rumination, and self-reflection as predictors of well-being. *The Journal of Psychology, 145,* 39-57.

Hausdorff, J. M., Levy, B. R. and Wei, J. Y. (1999). The power of ageism on physical function of older persons: Reversibility of age-related gait changes. *Journal of the American Geriatrics Society, 47,* 1346-1349.

Heatherton, T. F. and Polivy, J. (1991). Development and validation of a scale for measuring state self-esteem. *Journal of Personality and Social Psychology, 60,* 895-910.

Kennedy, Q., Mather, M. and Carstensen, L. L. (2004). The role of motivation in the age-related positivity effect in autobiographical memory. *Psychological Science, 15,* 208-213.

Kirk, R. and Chen, Y. "*Age Differences in Goal Concordance and Subjective Well-Being: The Differential Impact of Insight and Rumination.*" Preliminary Study, Bowling Green State University, 2012.

Levy, B. (1996). Improving memory in old age through implicit self-stereotyping. *Journal of Personality and Social Psychology, 71,* 1092-1107.

Levy, B. and Banaji, M. (2004). Implicit ageism. In T. Nelson (Ed.), *Ageism: Stereotyping and prejudice against older persons* (pp. 49-75). Cambridge, MA: The MIT Press.

Marcia, J. E. (1966). Development and validation of ego-identity status. *Journal of Personality and Social Psychology, 3,* 551-558.

Macnicol, J. (2006). *Age discrimination: An historical and contemporary analysis.* New York: Cambridge University Press.

Mather, M. and Carstensen, L. L. (2005). Aging and motivated cognition: The positivity effect in attention and memory. *TRENDS in Cognitive Sciences, 9,* 496-502.

Morton, L. W. and Weng, C. Y. (2013). Health and healthcare among the rural aging. In Glasgow, N. and Berry, E. H. (Eds.), *Rural aging in 21st century America* (pp. 179-194). Netherlands: Springer.

Nelson, T. D. (Ed.). (2002). *Ageism: Stereotyping and prejudice against older persons.* Cambridge, MA: The MIT Press.

Nelson, T. D. (2005). Ageism: Prejudice against our feared future self. *Journal of Social Issues, 61,* 207-221.

Nilly, M. and Winquist, J. (2002). Self-focused attention and negative affect: A meta-analysis. *Psychological Bulletin, 128,* 638-662.

Palmore, E. (2001). The Ageism Survey: First findings. *The Gerontologist, 41,* 572.

Piaget, J. (1975/1977). *The development of thought* (A. Rosin, Trans). Oxford, England: Basil Blackwell.

Piliavin, J. A. and Charng, H-W. (1988). What *is* the factorial structure of the private and public self-consciousness scales? *Personality and Social Psychology Bulletin, 14,* 587-595.

Rankin, J. L., Lane, D. J., Gibbons, F. X. and Gerrard, M. (2004). Adolescent self-consciousness: Longitudinal age changes and gender differences in two cohorts. *Journal of Research on Adolescence, 14,* 1-21.

Robins, R. W. and John, O. P. (1997). The quest for self insight: Theory and research on accuracy and bias in self-perception. In R. Hogan, J. Johnson and S. Briggs (Eds.), *Handbook of personality psychology* (pp. 649-679). New York: Academic.

Rupp, D. E., Vodanovich, S. J. and Crede, M. (2005). The multidimensional nature of ageism: Construct validity and group differences. *The Journal of Social Psychology, 145,* 335-362.

Sawaoka, T., Barnes, R. D., Blomquist, K. K., Masheb, R. M. and Grilo, C. M. (2012). Social anxiety and self-consciousness in binge eating disorder: Associations with eating disorder psychopathology. *Comprehensive Psychiatry, 53,* 740-745.

Scheibe, S. and Blanchard-Fields, F. (2009). Effects of regulating emotions on cognitive performance: What is costly for young adults is not so costly for older adults. *Psychology and Aging, 24,* 217-223.

Scheier, M. F. and Carver, C. S. (1981). Private and public aspects of the self. In L. Wheeler (Ed.), *Review of personality and social psychology* (Vol. 2). Beverly Hills: Sage.

Scheier, M. F. and Carver, C. S. (1985). The Self-Consciousness Scale: A revised version for use with general populations. *Journal of Applied Social Psychology, 15,* 687-699.

Schlenker, B. R. and Leary, M. R. (1992). Social anxiety and self-presentation: A conceptualization and model. *Psychological Bulletin, 92,* 641-669.

Sneed, J. R. and Whitbourne, S. K. (2003). Identity processing and self-consciousness in middle and later adulthood. *Journal of Gerontology, 58,* 313-319.

Sneed, J. R. and Whitbourne, S. K. (2001). Identity processing styles and the need for self-esteem in middle-aged and older adults. *International Journal of Aging and Human Development, 52,* 311-321.

Trapnell, P. D. and Campbell, J. D. (1999). Private self-consciousness and the five-factor model of personality: Distinguishing rumination from reflection. *Journal of Personality and Social Psychology, 76,* 284-304.

United Nations, Department of Economic and Social Affairs, Population Division (2013). World population prospects: The 2012 revision, key findings and advanced tables. (Working Paper No. ESA/P/WP.227). Retrieved July 31, 2013, from United Nations website: http://www.unfpa.org/pds/trends.htm.

Watson, P. J., Hickman, S. E., Morris, R. J., Stutz, N. L. and Whiting, L. (1994). Complexity of self-consciousness subscales: Correlations of factors with self-esteem and dietary restraint. *Journal of Social Behavior and Personality, 9,* 761-744.

Watson, P. J., Morris, R. J., Ramsey, A., Hickman, S. E. and Waddell, M. G. (1996). Further contrasts between self-reflectiveness and internal state awareness factors of private self-consciousness. *The Journal of Psychology, 130,* 183-192.

Whitbourne, S. K. (1987). Personality development in adulthood and old age: Relationships among identity style, health, and well-being. In K. W. Schaie (Ed.), *Annual Review of Gerontology and Geriatrics* (Vol. 7, pp. 189-216). New York: Springer.

Whitbourne, S. K. (1996). *The aging individual: Physical and psychological perspectives*. New York: Springer.
Whitbourne, S. K. and Collins, K. C. (1998). Identity and physical changes in later adulthood: Theoretical and clinical implications. *Psychotherapy, 35,* 519-530.
Whitbourne, S. K. and Sneed, J. R. (2004). The paradox of well-being, identity processing, and stereotype threat: Ageism and its potential relationships to the self in later life. In T. Nelson (Ed.), *Ageism: Stereotyping and prejudice against older persons* (pp. 247-273). Cambridge, MA: The MIT Press.
Whitbourne, S. K., Sneed, J. R. and Skultety, K. M. (2002). Identity processes in adulthood: Theoretical and methodological challenges. *Identity: An International Journal of Theory and Research, 2,* 29-45.
Whitbourne, S. K. and Van Manen, K. W. (1996). Age differences in and correlates of identity status from college through middle adulthood. *Journal of Adult Development, 3,* 59-70.
Wise, D. A. (Ed.). (2012). *Investigations in the economics of aging*. Chicago, IL: University of Chicago Press.

INDEX

#

A

B

C

J

L

M

N

O

P

Q

R

S

T

U

V

W

Y